Handbook of School Counseling

Handbook of School Counseling

Debra C. Cobia
Auburn University

Donna A. Henderson
Wake Forest University

Merrill
Prentice Hall

Upper Saddle River, New Jersey
Columbus, Ohio

Library of Congress Cataloging-in-Publication Data

Cobia, Debra C.
   Handbook of school counseling / Debra C. Cobia, Donna A.
Henderson.—1st ed.
       p. cm.
   Includes bibliographical references (p.) and index.
   ISBN 0-13-011010-8
     1. Educational counseling—Handbooks, manuals, etc.
   I. Henderson, Donna A. II. Title.
   LB1027.5 .C57 2003
   371.4—dc21

                                                    2002026422

Vice President and Publisher: Jeffery W. Johnston
Executive Editor: Kevin M. Davis
Associate Editor: Christina Kalisch Tawney
Editorial Assistant: Autumn Crisp
Production Editor: Mary Harlan
Production Coordination: Jan Braeunig, Clarinda Publication Services
Design Coordinator: Diane C. Lorenzo
Cover Design: Jason Moore
Cover Image: Corbis Stock Market
Text Design and Illustrations: Clarinda Publication Services
Photo Coordinator: Kathy Kirtland
Production Manager: Laura Messerly
Director of Marketing: Ann Castel Davis
Marketing Manager: Amy June
Marketing Coordinator: Tyra Cooper

This book was set in Goudy by The Clarinda Company. It was printed and bound by R. R. Donnelley & Sons Company. The cover was printed by Phoenix Color Corp.

Photo Credits: Scott Cunningham/Merrill: pp. 16, 53, 105, 171; Kathy Kirtland/Merrill: 71; Anthony Magnacca/Merrill: 37, 88, 145; Barbara Schwartz/Merrill: 126, 194; Teri Leigh Stratford/PH College: 212; Anne Vega/Merrill: 1.

Pearson Education Ltd.
Pearson Education Australia Pty. Limited
Pearson Education Singapore Pte. Ltd.
Pearson Education North Asia Ltd.
Pearson Education Canada, Ltd.
Pearson Educación de Mexico, S.A. de C.V.
Pearson Education—Japan
Pearson Education Malaysia Pte. Ltd.
Pearson Education, *Upper Saddle River, New Jersey*

Merrill
Prentice Hall

10 9 8 7 6 5 4 3 2
ISBN: 0-13-011010-8

To the Memory of Jean Houchins Cecil
. . . whose professional contributions to the fields of school counseling
and counselor education are beyond measure.
Her influence continues through those of us
whose personal and professional lives she touched.

and to . . .

Don Adams and J.D. and Chris Henderson
. . . whose unwavering support helped us turn this idea into a book.

Preface

Handbook of School Counseling emerged from conversations between two counselor educators. We had been teaching school counselors for over a decade and agreed with other school counselor educators around the country that we needed instructional materials reflective of the transformations that have taken place in the school counseling profession. The National Standards for School Counseling Programs developed by the American School Counselors Association (ASCA), school counseling specialty standards articulated by the Council for Accreditation of Counseling and Related Educational Programs (CACREP), the expanded view of school counselors' roles emerging from recent reform efforts, and program models frequently adopted by state departments of education have all informed the content and structure of this text.

The "Three Cs" model of school counseling (counseling, coordination, and consultation) has been updated and expanded over the past decade to include leadership, advocacy, and collaboration as primary school counselor roles. The addition of these roles, both in practice and in training, provides the school counselor opportunities to firmly establish links between the school counseling program and the total educational enterprise, thereby operationalizing the concept of school counselors working collaboratively with other educational professionals to maximize the academic, career, and personal/social development of all students.

Our goal has been to provide a book focused on teaching school counseling students how to develop, implement, manage, and evaluate a comprehensive developmental school counseling program that contributes to the mission of the school in meaningful and productive ways. To be successful in this task, we have used the specialty area content for school counselor preparation articulated by CACREP and the National Standards for School Counseling Programs adopted by ASCA and integrated them with the widely adopted organizational structure articulated by Norman Gysbers and Patricia Henderson.

Coverage

Handbook of School Counseling provides counselor educators with a text that emphasizes the school counselor's role in education with particular emphasis on placing counselor interventions in the school context.

The text covers the following areas of emphasis:

- **Foundations of School Counseling.** Chapters 1–2 are designed to increase students' understanding of the school environment and the school counselor's place in the total school program. Emphasis is placed on the development of the school counseling profession, factors that promote or inhibit learning, program models and their components, and skills needed by school counselors to successfully coordinate a program.

- **Contextual Dimensions of School Counseling.** Chapters 3–5 are designed to increase students' understanding of the school counselor's role as an educational leader, advocate, and change agent and of the school counseling program as an integral part of the school success of all students. Emphasis is placed on developmentally appropriate counselor skills and interventions in the context of the four program components: guidance curriculum, individual planning, responsive services, and system support.
- **Standards-Based School Counseling Programs.** Chapters 6–12 include studies in specific approaches used by school counselors to achieve program goals and objectives in elementary, middle, and secondary schools. Chapters provide concrete grade level examples of how sample programs are organized around implementation of the National Standards for School Counseling Programs (ASCA) and local needs assessment results. Each of the four program components—guidance curriculum, individual planning, responsive services, and system support— is described for each grade level.

Format

Information is provided in an easy-to-follow format with a logical structure from which to teach. The following sections are included in each chapter:

- **Case.** Real-world case studies introduce the major topics in each chapter. Real problems are posed that can be addressed by students after mastering the material covered in each chapter.
- **Chapter introduction.** Each chapter begins with a list of objectives keyed to the important concepts.
- **Margin notes.** Throughout the text, brief notes and questions challenge students to think critically about the material being presented. Also, active learning strategies are incorporated to challenge students to reflect on, discuss, identify, and apply the concepts they are studying.
- **Text boxes.** Concrete examples from real-life school counseling programs predominate.
- **Portfolio components.** At the end of each chapter, students are encouraged to complete one or more of the suggested activities for their professional school counselor portfolios. These activities can help students identify not only individual areas of strength but also challenges to their development as they progress through the text.

Features

Handbook of School Counseling offers the following special features:

- Provides a contemporary, integrated view of school counseling in a well-recognized organizational framework.
- Describes a practical, logical sequence for program development, implementation, and evaluation.
- Integrates real-life examples, thereby conceptualizing learning to the school environment.

- Uses active learning strategies throughout each chapter to develop competence and efficacy.
- Encourages reflection and planning for professional growth and development.

In addition relevant documents and forms that students may find useful as they plan, design, implement, and evaluate school counseling programs at all developmental levels are provided in the appendixes.

Instructor's Manual

The Instructor's Manual contains test questions and suggestions for additional classroom activities. Supplemental readings are also included.

ACKNOWLEDGMENTS

We wish to acknowledge the foundational work of Norman Gysbers and Patricia Henderson, who have provided an organizational structure for school counseling programs that is both practical and manageable. This program model is the one adopted, in some form, most frequently by those state departments of education that have adopted a program model. Additionally, the work of those committed professionals who contributed to the development of the ASCA national standards has moved the profession forward immeasurably. Our colleagues from around the country, who have gathered whenever possible to share ideas and discuss needs and trends in the profession, have been a major inspiration for this project. Finally, the students who give us feedback both before and after graduation about what they need from us to be better prepared to enter the profession continue to influence our thinking about school counselor preparation. Finally, no project of this magnitude is accomplished by the author alone. Kevin Davis, our editor with Merrill Publishing, has been patient, encouraging, and instructive throughout the development of this book. Our thanks and appreciation go to him and the entire team at Merrill for their efforts.

The feedback from reviewers of this text at all stages of its development has been invaluable. We extend a special thank you to Virginia B. Allen, Idaho State University; Duane Brown, University of North Carolina–Chapel Hill; Robert D. Colbert, University of Massachusetts–Amherst; Kathy Evans, University of South Carolina; Marijane Fall, University of Southern Maine; M. Sylvia Fernandez, Arkansas State University; Margaret Herrick, Kutztown University of Pennsylvania; Susan G. Keys, Johns Hopkins University; Lee A. Rosen, Colorado State University; and Sue A. Stickel, Eastern Michigan University.

Discover the Companion Website Accompanying This Book

The Prentice Hall Companion Website:
A Virtual Learning Environment

Technology is a constantly growing and changing aspect of our field that is creating a need for content and resources. To address this emerging need, Prentice Hall has developed an online learning environment for students and professors alike—Companion Websites—to support our textbooks.

In creating a Companion Website, our goal is to build on and enhance what the textbook already offers. For this reason, the content for each user-friendly Website is organized by topic and provides the professor and student with a variety of meaningful resources. Common features of a Companion Website include:

For the Professor—

Every Companion Website integrates **Syllabus Manager**™, an online syllabus creation and management utility.

- **Syllabus Manager**™ provides you, the instructor, with an easy, step-by-step process to create and revise syllabi, with direct links into Companion Website and other online content without having to learn HTML.
- Students may logon to your syllabus during any study session. All they need to know is the web address for the Companion Website and the password you've assigned to your syllabus.
- After you have created a syllabus using **Syllabus Manager**™, students may enter the syllabus for their course section from any point in the Companion Website.
- Clicking on a date, the student is shown the list of activities for the assignment. The activities for each assignment are linked directly to actual content, saving time for students.
- Adding assignments consists of clicking on the desired due date, then filling in the details of the assignment—name of the assignment, instructions, and whether it is a one-time or repeating assignment.
- In addition, links to other activities can be created easily. If the activity is online, a URL can be entered in the space provided, and it will be linked automatically in the final syllabus.
- Your completed syllabus is hosted on our servers, allowing convenient updates from any computer on the Internet. Changes you make to your syllabus are immediately available to your students at their next logon.

For the Student—

- **Counseling Topics**—17 core counseling topics represent the diversity and scope of today's counseling field.
- **Annotated Bibliography**—includes seminal foundational works and key current works.
- **Web Destinations**—lists significant and up-to-date practitioner and client sites.
- **Professional Development**—provides helpful information regarding professional organizations and codes of ethics.
- **Electronic Bluebook**—send homework or essays directly to your instructor's email with this paperless form.
- **Message Board**—serves as a virtual bulletin board to post—or respond to—questions or comments to/from a national audience.
- **Chat**—real-time chat with anyone who is using the text anywhere in the country—ideal for discussion and study groups, class projects, etc.

To take advantage of these and other resources, please visit the *Handbook of School Counseling* Companion Website at

www.prenhall.com/cobia

Brief Contents

Contents

C H A P T E R 1

The Profession of
School Counseling

======================= **CASE STUDY** =======================

UNDERSTANDING THE PROFESSION:
THE EXPERIENCE OF MARK

Mark, a counseling student, has completed most of his required academic work and is ready to begin his 600-hour internship, split between a secondary school and an elementary school. Mark knows from his experience that the local community has some racial strife and an economic underclass, and that a large percentage of students go from high school directly into the workforce. Mark assumes, as he has been taught in graduate school, that the counseling program will be designed to address these needs as well as those of economically advantaged, college-bound, academically proficient students. Mark's view of school counseling is influenced by the philosophy that school counselors bear some degree of responsibility for the academic, career, and personal/social development of all students.

During the second week of the internship, Mark expresses confusion during his group supervision seminar and asks for assistance from his peers and university supervisor. Specifically, he found that the counselors in his particular secondary school placement spend most of their time working with college-bound students in individual sessions, registering or withdrawing students, and preparing transcripts and letters of reference for college applications. These counselors and this particular counseling program emphasize preparing students to make vocational choices, with a great deal of attention to those who are preparing to enter colleges or universities. In the elementary school placement, greater emphasis is placed on classroom guidance aimed at developing academic, career, and personal/social competence in which all students participate. Additionally, there are numerous special programs for students with particular needs, such as those who have recently experienced a family loss. Mark asks, "Are all secondary counselors so burdened with administration and paperwork that they can only spend their counseling time with a relatively small percentage of the school population? If the counselors are not going to address student needs such as developing an appreciation for diversity or career planning for non-college-bound students, who will?"

Mark is frustrated because what he had been taught in graduate school did not seem to apply in the real world. He is also concerned about the large number of students who are not receiving guidance and counseling services, particularly those in traditionally underserved populations. Additionally, he is confused about the difference in philosophy and practice evidenced by elementary and secondary counselors within the same district. Mark's university supervisor determines that a review of the history of the counseling profession and a discussion of school counselors' ethical responsibilities to those they serve is in order.

What are the elements of a profession? A profession typically has an agreed on set of preparation standards and qualifications one must have to occupy the role of "professional" in a given field. These standards are based on an established literature that provides both theoretical and empirical support for the profession's existence. Additionally a profession governs itself, usually by establishing minimum standards of care or practice to which members of the profession subscribe.

Often these standards are articulated in ethical guidelines. Finally, there is consensus about the role, identity, and functions performed by a person who enters the profession (VanZandt, 1990). All these conditions are true for the profession of school counseling.

The American School Counselor Association (ASCA) has adopted a role statement that describes the role of a school counselor (see Appendix A). Once you graduate and assume the role of professional school counselor, you will be expected to function as a specialist in human behavior and relationships (American School Counselor Association [ASCA], 2000). You will be called on to provide assistance to students who are experiencing life transitions related to growth, family, or life circumstances outside the student's control and specific problems related to learning and behavior. You have had, or will have, a number of courses designed to assist you in working with students at all stages of development. In this book, we focus on the special skills and knowledge you will need to work effectively as a counselor in a school setting, managing a comprehensive, developmental school counseling program. To fully understand the profession, and some of the reasons for widely divergent practices, we believe it is important to place the current status of school counseling in a broader historical context.

After reading and discussing this chapter, you should be able to

- Identify the significant historical events that led to the current status of the school counseling profession.
- Describe the differences between philosophies of school counseling based on a services-oriented versus a comprehensive developmental approach.
- Explain the role of a school counselor in today's schools.
- Explain the ethical responsibilities of the school counselor toward students, parents, colleagues, community, profession, and self.

LEARNING FROM THE PAST

Mark might be able to reconcile the differences between his two different experiences of school counseling by considering the major historical events that influenced the development of school counseling as a profession. How could our professional history have led to two such different philosophies of school counseling? If we go back 100 years or so, we find "guidance" curriculum components delivered in the United States by teachers to help young people become moral, productive citizens (Baker, 2000). The need for this component emerged during the Industrial Revolution with the large-scale migration of families from agricultural communities to northeastern cities in search of better occupational opportunities (Cecil & Cobia, 1990). Previously, children reared in farming communities expected to become farmers themselves and may have had limited access to formal education. Consequently, little attention was given to occupational planning. As these children migrated to cities and enrolled in public schools, school personnel quickly became aware of the need to provide them information about possible occupations and teach them the skills necessary to make decisions about their futures.

In 1907, Jesse B. Davis, a high school principal in Grand Rapids, Michigan, set aside one session of English class each week for guidance. Believing that individuals could only make responsible choices about their future if they had information about themselves and about the vocations they were considering, Frank Parsons organized the Vocational Bureau of Boston in 1909 to make career information available to out-of-school youth (Baker, 2000). Davis and Parsons have been identified as the fathers of school guidance (Aubrey, 1982). In 1913, the National Vocational Guidance Association (NVGA) was founded and in 1915 began to publish a bulletin that later became the current *Journal of Counseling and Development* (Gladding, 1996). This bulletin was the beginning of a professional literature devoted to what we have come to call *counseling*. Adding momentum to the guidance movement was the passage of the Smith-Hughes Act of 1917 that provided funding for vocational education in public schools.

> The long-standing assumption that guidance was a function of teaching and could only be provided effectively by classroom teachers was based in this early history of the guidance movement.

Another significant influence on the development of school counseling was the emphasis on testing and measurement. During both World Wars I and II the armed forces developed and used instruments designed to measure individual personality traits, skills, and aptitudes (Myrick, 1987). These instruments were used to test and place inductees in jobs for which they demonstrated the most ability and to ensure the best use of all available human resources. Instruments developed, especially in the areas of career interest and aptitude, were based on the trait and factor models introduced by Parsons and further developed by E. G. Williamson during the 1930s (Gladding, 1996). Guidance personnel embraced the use of tests, believing that an emphasis on precision and science legitimized their programs (Baker, 2000).

After World War II, society was rapidly changing and traditional values were being challenged. The need for mental health services was recognized, and there was a corresponding need for people who could provide such services. Training programs for counselors and counseling psychologists experienced rapid growth. Keep in mind that the principal theoretical influences on counseling up to this point had been trait and factor approaches and Freudian analysis. Because such approaches were not helpful to all persons seeking assistance, Carl Rogers had articulated a person-centered versus counselor-centered approach to counseling in 1942 (Gladding, 1996). Thus, a more humanistic theoretical perspective influenced the preparation programs for counselors and counseling psychologists that emerged during the 1940s, 1950s, and 1960s. After the publication of Rogers's fist book, the term *guidance* was replaced by an emphasis on counseling, of which guidance may be a part (Gladding, 1996).

> Initial, wide-scale entry of school counselors into secondary schools was to identify academically talented youth and help them get into colleges and universities. How do you think this event influenced the philosophy of school counseling in the secondary school where Mark is placed?

In 1957, the Union of Soviet Socialist Republics (USSR) launched Sputnik, the first artificial satellite. American citizens were shocked that the USSR had developed this technology and launched into space before the United States. In response, Congress passed the National Defense Education Act in 1958 (NDEA). Part of this bill provided funding to put in every high school school counselors who were specially trained to identify and encourage talented youth to attend college. Special emphasis was placed on those students who showed promise in math and science, for they were perceived as our future technological saviors.

The NDEA also provided funds to colleges and universities to develop programs to train school counselors. Counselor preparation varied widely and was directed toward secondary school personnel. The preparation programs often required as few as five additional courses for teachers holding master's degrees in any field of education to gain certification in school guidance and counseling. The early counselor preparation programs were quite experimental, for there was no research or professional consensus about what kind or how much preparation was necessary to be a qualified or effective school counselor. A common thread was that all school counselors came from the teaching ranks, continuing the perspective that preparation for teaching was the foundation for guidance.

A major step in the evolution of school guidance and counseling as a profession distinct from teaching was the establishment of the American School Counselor Association (ASCA) in 1958 as a division of what was then called the American Personnel and Guidance Association, now the American Counseling Association (ACA) (Myrick, 1987). With nationally recognized leadership in school counseling, a commission was created to study the role and function of school counselors. As chair of the committee, Gilbert Wrenn (1962) submitted a written report in 1962 entitled *The Counselor in a Changing World*. This report identified the goals of the school counseling profession. The goals centered on the personal development of students, and the commission recommended that counselors add the identification of the developmental needs of students to their emphasis on vocational guidance and testing. Further, the report suggested that counselors use various interventions such as individual and group counseling to help meet those needs. The timing of this report was quite remarkable in that the federal government extended the NDEA in 1965 to provide funds for training elementary school counselors. The report submitted by Wrenn on behalf of the commission provided a valuable resource for persons who were preparing counselors with NDEA funds in intensive summer institutes and greatly influenced contemporary models of counselor preparation and practice.

From the early 1960s to the present, school counselor preparation and practice have changed dramatically. The emphasis on human growth and development suggested by Wrenn and his colleagues has continued to gain momentum and is now widely accepted as the foundation for the profession. The preparation of school counselors has received professional consensus, as evidenced by the establishment of the Council for Accreditation of Counseling and Related Educational Programs (CACREP) as an affiliate organization of ACA (Gladding, 1996). CACREP refined the national standards proposed by the Association for Counselor Education and Supervision (ACES) in the early 1970s. National standards for the accreditation of school counseling programs, as well as other counseling specialties, was an important step in having counseling recognized as a distinct profession. Instead of adding five courses to an existing master's level teaching certificate, persons enrolled in CACREP accredited school counseling programs were engaged in studies requiring a minimum of 48 semester hours or 76 quarter hours including extensive supervised clinical experiences through practicum and internship placements in school settings. Further defining the goals, objectives, and responsibilities of school counselors, ASCA developed *National Standards for School Counseling Programs* (Campbell & Dahir, 1997). The standards clearly articulate expected student outcomes in academic, career, and personal/social development for those students who have participated in a comprehensive developmental program of school guidance and counseling (see Appendix B).

> With limited preparation, persons will naturally assume responsibilities for which they feel prepared. For school counselors trained during the early years, this often meant vocational guidance, college placement, and quasi-administrative tasks such as scheduling, registration, records maintenance, and testing.

In addition to the influences of professional associations and accrediting bodies, training, preparation, and previous professional experiences, persons aspiring to be school counselors are governed by the requirements for certification by their state department of education (SDE). To practice as school counselors, persons must meet the minimum qualifications established by their respective SDE. Unfortunately, SDE regulations have not always kept pace with the meaningful changes in the profession at large. As a case in point, the state where Mark is working certified teachers with a master's degree in any field of education who had 3 years of teaching experience with only five additional courses until as recently as 1994. Typically included in the coursework was an introduction to guidance course, an assessment course, a career or vocational guidance course, counseling theories, and internship requiring as few as 100 hours of supervised practice. In contrast, Mark is attending a 78 quarter hour program with preparation in human growth and development, group counseling, career counseling, social and cultural implications for counseling, appraisal, helping relationships, research and evaluation, and professional orientation. In addition, he took special coursework related to the work of a school counselor and will spend approximately 1 year in the schools for supervised practicum and internship prior to his graduation.

> How might this historical account help Mark understand the frame of reference of those counselors with whom he currently works, both elementary and secondary? Based on this information, how might Mark reconsider his view of the counselors?

WORKING IN TODAY'S SCHOOLS

Now that we have a historical context for understanding the development of school counseling, let us turn our attention to the current status of the profession. The school counselor is one professional among many working in today's schools to promote the academic success of all students. What do we mean by academic success? Basically, we are referring to what one should be able to do upon graduation from high school. The educational outcomes of American education have been much debated in both public and private sectors (Dahir, Sheldon, & Valiga, 1998). Reform efforts sparked by these debates have led to the development of national standards across academic disciplines and, most recently, in school counseling. The standards (Campbell & Dahir, 1997) advocate a shift from the service/activity approach practiced by the counselors in Mark's school to a programmatic approach that is "comprehensive, developmental and measures program effectiveness and the achievement of attitudes, skills and knowledge by students" (Dahir, Sheldon, & Valiga, 1998, p. 3).

In 1997, the ASCA revised its position statement, "The Professional School Counselor and Comprehensive School Counseling Programs," originally adopted in 1988 (ASCA, 2000). The position asserted by ASCA is that the school counseling program is an integral part of the total school program. Similar to other educational programs, the program is based on specific goals and objectives, specifies desired student outcomes as a result of participating in the program, includes activities designed specifically to achieve outcomes, and is delivered and evaluated by professionally credentialed personnel. The program "assists students in acquiring and using life-long skills through the development of academic, career, self-awareness, and interpersonal communication skills" (p. 51). Further, the position is taken that an effective school counseling program is based on collaboration between school counselors and other educators. How does this collaboration occur? School counselors are an indispensable part of a total educational team consisting of teachers, administrators, and families. Counselors work collaboratively with the other team members to help students acquire the aforementioned skills. A sample philosophy statement for a comprehensive, developmental school counseling program is found in Paisley and Hubbard (1994):

> The school counseling program is a comprehensive, developmental program that is an integral part of the total learning experience for all students. The program includes developmental, preventive, and remedial components to promote skills for living and success in schools. The focus of the counseling program is on the total child or adolescent and recognizes cognitive, affective, social and physical dimensions. Students can benefit from a proactive school counseling program designed to promote personal-social, educational and career development. This orientation maximizes student potential to become fully functioning and contributing members of society. (p. 208)

What do you suppose the philosophy statement at Mark's school would look like? How would the philosophy differ from the one articulated by Paisley and Hubbard?

WHAT DOES THE COUNSELOR DO?

Mark's understanding of the activities of counselors can be enhanced by the profession's definition of a school counselor's role (see Appendix A). As one can see by reading the role statement (ASCA, 2000), ASCA outlines the work of the professional school counselor as involving three functions and four primary interventions. According to this statement, school counselors act as student advocates as they develop and implement school counseling programs. They accomplish this by using the primary interventions of individual and small group counseling; large group guidance; consultation with parents, teachers, and others; and coordination of the program. As educational team members, school counselors focus their activities on facilitating the educational process and the opportunities for student success. The following sections of this book will expand the definitions and applications of the roles and interventions in the ASCA role statement.

Other authors provide summaries of the practices of school counselors that embellish the ASCA statement. Schmidt (1999) discusses counseling, consulting, coordinating, and appraising as the essential services provided by school counselors. Myrick (1993) adds peer facilitator programs and projects to the school counselor intervention list. Gysbers and Henderson (2000) describe the elements of a comprehensive program as the guidance curriculum (large group guidance), individual planning (advising and assessing), responsive services (counseling, consulting, and referring) and system support (managing, outreach, and public relations). Finally, Baker (2000) includes social action and accountability as counselor responsibilities. These authors help us identify the congruence that exists in interpreting the professional responsibilities of the school counselor and present explanations that emphasize particular components of those duties.

The ASCA role statement recommends that school counselors spend 70 percent of their time in direct services to students. What activities in Mark's elementary and secondary schools might be considered direct services? What program components are emphasized?

HOW DO SCHOOL COUNSELORS UNDERSTAND THEIR RESPONSIBILITIES?

As Mark struggles to understand the differences between his views and those of his supervisors, he needs to study the ethical standards that guide the professional school counselor. Both the general professional ethics of the American Counseling Association and the specific professional ethics of the American School Counselor Association provide these frameworks. The ASCA (2000) ethical standards (see Appendix C) are organized around the responsibilities a professional school counselor has to students, parents, colleagues and professional associates, the school and community, self, and the profession. This organization identifies the variety of people to whom counselors are accountable. In most instances, counselors work with parents, teachers, and administrators in a consultant role to assist the student (counselee). However, under some circumstances, such as when running a parenting group, the parents would be considered counselees. The same holds true for teachers or other adults for whom the counselor becomes a referral interviewer. The discussion below is intended to highlight the ethical standards detailing these and other complexities of a school counseling practice. The prominent ethical issues are discussed in more detail in the following sections.

Responsibilities to Students

COUNSELOR FOCUS

The primary ethical obligation of the school counselor centers on the counselee. Each client receives the counselor's respect and acceptance as a unique person. The counselor is charged with providing a program designed to encourage and enhance the educational, career, emotional, and behavioral needs of the student. Counselors stay informed of laws, regulations, and policies to ensure that the rights of the counselee are met. They also refrain from imposing their personal beliefs and values on their counselees.

How does this focus correspond with the philosophy statement you developed for Mark's school?

COUNSELING PROCESS

Professional school counselors are deliberate in providing information and in planning the counseling process. School counselors tell counselees about the purposes, goals, techniques, and rules of procedure at the beginning of a counseling relationship. Counselees are given written statements that explain the limits of confidentiality, privileged communication, legal restraints, and the possible necessity for consulting with other professionals. This document (following) is called a professional disclosure statement and also includes information about the counselor and his or her philosophy of counseling.

Riverside/Middle School
School Counseling Program Disclosure Statement

We have developed this statement to tell you about the counseling program at Riverside and about our role in your educational development. We hope that after reading this statement you will have an understanding of the ways we provide assistance to students in achieving their full academic potential. If you ever have questions about what you read here, please ask us so that we might provide answers.

Counseling Approaches and Background

Mr. I. M. Harris, M. Ed., School Counselor. This is Mr. Harris' fifth year as a school counselor. His approach is based on helping students identify those issues and emotions in their lives that may interfere with their ability to learn. He uses a variety of methods to help identify these barriers, and then helps students, teachers, and families develop plans to address the issues so that students are free to pursue their academic goals.

Ms. H. R. Patterson, M.Ed., School Counselor. Ms. Patterson has been a school counselor for 12 years. Her approach is based on helping students identify the thoughts they are having that may lead to distress and interfere with their ability to learn. She uses methods that help students identify these thoughts, and then helps students, teachers, and families develop plans to change the thoughts so that students are free to pursue their academic goals.

Appointments

Counselors are assigned to work with students and teachers in grade-level teams. You can make an appointment with your assigned counselor, or, if he or she is available, you may walk in without waiting for service. If you need to see a counselor right away and your assigned counselor is not available, the other counselor will be happy to assist you. Counselors are also available for after-school appointments on the second and fourth Wednesday of each month until 7:00 P.M.

Confidentiality

The information shared between a student and a counselor is confidential. Confidential means that, except under specified circumstances, what you tell your counselor will not be shared with others. The exceptions, or conditions under which your counselor may share information about you with someone else, are listed below:

- If you ask your counselor to tell someone else
- If your counselor believes that you are in some danger from others or that you present a danger to others or to yourself
- If a judge orders your counselor to tell others

- If you report behavior in violation of school policy that your counselor is required to tell the school administration (identified in your student handbook)
- If your counselor needs to consult with someone else to provide better service (with your permission)

Benefits

You may experience increased understanding of the issue(s) that brought you to counseling and you may feel better because you have talked things over with someone who will try to help you resolve your concerns. If you achieve the goals that you and your counselor set together, you may feel confident and successful about your accomplishments.

Risks

Entering into a counseling relationship may create some anxiety for you. You may be challenged to think about yourself in ways that are not comfortable.

The counselor and counselee develop counseling plans jointly. The plans conform to the abilities and circumstances of both and are monitored regularly. Counselors have an ethical obligation to evaluate the ongoing effectiveness of the plan and to adapt the plan as necessary to increase the potential for achieving counseling goals.

CONFIDENTIALITY

Confidentiality implies an assurance to the client that what is communicated in a counseling relationship will not be repeated except in those limited circumstances noted in the disclosure statement. A counselor actively protects the privacy of a counselee's communications and is guided by federal and state laws, written policies, and applicable ethical standards. Professional school counselors who decide to reveal information to others must inform counselees of actions they will be taking to protect counselees and must attempt to obtain the informed consent of counselees.

School counselors have several challenges in honoring the ethical obligation of confidentiality. In fact a federal district court decision documented the competing constitutional rights of children, parents, administrators, and teachers in schools (American Counseling Association, 1993). In the United States, the protection of children's rights often depends on interpretations made by their parents, guardians, or the courts (Remley, 1985). In some states children are granted privileged communication, a legal status protecting their communications from being disclosed in court. Fischer and Sorenson (1996) report that students in schools in approximately 18 states are granted the legal right of privileged communication when talking with a school counselor. Restrictions to these laws vary across the states. School counselors should investigate the laws and restrictions that exist in the states in which they are employed (Waldo & Malley, 1992) to determine the protection their counselees are afforded by state statute. They should also educate other school personnel and parents about the meaning and implications of these laws for the counselor's work (Welfel, 1998).

As one can see from the exceptions to confidentiality discussed above, a counselor discloses information to prevent clear and imminent danger to the counselee or to others. Counselors discuss information when legal requirements dictate that the confidential communication be revealed. The current ethical standards state that a counselor may also disclose information to a third party who is at a high risk of contracting a communicable and fatal disease as a result of relationship with the counselee. This type of disclosure occurs only after the counselor has determined that the third party has not been informed of this danger by the counselee. In all cases careful deliberation and, if possible, consultation with other professionals is advised before the information is revealed. Counselors must consider whether the implications of eating disorders, substance abuse, reckless sexual behavior, cult membership, criminal activity, and other dangerous activities constitute a grave enough threat to self or others to warrant a breach of confidentiality. Counselors who want more information on making these difficult decisions are referred to Isaacs (1997), Isaacs and Stone (1999), and Henderson and Fall (1998).

Another exception to the standard of confidentiality is the reporting of child abuse and/or neglect. All states dictate some type of reporting for these cases although standards vary from state to state. Counselors must know the requirements of the laws in their states and the procedures in their districts. These guidelines are revised often and must be monitored regularly. Sandberg, Crabbs, and Crabbs (1988) offer suggestions about the legal issues involved in reporting child abuse.

> Secure a copy of the statute mandating the reporting of child abuse in your home state. In the larger group, discuss the similarities and differences among the statutes. Based on reporting procedures described, develop a reporting system or protocol that might be used in your school counseling program to ensure that all requirements for reporting suspicions of child abuse are met.

DUAL RELATIONSHIPS

Whenever a counselor is involved with a counselee in more than one capacity, dual relationships can occur (Fisher & Hennessy, 1994). Counseling relatives, close friends, children of close friends, or associates are examples of situations with possible dual relationships. Ethical standards state that school counselors avoid dual relationships. In these situations, incompatible roles have the potential to limit the effectiveness of the counseling relationship (Corey, Corey, & Callanan, 1993). If unavoidable, counselors take action to eliminate or reduce the potential for harm in a dual relationship by providing informed consent, seeking consultation and supervision, and documenting their actions.

GROUP WORK

When offering group counseling, the counselor establishes and stresses a norm of confidentiality but clearly states it cannot be guaranteed. The professional school counselor begins forming a group by screening prospective group members. As the group proceeds, the counselor stays alert to the needs and goals of group participants. Counselors also provide reasonable precautions to protect participants from physical and psychological damage resulting from group interaction.

RECORDS

A counselor maintains and protects student records as required by laws, regulations, institutional procedures, and confidentiality guidelines. Federal laws that safeguard the privacy of student information include the Family Educational Rights and Privacy Act (FERPA, 1974), the Grassley Amendment (1994) to the Goals 2000, Drug Abuse Office and Treatment Act (1976), and Individuals with Disabilities Education Act (IDEA, 1997). FERPA (1974) establishes guidelines for the accessibility as well as the disclosure of student records. The protection of privacy for students who participate in surveys, analysis, and evaluation is detailed in the Grassley Amendment (1994). The Drug Abuse Office and Treatment Act (1976) protects the confidentiality of records of people receiving treatment for drug and alcohol abuse. Finally, security for the records of students who receive special education services is outlined in the Individuals with Disabilities Education Act (IDEA) (1997).

Counselors are encouraged to keep counseling records in addition to student's cumulative records (ASCA, 1999a). Information in the counseling records should include evidence of disclosure, the counseling plan, notes of ongoing contact, decisions made regarding counseling process, relationship, and referrals. The notes should be objective and accurate and include the time and circumstances of the session. Well-kept notes will demonstrate whether the quality of counseling provided was consistent with the established standards of practice for school counselors. The records should be maintained in a locked file cabinet in the counselor's office, never in the student's cumulative file. The counselor does not share these notes with others.

TESTING

According to the ethical standards, a professional school counselor subscribes to standards regarding selection, administration, and interpretation of testing materials. A counselor recognizes that computer-based assessment requires specific training. In the testing process, counselors are obligated to provide an understandable explanation of the nature, purposes, and results of the assessment measures. Counselors are cautioned to avoid the misuse of results and interpretations and to pay particular attention to the representation of the norm group on which the instrument was standardized. School counselor competencies in assessment and evaluation, developed by the Association for Assessment in Counseling (1998) and endorsed by ASCA, identify minimum standards for school counselors in the area of testing and assessment (see Appendix D).

COMPUTERS

Professional school counselors ensure that computer applications suit the individual needs of a counselee. They explain the benefits and limitations of computer programs to counselees. Counselors determine that counselees understand how to use the computer program and provide follow-up counseling assistance. Counselors ensure that underrepresented groups have equal access to computer technology and are not subjected to information that is discriminatory. Sampson and Pyle (1988) discuss ways to protect the data stored on the computer. Counselors who communicate with counselees via a computer follow ACA Ethical Standards for Internet On-line Counseling (http://www.counseling.org).

PEER HELPER PROGRAMS

School counselors are responsible for anyone who participates in peer helper programs that are under their direction. Counselors protect the welfare of all the students who are involved at all times. The National Peer Helper Association Web site includes more specific guidelines for developing and implementing peer helper programs (http://www.peerhelping.org).

Responsibilities to Parents

PARENT RIGHTS AND RESPONSIBILITIES

A professional school counselor respects the rights and responsibilities of parents for their children. A counselor tries to build a collaborative relationship with parents to enhance the development and welfare of the counselee. Counselors work with sensitivity to the cultural and social diversity among families and adhere to laws and local guidelines when helping parents.

PARENTS AND CONFIDENTIALITY

Parents are provided with an explanation of the role of the professional school counselor that emphasizes the confidential nature of counseling. Counselors provide accurate, comprehensive, and relevant information in a manner consistent with all ethical guidelines and make reasonable efforts to honor the requests of parents and guardians for information while protecting the counselee.

Responsibilities to Colleagues and Professional Associates

PROFESSIONAL RELATIONSHIPS

The boundaries and levels of the counselor's professional role are well established and maintained in working with faculty, staff, and administration. Colleagues are viewed as competent professionals and are treated with respect, courtesy, and fairness.

SHARING INFORMATION

As stated previously, a counselor educates other professionals about confidentiality. If information necessary for assisting the counselee is provided, the counselor ensures that it is accurate, objective, concise, and meaningful. After the parent and student consent, professional school counselors may inform other mental health professionals if one of their counselees is also receiving services in the school.

Responsibilities to the School and Community

SCHOOL

School counselors defend an educational program from anything that might interfere with the best interest of the students. Accordingly counselors honor the confidentiality between themselves and their counselees but report situations that may be disruptive or damaging to appropriate officials. Recent legislation in some states aimed at limiting school violence creates strict reporting criteria for threats. School counselors must monitor their state and district policies regarding these procedures.

The scope of a school counselor's duties is clearly articulated in this section of the ethical standards. Counselors help in developing (1) appropriate curricular and environmental conditions, (2) developmentally correct educational procedures and programs, and (3) a system of evaluation for school counseling programs, services, and personnel. The results of the program evaluation guide the planning process for the school counseling program.

COMMUNITY

To promote the best interest of counselees, the professional school counselor collaborates with others in the community without expectations of reimbursement.

Responsibilities to Self
COMPETENCE

If Mark's supervisors were certified under the minimum requirements previously described, what professional development activities might they pursue to update their knowledge and skills? Working in small groups, discuss potential professional development goals for yourselves during your school counselor training. Project 5 years into the future and identify professional development goals you may be working toward.

Counselors practice within the limits of personal competence and take responsibility for their actions. Counselors monitor themselves and diligently protect counselees from harm. Counselors maintain professional competence and up-to-date knowledge, recognizing the life-long process of professional growth. Counselors also recognize ways their own personal values and beliefs affect the counseling process and use this awareness as well as their understanding of diverse cultural backgrounds when working with counselees.

Responsibilities to the Profession
PROFESSIONALISM

Professional school counselors accept these ethical policies and procedures as well as relevant statutes, conducting themselves in ways that advance individuals, ethical practice, and the profession. Clear distinction is made between actions and statements made as a private individual and those made as a representative of the school counseling profession. The school counselor does not use the professional position for unjustified personal gains, unfair advantage, sexual favors, or unearned goods or services. School counselors conduct and report research appropriately, always ensuring the privacy of any participants. Finally counselors are affiliated with professional associations and make contributions to the development of the profession.

In the preamble of ASCA code of ethics the following assumptions are listed as the foundations for the responsibilities discussed in the standards:

1. Each person has the right to respect and dignity as a human being and to counseling services without prejudice as to person, character, belief or practice, regardless of age, color, disability, ethnic group, gender, race, religion, sexual orientation, marital status or socioeconomic status.
2. Each person has the right to self-direction and self-development.
3. Each person has the right of choice and the responsibility for goals reached.

4. Each person has the right to privacy and thereby the right to expect the counselor-counselee relationship to comply with all laws, policies, and ethical standards pertaining to confidentiality. (ASCA, 2000, p. 25).

School counselors are confronted with many situations that require difficult decisions. Counselors who remember the rights cited above and who study the definitions of ethical behavior provided in the standards will be better prepared to resolve those situations using their careful judgement to preserve the best interest of the student.

SUMMARY

After a review of the history, philosophy, definitions, and standards of the school counseling profession, Mark will have gained a broader perspective on the many influences that go into the development of a school counselor's philosophy. Examining the current context for counseling in schools should help him understand the role of a school counselor as he enters the profession. Hopefully this experience will also emphasize for him the need to update his knowledge and skill throughout his career. An understanding of the ethical guidelines that govern the practice of school counselors should lead to greater awareness of his responsibilities to students, parents, colleagues, community, self, and profession.

More than any other counseling specialty, school counselors have opportunities to serve an array of clients in a variety of ways. Schools are a microcosm of society with the strengths and challenges of the larger world impacting each school. As they encounter these multiple demands, school counselors who are informed about the history, definitions, and standards of the school counseling profession continually strive to improve their practice.

PORTFOLIO COMPONENTS

1. Prepare a reflection statement by describing your motivation for seeking entry into the school counseling profession. Include a summary of your interpersonal and intrapersonal strengths that will help you become a competent school counselor. Also, identify any limiting factors and describe how you will compensate for or overcome them.
2. Adapt the disclosure statement provided in this chapter to reflect your own qualifications, beliefs, and organizing strategies. Make sure the reading level and language are appropriate to the grade levels in your ideal school.
3. Review the ASCA role statement (sec Appendix A) and identify any aspects that are different from your previous perceptions of a school counselor's role. Reflecting on these differences, speculate about how you came to hold these beliefs. How might your awareness of these preconceptions influence your training experiences?

The School Counselor: Promoting Academic Excellence for All Students

CASE STUDY

IDENTIFIYING BARRIERS TO ACADEMIC SUCCESS

Ms. Irma Roccone has been a counselor at Warm Springs Middle School for 10 years. The school counseling program is integrated into all parts of the school with all school personnel involved. Ms. Roccone recognizes the need for careful organization and focused management of the counseling plans. She coordinates the many activities that are ongoing in Warm Spring's counseling program. Her days are spent counseling students and working collaboratively with teachers, parents, and administrators. Throughout the school year Ms. Roccone monitors the progress and outcome of the activities and makes modifications as necessary. Overall, she and her colleagues are pleased with the implementation of the counseling program, ongoing evaluations, and resulting improvements.

As the program has become easier to manage, Ms. Roccone made two decisions. One, she is going to focus each year on a selected group of students who are not realizing their potential. In the current school year she is targeting a group of seventh-grade girls whose grades have slipped from Bs and Cs to Cs and Ds in their language, math, and science courses. Two, she will supervise a school counseling intern from a neighboring university who is expected to participate in all aspects of the school counseling program.

Ms. Roccone would like assistance from the intern, Earl Truman, with her goal of compiling a more complete assessment of the resources and needs of students in her school and district to supplement what she had done in some earlier years. For the specific group of students targeted this year, she gathered information from the students' files, from observations, and from conversations with their teachers. She also talked with each of the seventh-grade girls. She has asked Mr. Truman to help gather information about school policies and procedures, as well as social and environmental issues and contexts that may be affecting the girls'

performance. She knows that this information will be invaluable to them as they plan interventions and identify resources that may help the girls return to previous levels of academic success.

Ms. Roccone sees some patterns in the information gathered about the girls so far:

- All the girls live within a few blocks of each other in a part of town that is crowded with many rental properties that are poorly maintained. The neighborhood has few places for young people to gather safely and little public transportation available.

- Lucia had once been part of this close-knit group but is being left out of some of their new activities. She goes home to care for her grandmother after school and is unavailable for hanging out at the mall. Lucia is concerned about her friends' behaviors but also sad to be excluded.

- Tia at one time had the highest grades of the five girls. She is now in danger of failing two courses for the semester. She told Ms. Roccone that she is in love with someone and that school is a bore. Ms. Roccone knows that the young man with whom Tia is involved dropped out of high school 2 years earlier.

- Theresa has been picked up for shoplifting and is waiting to find out whether she is going to trial. She is convinced she can beat the charge.

- Sophie quit the volleyball team in midseason and refuses to talk to any adults about her reasons. She and Tia now spend their afternoons with Tia's boyfriend and his crew.

- Jacky causes more school disruptions than the others. She defiantly challenges all the teachers on her grade-level team and belittles her classmates. She has spent 4 days in-school suspension this semester. Her misbehavior seems to be escalating as her grades drop.

Ms. Roccone knows human development and counseling theories. She has also studied extensively children's mental health and risky behavioral patterns. She uses information from those fields daily. She recognizes also that children exist within multiple systems, such as family, community, peers, and school. The effectiveness of program planning and implementation efforts that focus only on the individual student and ignore the impact of the external systems are limited. Therefore, with her we will consider ways to understand the academic setting and curriculum; social, cultural, diversity, and equity issues relevant to academic achievement; the role of school counseling; and strategies and resources supporting school success of students and families.

After reading and discussing this chapter, you should be able to

- Describe the structure and governing of the education system in the United States.
- Recognize factors related to academic success and barriers to academic development in institutions, communities, families, and environment.
- Identify educational strategies and community resources that promote academic success.

THE EDUCATIONAL ENTERPRISE

The American School Counselor Association (1999c) role statement on professional school counseling contains these words: "Above all, school counselors are student advocates who work cooperatively with other individuals and organizations to promote the development of children, youth, and families in their communities" (p. 2). School counseling programs contribute to school effectiveness. School counseling increases students' ability to concentrate, study, and learn. Students who attend schools that have counseling programs earn higher grades, report fewer classroom disruptions, and show improved peer behavior (Lapan, Gysbers, & Sun, 1997; American Counseling Association [ACA], 2000). Gerler, Kinney, and Anderson (1985) report that underachieving students who receive counseling improve in classroom behavior and in mathematics and language arts grades. A school counseling program is an essential part of the learning environment of schools.

To accomplish their goal of being a student advocate, counselors increase their knowledge of the educational enterprise. School counselors need to understand the purposes of schooling, the responsibilities of different governing bodies, and the roles of many school personnel. Mr. Truman's next task is to look at the existing structures in Warm Springs that support or inhibit students' success.

Purposes of Schooling

Some basic assumptions have guided education in the United States. These assumptions were stated in 1908 by the National Education Association Commission on the Reorganization of Secondary Education when it recommended that secondary education should "develop in each individual the knowledge, interests, ideals, habits and powers whereby he will find his place and use that place to shape both himself and society toward ever nobler ends" (as cited in Ballantine, 1997, p. 130).

Within this statement the purposes of education relate to intellectual, economic, political, and social purposes. Schooling is ultimately designed to help students increase their cognitive knowledge and skills, an intellectual goal. Education also provides students with the credentials they need to practice their careers, which in turn advances the nation's economic growth through a skilled labor pool. Goldberg (2000) identifies those skills that the business community asks for in employees: to be motivated, creative, well educated, constant learners, excellent communicators, and able to work in groups. Patriotism, law and order, leadership building, and knowledge of the governmental systems within the nation are the political functions of the educational enterprise. Schools also provide places in which cultural ideals are transmitted. Schools are optimally places that encourage cultural pluralism: "the maintenance of diversity, a respect for differences, and the right to participate actively in all aspects of society without having to give up one's unique identity" (Sleeter & Grant, 1988, p. 170). In schools young people hopefully learn to be responsible citizens. Although these general intellectual, economic, political, and social purposes serve as guideposts, different ways of translating the goals into operating principles occur at both the state and the local level. Recognizing the roles of state and local agencies and personnel will provide Ms. Roccone more ways of incorporating those influences into the goals for a school counseling program.

School Structures

The primary responsibility for public education rests with the state. Each state has a reference to education in its constitution that outlines who makes what decisions and how. A clause common in all state constitutions refers to the obligation of each state to maintain a free system of public schools open to all students in the state (Pipho, 2000a). A K–12 grade structure exists in all states. All states have similar standards for licensing teachers (Webb, Metha, & Jordan, 1996), and national standards for teaching excellence are available for some subject areas. In the fall of 1999 about one out of every four persons in the United States participated in formal education as a student or an employee (U.S. Department of Education, 2000), a fact that highlights the enormous effort of educating students. American education includes 50 state educational agencies, approximately 15,000 school districts, and around 80,000 schools.

Governors, state legislatures, and state and local school boards set educational policies. The federal government has a more limited role, mainly contributing funds for programs and services for special populations such as students with disabilities and youth who are educationally disadvantaged. A recent multiyear study of school governance resulted in the following possible model for schools:

- The state creates a context for schools and districts to excel;
- The district creates an environment that allows schools to focus on teaching and learning; and
- The school creates an environment focused on teaching and learning and is held accountable for the results. (Pipho, 2000b, pp. 341–342)

At the state level the administration of schools generally includes a state board of education that makes policy, a state department of education that serves as an administrative agency, and a chief state school officer who is the executive officer of the state board as well as an administrator of the state department.

State boards of education oversee state standards and district policies, especially those that depend on state funds. These boards determine minimum standards for teacher licensing, graduation, the length of the school day, and the number of school days in a year. State boards of education may also establish policies, provide technical assistance, monitor schools, and provide others with information about schools (Webb et al., 1996).

Gysbers, Lapan, and Jones (2000) surveyed state school boards to determine the nature, structure, and content of policies for counseling programs across the country. In their analysis of 24 state school board association policies, they concluded that those policies are outdated and are not written to recognize counseling as an integral school program. They provide a sample policy statement from the Missouri School Board that can serve as a template for rewriting less inclusive policies.

Local school boards oversee the operation of the school system within which an individual school exists. Some of the duties of those boards include hiring, determining salaries and contracts, and providing transportation, budgets, and building facilities. Often the board delegates the administration and teaching aspects of its duties to the superintendent and devotes its attention to policy concerns, much like a board of directors of a corporation.

> Determine whether the state and local school board members in your area are elected or appointed to those positions. Discuss the advantages and disadvantages of each way of selecting board members.

Henderson and Gysbers (1998) explain the different ways a counseling program may be placed in the organization of the school district. The placements reflect the district's concept of the mission of counseling. According to Henderson and Gysbers, if the counseling program is perceived to be student centered and based on a developmental perspective, it will be placed with the instructional components. If the program is perceived as student centered with priority given to responsive services, the counseling program may be placed within the student services part of the structure. Finally if the school counseling program is centered on operations and reactive to the demands of administrators and teachers, it may be aligned with the administrative part of the structure. Gysbers and colleagues (2000) argue that local school boards should revise policies for counseling programs to provide a sound organizational structure for counseling programs. Those policies would allow counselors to work closely with teachers and parents within the framework of a comprehensive counseling program focused on critical aspects of student development. Adelman and Taylor (1998) also urge school boards to revisit all policies that similarly fragment and therefore reduce the impact of programs and services.

School Administration

Superintendents manage school systems. They serve as conduits among schools, the school board, and the community. They operate as the chief executive officer of a school system, supported by a staff of specialists in curriculum and instruction, business services, personnel services, and special services.

The smallest but most critical unit in a school district is the individual school. The principal is the designated leader of the school and the person charged with the primary responsibility for its success or failure. Principals use leadership, management, and planning skills as they support teachers, manage the budget, oversee school personnel, work with students, and interact with the public along with other day-to-day responsibilities. The level of the school, the types of students who attend, the size and location of the school, and the district all interact in affecting the way a principal carries out that role. Ballantine (1997) summarizes the following as behaviors of effective leadership of principals in schools that have raised student achievement:

- Leaders are concerned with instruction.
- They convey their views about instruction.
- They take responsibility for instruction-related decisions.
- They coordinate the instructional program.
- They emphasize academic standards.

As a professional school counselor, Ms. Roccone can find many ways to support her building leader in these practices. As an intern supervisor, she models collaboration and support as important aspects of building strong, mutually respectful relationships with school administrators.

School Personnel

Other school staff positions include specialists and services workers such as office workers, media specialists, school psychologists, special education teachers, maintenance personnel, paraprofessionals, food service workers, bus drivers, and nurses. All school personnel affect the education of children, and all should be involved in creating environments that allow young people to be active learners, respected participants, and caring citizens. Ms. Roccone recognizes that any of the Warm Springs staff may be valuable resources for her targeted group members and their families. For example, office workers are often the first people to greet parents when they visit the school. If the main office is staffed with warm and caring persons, parents or guardians who may otherwise view schools as inhospitable (e.g., parents who did not consider their own school experiences to be successful) may come to experience schools as warm and inviting environments.

Other noncertificated personnel may form positive, lasting bonds with students who have few such relationships with adults. These significant adult figures have the opportunity to exert positive influence on the school behaviors of the youths with whom they become involved. For example, if one of the girls has an interest in food preparation, Ms. Roccone may be able to establish a mentoring relationship with the head of the cafeteria workers where the student might learn about menu planning, food selection and preparation, service, and so on. This experience might lead the student to an exploration of career opportunities in the food service industry and could result in a renewed commitment to academic pursuits.

Teachers stand in the center of the work of schools. They work in many ways to share their knowledge and skills, create and use learning environments, and control the teaching process so that pupils can learn. Sometimes they have more contact with students than parents do. Their commitment, energy, and expectations play crucial parts in the academic accomplishments of their students. They teach children how to learn, how to hope, and how to be members of society. The behaviors and attitudes they demonstrate in their classrooms affect many areas of the student's development. A teacher is expected to be an instructional leader, a classroom

List all the school staff for one of the schools in which you were a student between grades kindergarten through 12. Talk about the ways each of these influenced your school day.

manager, and a caring person. According to the U.S. Department of Education (2000), effective teachers set and communicate high standards, explain and demonstrate what is expected, assign meaningful homework, and help students with study skills. In Warm Springs Middle School, teachers have formed interdisciplinary grade-level teams to work together to achieve their mutual goal of providing effective educational programs and services (Friend & Cook, 2000).

Mr. Truman meets with the seventh-grade team to discuss ways in which the various teachers who interact with the girls targeted by Ms. Roccone might assist in her efforts to get them back on track academically. One of the team members is also the volleyball coach, a person the team believes to be a major resource for Sophie. The team considers ways to try to reconnect Sophie with the team. The group recognizes the relationship between participating in extracurricular activities and school bonding for students at risk of school failure.

Ms. Roccone recognizes the interactive relationships that exist at all levels of schooling. She knows that different school counseling initiatives require working at different levels. Her program concern may need to be addressed by a policy group at the state or local level. A consortium of five groups concerned with school counseling—National Association for College Admission Counseling, American Counseling Association, The Education Trust, American School Counselor Association, and Sallie Mae (2000)—suggests the policies listed in Figure 2.1. Some of these policies may be appropriate to the concerns at Warm Springs School or the school counselors in that school district.

Finally knowing the roles of the many people involved in the educational enterprise allows her to access the information and resources she may need to assist all of those within the scope of her program. She will continue to lobby for professional development to support teachers and to provide them pertinent resources she gathers at their request. Her recognition of the formal roles and structures involved in education will help her with program planning and change initiatives as well as with her daily activities. She also knows that she must be aware of the more informal aspects of schooling.

> Consider the information provided for Jacky and Lucia. What additional resources might the grade-level team identify for each of them?

Curriculum and Climate

Most state governing bodies provide a formal curriculum that guides the focus of instruction for the school district. That curriculum provides a broad outline of the learning content, outcomes, and standards for students.

HIDDEN CURRICULUM

Hidden curriculum refers to the unintended effects of schooling. Apple (1988) identifies three areas of the hidden curriculum. One involves the social messages presented in textbooks and other curriculum material. Another area includes the norms and values that are expressed in the regulations, rituals, structure, and interactions in the school. These allow students ways to cope with power, praise, reward, criticism, and authority (Apple, 1980); to move through social and physical spaces (Bowers, 1984); and to learn the value of competition, obedience, use of time, and seriousness of purpose (Webb et al., 1996). A third area of the hidden curriculum is the information that is excluded from the formal curriculum, either on purpose or unintentionally.

FIGURE 2.1   School Counseling Program Policies per the National Association for College Admission Counseling

The Role of School Counseling in Preparing Students for the 21st Century

Policies that Foster Effective School Counseling Programs

School Counseling Program and School Counselors are not interchangeable terms. Although the school counselor is a vital part of a school counseling program, the individual is not the program. A school counseling program has a curriculum, goals, objectives, and outcomes just as other educational programs do. School administrators, classroom teachers, students, parents, and the community at-large all have important roles in the delivery of successful school counseling programs that will reap benefits for students. We recommend:

At the national level—

- The federal government identify and disseminate information about effective models for school counseling programs and for high quality school counselor preparation and professional development.

- The federal government support research on school counseling programs, including studies on programs and practices that increase school success for all students. Information on school counseling should be collected as part of the core data elements at the National Center for Education Statistics.

- The federal government fund initiatives that support school counseling, including professional development (both pre-service and in-service), student services, and capacity building.

At the state level—

- States develop standards for school counseling programs that are aligned with the state's vision for student success, including academic standards, graduation requirements, postsecondary options, and personal, social attributes.

- States ensure that school districts have the resources to implement school counseling programs that meet the state standards.

- States require that school counselors meet certification requirements that include completion of an approved graduate program.

- States recognize only school counselor preparation programs that provide the knowledge and skills needed for new professionals to implement the state standards.

At the local level—

- Students have access to counseling programs that are part of the education program of the school system.

- Students have access to counseling programs that are approved by the school board and, at a minimum, should feature measurable results, access to students, parental involvement, highly qualified, professional staff, and strong administrative support.

- Students have access to counseling programs that have adequate fiscal, human and technological resources to implement the school counseling program.

Adults can use the power of the hidden curriculum by becoming more conscious of it, examining the assumptions within the materials and practices used, and finding ways to take advantage of these opportunities for learning (Apple, 1988; Webb et al., 1996). For example, Warm Springs School has a committee in place to review and adopt textbooks. Ms. Roccone wants to use the process they have in place to review the supplemental materials she has been using in the guidance curriculum. She will create a checklist to use as she plans for classroom presentations. She will also work on a method to review the other material in the counseling office.

From her recently developed profile of the student population, Ms. Roccone realizes that the school now includes more students from working- and middle-class parents. She wonders if some teacher expectations for the students have been lowered. Again, the grade-level teams are excellent resources for gathering this information and making recommendations about procedural changes if they are needed. For example, asking the team members to review the types of texts used, homework assigned, grades typically earned, and general expectations of performance of specific student groups would provide Ms. Roccone with some beginning information. The teachers may also begin to identify some patterns of student achievement that they may not have noticed previously. Additionally, she asks Mr. Truman to review the cumulative records of students in question to examine the types of courses they are being encouraged to take when they leave the middle school and move into ninth grade. Specifically, how many of them are being routinely registered in lower level classes that do not prepare them for postsecondary education opportunities such as college? This information helps Ms. Roccone, Mr. Truman, and the grade-level teams discuss possible changes that will hopefully result in higher expectations for all students. Additionally, Ms. Roccone and Mr. Truman will be discussing ways that they might further influence course selection during preregistration periods.

SCHOOL CLIMATE

The term *school climate* incorporates many factors within a school and has been defined as "how people feel about the qualities of a school and the people in that school" (Kaplan & Geoffroy, 1990, p. 8). School climate has been credited with predicting school adjustment in urban, minority, and low-income children (Esposito, 1999); teacher satisfaction and sense of efficacy (Taylor & Tashakkori, 1995); counselor self-efficacy (Sutton & Fall, 1995); and school disorder (Welsh, 2000). Gottfredson (1988) discusses how a positive climate can reduce delinquency.

Ms. Roccone has prepared the people with whom she works for creating a positive school climate by teaching them about Purkey's invitational learning (Purkey & Schmidt, 1990; 1996; Purkey & Novak, 1996). Purkey offers a blueprint for counselors, teachers, principals, supervisors, superintendents, and others to create physical and psychological environments that encourage development that he refers to as invitational learning. The goal of invitational learning is to build an optimally inviting environment for each person in the school. To accomplish this counselors and educators learn invitational behaviors and assist students in relating to the school. Students can then develop a sense of control over their lives, invest in their futures, and cope with school expectations. The method, according to Purkey (Purkey & Novak, 1996;

Purkey & Schmidt, 1996), is a system of beliefs and a guide to professional practices. The process is based on four elements that interact and lead to inviting relationships.

- **Respect.** An appreciation of each person and every culture; the belief that people are able, valuable, responsible, capable of self-direction, and deserve to be treated accordingly.
- **Trust.** The belief in the interdependence of humans; a high priority on human welfare; and the idea that education should be a collaborative, cooperative activity in which the process is as valuable as the product.
- **Optimism.** The notion that people have untapped potential in all areas, displayed by a confidence in and perseverance with people.
- **Intentionality.** The potential of human beings is best realized by places, policies, programs, and processes designed to affirm human worth and to invite development and by people who are deliberately inviting with themselves and with others.

In the interconnectedness of schools everything and everyone contributes in creating an environment that invites all to reach their potential. This includes arranging the following five factors:

- **Places.** Structuring an attractive and efficient physical environment that is functional, clean, warm, and accessible creates a setting for inviting behavior. This relates to building a school climate in physical ways (Esposito, 1999; Welsh, 2000; Bulach & Lunenberg, 1995; Freiberg, 1998).
- **Policies.** School personnel can influence regulations, plans, rules, and mandates that encourage student responsibility and participation. Inviting schools write inviting policies related to admission, enrollment, attendance, promotion, grading, discipline, and inclusion.
- **Programs.** Counselors help develop, monitor, and advocate for programs founded on the assumptions of invitational learning such as peer helpers, faculty mentoring, and other collaboration efforts. For example, counselors and other school staff encourage enrichment activities, multicultural emphasis, parental involvement, community service, recognition, and cocurricular programs.
- **Processes.** Invitational learning assumes that the processes influence quality of life. School characteristics such as clarity and fairness in rules, order, and expectations are important to processes. In their work, counselors who establish norms of collegiality, professional development, mutual assistance, and ongoing discussions with other educators contribute to inviting schools. Everyone in school works to build relationships that are inclusive, integrative, and cooperative. Everyone helps build positive climates. They all work to demonstrate respect for all students and give attention to their needs.
- **People.** Invitational learning is based on valuing systems, regulations, and policies by putting people first. The interactions in schools among all the educators and between educators and students determine the success of the inviting learning community.

Ms. Roccone acknowledges that all five of her targeted students have teachers on their team who arrived after the school incorporated these ideas. She has decided to be more consistent about helping with some annual training for incoming teachers and staff and to offer refresher opportunities for others. She is convinced that the attitudes of invitational learning help create environments that overcome some of the barriers to learning that students encounter. She has now looked at the ways a school system's structure and personnel affect learning. She has considered the aspects of hidden curriculum and school climate. She will now consider some specific issues related to success in education as she considers other ways to help these girls.

CONTRIBUTORS TO ACADEMIC SUCCESS

During a school day how many things occur that increase the chances of children's learning well and developing positively? How many of the events lead to less desirable outcomes? Ms. Roccone and Mr. Truman discussed some of the factors that contribute to academic success. Rak and Patterson (1996) define resilience as

> the capacity of those who are exposed to identifiable risk factors to overcome those risks and avoid negative outcomes such as delinquency and behavior problems, psychological maladjustment, academic difficulties, and physical complications. (p. 368)

Some personal, family, and environmental factors have been identified as contributing to resiliency. Some of the personality traits that resilient children demonstrate include an active approach to problem solving, social competence, optimism, a proactive perspective, and a friendly nature (Rak & Patterson, 1996). Other characteristics of resilient children include receiving affection and support from caregivers. Support from individuals and from institutions such as schools also contributes to resilience (Masten & Coatsworth, 1998). Counselors recognize that protective factors such as the child's temperament, multiple sources of support, and positive role models in the community help young people overcome barriers and succeed.

Another way to define children's assets has been provided by the Search Institute (2000), a nonprofit organization devoted to improving the well-being of young people through research, effective communication, and tools for practice. That group created the *Search Institute Profiles of Student Life: Attitudes and Behaviors* (1999), a survey designed to explain the developmental strengths of children. By using data from the questionnaire, researchers identified 20 external and 20 internal assets across eight areas. Those assets are listed in Table 2.1.

According to this study, external assets include the positive experiences and support young people receive from their social environment of family, peers, and institutions such as schools. Adults who recognize the importance of support, empowerment, boundaries and expectations, and constructive use of time will strengthen a young person's external assets. Internal strengths are the personal characteristics that guide young people in their choices and that create their sense of purpose and focus. Those identified characteristics include a commitment to learning, positive values, social competencies, and a positive identity (Benson, Galbraith, & Espeland, 1998).

McWhirter, McWhirter, McWhirter, and McWhirter (1998) have also summarized the positive skills of young people that increase their opportunities to succeed. These skills include patterns of attitude, habits, preferences, and other behaviors. McWhirter and colleagues base their approach on the assumptions that all young

TABLE 2.1 Developmental Assets

Internal Assets	External Assets
Commitment to Learning	*Support*
• Achievement motivation	• Family support
• School engagement	• Positive family communication
• Homework	• Other adult relationships
• Bonding to school	• Caring neighborhood
• Reading for pleasure	• Caring school climate
	• Parent involvement in schooling
Positive Values	
• Caring	*Empowerment*
• Equality and social justice	• Community values youth
• Integrity	• Youth as resources
• Honesty	• Service to others
• Responsibility	• Safety
• Restraint	
	Boundaries and Expectations
Social Competencies	• Family boundaries
• Planning and decision making	• School boundaries
• Interpersonal competence	• Neighborhood boundaries
• Cultural competence	• Adult role models
• Resistance skills	• Positive peer influence
• Peaceful conflict resolution	• High expectations
Positive Identity	*Constructive Use of Time*
• Personal power	• Creative activities
• Self-esteem	• Youth programs
• Sense of purpose	• Religious community
• Positive view of personal future	• Time at home

Reprinted with permission. From A positive look at today's youth. *The Child Indicator, 2,* (Minneapolis, MN: Search Institute). © Search Institute, 2000. www.search-institute.org

people have the capacity to become more mature, to have an interest in learning, and to function competently. They identify five characteristic skills for children to have a high potential for success: critical school competencies, concept of self and self-esteem, communication with others, coping ability, and control.

Critical school competencies include basic academic skills in reading, writing, and mathematics as well as academic survival skills or habits that make it possible to learn. Staying with a task, following directions, and writing legibly are examples of the academic survival skills. The concept of self and self-esteem are the perceptions people have about themselves and the value they place on that self-concept. Communication with others allows students to achieve and maintain positive interpersonal relationships. The ability to cope effectively with anxiety and stress is a fourth essential skill and includes how one deals with conflicts. Finally McWhirter and colleagues discuss having decision-making skills, being able to delay gratification, and having a purpose in life as the skill of control. The counselors at Warm Springs

Using the list of 40 assets and the list of 5 competencies, rate yourself on the presence and strength of each. From the information you have, what assets and competencies can you identify for the five girls? Which assets and competencies might Ms. Roccone wish to increase among her targeted students?

realize that young people come to school with external and internal strengths and that certain skills can enhance those assets. Knowing what children need to succeed academically allows educators to focus on increasing those skills and assets along with the basic academic skills necessary for school success.

BARRIERS TO LEARNING

The Achievement Council explains that equity can be "an operational principle for shaping policies and practices which provide high expectations and appropriate resources so that *all students achieve at the same rigorous standard—with minimal variance due to race, income, language or gender*" (Johnson, 1996, p. 3). This group endorses the following principles:

> All schools can create a high-achievement culture that provides access and equity for all students ensuring that:
>
> - Students receive a rigorous core curriculum full of concepts and ideas that are drawn from the best sources to stimulate analysis and awareness of world culture.
> - Students learn in heterogeneous groups for most activities; the school does not label students as high or low ability but encourages students who have mastered advanced skills to help others learn them.
> - Teachers, administrators, students and parents build a community of education that jointly establishes a vision. Teachers and administrators translate the vision into a cooperative action plan.
> - The focus of the school is on intellectual activity supported by the flow of time and money accordingly.
> - Teaching and learning are active and personal. Teachers and students are engaged collaboratively in intellectual inquiry.
> - Teachers and other school personnel routinely examine instructional practice, experiment with new approaches and analyze their effects, constantly seeking better results for all learners.
> - The entire school community provides
>   - Time and opportunities for school staff and parents to improve their skills
>   - Time for adults and children to discuss and solve their personal problems. (Johnson, 1996, p. 5)

Some groups of students have more barriers than others in completing their education. Mortenson (2000b) provides a list of barriers to postsecondary education, which are summarized in Figure 2.2. Pupils can achieve high school graduation with varying degrees of knowledge and skill, depending on the curriculum they complete. They may receive a college preparation diploma or be a graduate of the general high school curriculum. They may be a recipient of the GED or receive certificates of achievement. Those who complete college preparation coursework have more opportunities. The life-long implications of limited education are illustrated in the earning potential related to educational level in Figure 2.3. (Mortenson, 2000a) These implications are compounded by the decline of low-skilled jobs and the need for the enhanced skills noted by Goldberg (2000).

Ms. Roccone does not want to underestimate the academic capacity of any student. She will next review whether this might be occurring with her targeted

With your classmates, discuss the school counselor's role in holding high expectations for students.

FIGURE 2.2   Barriers to Postsecondary Education

Academic

Course-taking in high school
Study skills
Commitment

Financial

Type of financial aid
Amount of aid

Geographic

Place bound
Cultural divides

Information Technology

Computer/Internet access and use

Parents

Dysfunctional families
Uninformed parents
Preoccupied parents

Cultural

Aspirations
Language

Functioning

Learning disabilities
Behavioral disorders
Health-related disabilities

Institutional

Admissions criteria
Academic and social
environment

K–12 Education Reforms

High-stakes testing

Social

Community values
Peer pressures

Source: From Mortenson, T. (2000b). Postsecondary education opportunity. *The Mortenson research seminar on public policy analysis of opportunity for postsecondary education, 92,* p. 11. Reprinted by permission.

students. She recognizes that gender, race/ethnicity, and socioeconomic status affect the opportunities provided to some students. She knows school practices of tracking students into vocational or special education courses may create differences in opportunities for education beyond high school. She realizes that school personnel must be aware of these possibilities and work to create environments in which more equitable conditions exist. A brief overview of these conditions is next.

Gender

Girls' school performance exceeds boys' in speaking, reading, and counting in the early grades, but by the time they graduate from high school, females perform more poorly than males in mathematics and science (Robinson & Howard-Hamilton, 2000; American Association of University Women [AAUW], 1992). Part of this discrepancy may be attributed to gender bias in the classroom, specifically to the amount and kind of attention girls may receive from teachers. Some proposed explanations for gender differences in achievement include race, biology, sociology, self-esteem, and attitudes toward certain topics (Brusselmans-Dehairs, Hencry, Beller, & Gafni, 1997). The International Association for the Evaluation of

FIGURE 2.3 Estimated Earning Potential

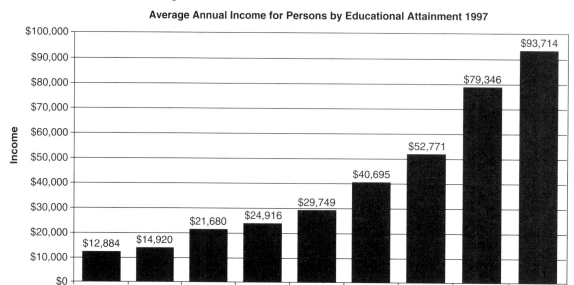

Average Annual Income for Persons by Educational Attainment 1997

Source: U.S. Census Bureau published by Postsecondary Education Opportunity. Reprinted by permission.

Educational Achievement conducted a cross-national comparative study in many areas and concluded that the "gender differences in ability and achievement are mainly due to societal and cultural influences and not to biological causes" (Brusselmans-Dehairs et al., 1997, p. 19).

Ms. Roccone has some hypotheses about how gender may be contributing to the decline in grades for her targeted group. The seventh-grade girls may be experiencing lower expectations from their teachers. Perhaps the different types of attention they receive in classes are undermining their desire to achieve. The research Mr. Truman is doing regarding students from middle- and working-class families can be extended to include a review of the records of all girls in the middle school. If there are indications that girls are generally performing at levels lower than boys, the grade-level team can be presented with the data so that they may plan strategically to address the issues of gender inequity. If the problem seems to be widespread, some in-service training may be appropriate.

Another guess is that the messages the seventh-graders are incorporating about gender roles may direct their aspirations away from careers outside the home. Tia's relationship with her boyfriend may be influencing that belief. Sophie also seems to be withdrawing from activities that do not revolve around the group of men led by Tia's boyfriend. Resources for addressing these issues should include those focusing on exploration of girls' futures, post–secondary education, and occupational opportunities. The connection between education and participation in the economy must be emphasized (Ballantine, 1997).

Race/Ethnicity

The race and ethnicity of students affect the educational opportunities they receive. In 1999, 20 percent of Latino teens dropped out of school compared with 7 percent of white teens and 13 percent of African American teens (Annie E. Casey Foundation, 2000). Based on these and other statistics Ms. Roccone has heightened concern for Lucia, Tia, and Theresa who have Latino backgrounds. Lucia arrived from Haiti 4 years ago and has overcome the language difficulty but has lost her support group in her exclusion from these seventh-grade girls. Tia and Theresa have been raised in the United States by parents who immigrated. Ms. Roccone will investigate their educational hopes more fully. She acknowledges that the interplay of expectations based on gender and ethnicity may be large parts of academic difficulties for all the girls.

Banks (2000) suggests that students who are socialized in low-income, predominantly minority communities learn behaviors, communication styles, and values that do not correspond to the prevailing culture in schools. The school population of Latino students has increased significantly in the last 5 years. Three of the girls Ms. Roccone has targeted for intervention have Latino backgrounds. Teachers have often expressed concern that they may not be adequately addressing the needs of these students. Students and parents have indicated that they do not feel understood or valued in their new community.

Ms. Roccone has decided to discuss with her principal the need for more support for these students. She wants to identify ways she might be involved in those efforts. Ms. Roccone has also met with the systemwide coordinator of programs for students for whom English is a second language. He is a potential resource for introducing new programs and securing more instructional materials for these students. Additionally, she has identified several potential multicultural education trainers to work with teachers and others in the school to help them understand some of the specific needs of these students and families. She is also considering asking well-established Latino families to serve as volunteer "hosts" for newer families when there are open houses and teacher conferences scheduled at Warm Springs. Obviously Ms. Roccone knows with whom she should discuss her concerns, what kind of information is needed to inform the decision makers of the need for change, and the types of proposals likely to meet with success.

> For more information about how to help teachers respond more effectively to these students, study Philips's (1983) research on the participation structures of Native American students, Au's (1980) study of Hawaiian students, Heath's (1983) explanation of the language socialization patterns in an African American community, and Lee's (1993) research of African American language usage as well as Ladson-Billings's (1994) study of eight teachers who use culturally congruent teaching in their classrooms.

High-Poverty Schools

Poverty affects the schools the students attend. Roos (1998) describes three ways that the distribution of financial resources contributes to differences in student outcomes. He recognizes that the single most important thing a school district can offer for student success is a skilled and well-trained teacher. A lower standard for teachers creates achievement problems for students (Riley, 1997). High-poverty schools are more apt to be overcrowded, too large, and outdated. Riley also reported that student achievement and behavior have been tied to school building conditions and overcrowding. Roos made a final point about the disparities that exist: school districts often spend less per pupil for students in inner-city schools. Haycock (2000) contends that some students get lower quality instruction as a result of going to school in poor school districts. McCaslin and Good (1996) recognize that the majority of minority students attend schools that are underfunded. The U.S. Department of Education (1998) reported the following achievement trends in high-poverty schools (75 percent of students receive free and reduced-price lunch) and low-poverty schools (25 percent or fewer students receive free and reduced-price lunch).

- The gap in math and reading achievement for 9-year-old students in high- and low-poverty schools is significant, although there are some recent signs of improvement.
- In math, there has been an upward trend in achievement for 9-year-old and fourth-grade students in high-poverty schools on National Assessment of Educational Progress (NAEP) since 1992.
- Reading presents a more complicated picture. The gap in reading performance between students in high- and low-poverty schools is dramatically larger than the gap in math, and NAEP reading scores have been stagnant, with no significant improvements across levels of school poverty.

Although Warm Springs School does not meet the criteria for a high-poverty school (with 60 percent of the students receiving free and reduced-price lunch), the school does incorporate the characteristics that identify top-performing, high-poverty schools:

- Using state standards extensively to design curriculum and instruction, to assess student work, and to evaluate teachers;
- Increasing instructional time in reading and math to help students meet standards;
- Devoting a larger proportion of funds to support professional development focused on enhancing instruction;
- Implementing comprehensive systems to monitor student progress and providing extra support to students as soon as it is needed;
- Focusing efforts on involving parents on helping students meet standards; and
- Having state or district accountability systems in place that have consequences for the adults in the schools (*Dispelling the Myth*, 1999).

Socioeconomic Status

Socioeconomic status also affects learning. Determining social class includes variables such as income, housing, membership(s) in organizations, occupation, formal education, race, ethnicity, and gender (Rich, 1992). The social class system in the United States is usually described in five groups: upper class, upper middle class, lower middle class, working class, and lower class. Among other things the distinctions between these groups relate to level of income, wealth, and status. Socioeconomic status affects school achievement and completion more than any other variable (Conger, Conger, & Elder, 1997). Coleman et al. (1966) documented the relationship in his report *Equality of Educational Opportunity* by recognizing the educational and social class background of the family as the most important variable in the difference in test scores. The educational and social class background of the other children in the school was the second most important variable. This study has been criticized as flawed, but the conclusions about the importance of students' families and backgrounds of peers have been supported in other research (Jencks et al. 1979; Ballantine, 1997; Brooks-Gunn, Klebanov, Liaw, & Duncan, 1995).

In *Kids Count Data Book* the Annie E. Casey Foundation (2000) reports that about 9.2 million children live in families overwhelmed by factors such as a lack of education and employment experience, single parenthood, and welfare dependency. This report suggests that many of the poorest families struggle to survive in communities that often contribute to the distress of poverty rather than lessen its effects. Those communities lack public resources and economic investment and are maintained by political powers that sometimes keep the families isolated. The families do not have cars to get to work, phones to link with family and neighbors, or computers to navigate the information superhighway. This disconnection from economic opportunity, distance from social supports, and separation from services and institutions perpetuates the day-to-day difficulties of the families, difficulties that affect the schooling of the children.

The seventh-grade students live in a disconnected neighborhood. Financial resources are scarce and families are isolated. Conditions of poverty are common. Currently no one in Theresa's family is working. Lucia's mother is a single parent who has two jobs as she tries to support her three children and aging mother. Jacky lives with her brother who has recently lost his manufacturing job.

Ms. Roccone has learned about the resources available in her community to assist families in need. When possible, she helps connect families with the assistance available from federal, state, and local governments; churches and civic groups; and other organizations dedicated to providing assistance to those in need. She maintains a contact list of people in the various agencies and groups so that she can refer families directly, rather than to impersonal voice mail systems. The types of support services on her list include those related to short- and long-term unemployment; job training programs and educational opportunities for nontraditional students; local employers; aid for families with dependent children and other social services; medical and legal services; mental health agencies; housing; emergency food, shelter, and clothing; domestic violence shelters; day care and after-school care facilities; churches; and the Salvation Army and other charitable organizations that operate in the Warm Springs community. Getting to know the families and circumstances of the targeted girls allows Ms. Roccone to connect them with the appropriate community resources. Her practice demonstrates a school counselor acting on the recommendation of other child advocates. For example, the Casey Foundation contends that helping families in poverty connect to resources will alleviate the plight of the poorest neighborhoods as well as the educational opportunities for the children.

Difficulty in Performing

Other children who have barriers to success are those who have difficulty performing everyday activities, such as communicating, moving, or taking care of themselves, or who have learning difficulties. These difficulties include specific learning disabilities, speech or language impairments, mental retardation, serious emotional disturbance, hearing impairments, orthopedic impairments, other health impairments, visual impairments, autism, and multiple disabilities. In *America's Children: Key National Indicators of Well-Being,* the Federal Interagency Forum on Child and Family Statistics (1999) reports that 12.3 percent of noninstitutionalized children ages 5 to 17 have some of these problems. During the 1998–1999 school year children ages 6 to 21 served under the Individuals with Disabilities Act numbered more than 5.5 million (Office of Special Education Programs [OSEP], 2000). Within this group 16 percent of boys have difficulty in at least one area compared with 9 percent of girls. Children in families with lower socioeconomic status are more likely to have difficulty. African American and Latino students are more likely to be categorized as mildly mentally retarded and as having emotional/behavior disorders, and a disproportionate percentage of Latinos students are in special education programs for students with speech and language problems (Banks, 2000; Artiles & Trent, 1994).

In 1997–1998, only 25.5 percent of students with disabilities who were 17 and older graduated from high school with a standard diploma. Those graduation rates for students with disabilities vary by type of disability. Those least likely to graduate were students with mental retardation, multiple disabilities, and autism. The percentage of students with disabilities graduating also varies by state and ranges from a low of 6.8 to a high of 45.4 (OSEP, 2000). In one study only 56 percent of high school dropouts who had learning disabilities were employed (Sitlington & Frank, 1993).

Parette and Hourcade (1995) identify three types of barriers against people with disabilities: physical barriers, policy and procedural barriers, and attitudinal barriers. They outline strategies for school counselors to eliminate those difficulties. Glenn (1998) edited a special issue of *Professional School Counseling* that provides many options for counselors as they work with children and adolescents with disabilities.

Ms. Roccone wonders if Theresa and Lucia may have been overlooked for assessment of learning problems. After investigating their records she found that both have gaps between their achievement test scores and their ability test scores, strong predictors of learning difficulties. Ms. Roccone will gather more information herself, confer with their teachers and parents, and then decide whether further assessment is needed.

STRATEGIES

To respond to the many conditions and circumstances that related to low academic performance, researchers and educators are constantly seeking solutions for those students negatively affected by these conditions. For example, Zeichner (1995) summarizes key elements that enable all students to achieve high standards:

- High expectations for all students
- Cultural congruence in instruction
- Teacher knowledge and respect for cultural traditions
- Teaching strategies that promote meaningful participation

Johnson (1996) reports that those four elements are not independently sufficient to overcome the gaps in achievement among groups of children. Societal, economic, and technological differences in access, allocation, and attitudes also affect learning. Teachers need training in how to address cultural backgrounds, clarity about the appropriate standards for children, opportunities to reflect on classroom practices, and time to incorporate what they learn.

The U.S. Department of Education (1991) outlined suggestions for school counselors in ensuring equal educational opportunity. Those ideas include counselors doing the following:

- Notify students and parents of their protections under the civil rights laws.
- Analyze course enrollment data to identify disproportionate enrollment of minorities, women, and students with handicaps.
- Identify discriminatory practices in existing counseling program policies and procedures.
- Establish goals, objectives, and action steps in school district counseling plans in response to identified career needs of minorities, women, and students with handicaps.
- Implement ongoing career counseling programs to meet students' needs.
- Ensure effective communication with students who have limited English proficiency and who have handicaps.
- Provide support for teachers, parents, and students through counseling and consultation.
- Assist students in job search skills.
- Review counseling materials for stereotypes.
- Identify role models of minorities, women, and people with handicaps who are in occupations in which they are traditionally underrepresented.
- Coordinate counseling activities with other school, community, and agency resources and activities.
- Support the establishment of an equity advisory council to obtain assistance in implementing nondiscriminatory counseling services (p. 6–7)

These guidelines provide Ms. Roccone with a checklist of specific strategies for guiding her efforts in equal educational opportunities. She may also refer to Johnson (1996) as a resource to guide her and Warm Springs School in ways to measure equality in the school.

> Design a series of information sessions for teachers on barriers to learning. Determine the categories you would include, the school data you would need for illustrating the concepts, and the practices you would want teachers to incorporate into their classes.

> Compile a checklist of strategies based on the list provided above. Include a specific action to illustrate each strategy.

SUMMARY

Ms. Roccone and Mr. Truman have gathered data about several student groups in their school and have already begun to review related information about strategies for change as well as to generate ideas about specific interventions they could use with the girls Ms. Roccone targeted for intervention this school year. The influences of family, peers, socioeconomic status, and gender are considered carefully in terms of the overall school climate and curriculum. Any interventions or plans initiated will be based on the collaborative efforts of counselors, teachers, other school personnel, and community resources.

PORTFOLIO COMPONENTS

1. Complete a profile of a school that describes the organizational structure, school climate, and equity standards and strategies.
2. Develop a form for monitoring the academic achievement of a group of students—for example, those who receive free lunch, those who live in particular neighborhoods, and so on.
3. Explain ways you will assess barriers to learning in a school.

Comprehensive School Counseling Programs: Planning, Implementation, Evaluation

═══════════════════════ **CASE STUDY** ═══════════════════════

MS. WEST'S FIRST SCHOOL COUNSELING JOB

Ms. Martha West recently accepted a school counseling position to work in a suburban school system in the southeast. The school to which she was assigned, Kingston Court Elementary (KCE), serves approximately 900 students in grades three through five. The staff includes 40 classroom teachers, 5 teachers of students with special needs, 3 administrators, 2 counselors, a nurse, an attendance officer, a sheriff's deputy, a registrar, an attendance clerk, 3 secretaries, 5 cafeteria workers, 4 custodial staff, and 9 bus drivers. The school counselor Ms. West replaced retired with 12 years of service at KCE. Her colleague, Ms. Nancy Jones, has been at KCE for 10 years. When Ms. West interviewed with the principal of KCE, she was told that the school counselors are involved in conflict-resolution programs and in prevention programs aimed at reducing school violence and preventing substance abuse. They are also in charge of the crisis response and student assistance teams.

Ms. Jones was oriented Ms. West to her new position. Each grade level includes 12 sections and is divided into two teams of six teachers each, their students, and students' parents. Ms. Jones is responsible for the all of the teams in grade three and one of the teams in grade four. Ms. West is responsible for the other grade four team and all of grade five teams. Ms. Jones emphasized the following responsibilities: scheduling all parent conferences, chairing meetings related to serving low-achieving students and students with special education needs, calling the parents of students with excessive absences, gathering homework assignments and instructional materials for students who are absent due to illness, providing individual counseling services for members of their teams, and determining the appropriate academic placement for new students.

Ms. West asked to see the school counseling programs' mission statement and program goals, the role statement for the school counselor, data from the most recent needs assessment, and a copy of the most recent program evaluation. Ms. West was informed that counselors at KCE had traditionally responded to individual student needs as they arose. Further, KCE had no "formal" role statement for the school counselor, nor was there needs assessment data available. The recently retired counselor had been intending to write up their program goals, but simply had not found the time to do so before she retired. Ms. Jones states, "There are a lot of needs in this school that go unmet. When I came here 10 years ago, I was enthusiastic about adding preventive activities, but the program and counselor were both well established and well liked. I basically stepped into an existing role that eventually came to fit."

Ms. West left the school after her orientation feeling confused and challenged. She had expected to walk into a well-established developmental comprehensive program with specific goals and objectives articulated. Instead, she found a loosely organized set of services aimed primarily at remediation.

What constitutes an effective school counseling program? Borders and Drury (1992) reviewed the counseling models appearing in the school counseling literature over the past few decades. They found that effective guidance and counseling models were

1. Independent education programs; comprehensive, purposeful, sequential, and guided, in part, by outcomes.
2. Integral to the primary educational mission of schools; that is, they support, facilitate, and encourage classroom instruction and student achievement.
3. Established with developmental theory and research in mind.
4. Designed to serve all students in an unbiased way.

Henderson (1996) further characterizes effective guidance programs as those that include a curriculum designed and organized to teach students basic life skills and provide guidance to students as they establish educational and career goals.

We believe that the best way to introduce a comprehensive school counseling program is to invite you to read the position statement developed by the American School Counselor Association (2000), following. This statement provides an excellent framework for understanding the foundation and components of programs, the school counselor's role within the program, and how the program contributes to the overall educational mission. We hope you will refer to the mission statement frequently as you read about the nuts and bolts of program planning and implementation.

The Professional School Counselor and Comprehensive School Counseling Programs
(Adopted 1988; revised 1993, 1997)

The American School Counselor Association (ASCA) Position

ASCA endorses comprehensive school counseling programs that promote and enhance student learning. The program's focus is on the three broad and interrelated areas of student development: academic, career and personal/social development. Each encompasses a variety of desired student learning competencies, which forms the foundation of the developmental school counseling program. The professional school counselor uses a variety of activities and resources to promote the desired student development. Professional school counselor responsibilities include organization, implementation and coordination of the program.

The Rationale

A comprehensive school counseling program is developmental in nature. It is systematic, sequential, clearly defined and accountable. The program's foundation is developmental psychology, educational philosophy, and counseling methodology. Proactive and preventive in focus, the school counseling program is integral to the educational program. It assists students in acquiring and using lifelong skills through the development of academic, career, self-awareness and interpersonal communication skills. The goal of the comprehensive school counseling program is to provide all students with life success skills.

The school counseling program has characteristics similar to other educational programs, including a scope and sequence, student competencies or outcomes, activities and processes to assist students in achieving the outcomes, professionally credentialed personnel, materials and resources and national standards for evaluation.

We recognize that our educational system is being challenged by the increasing needs of today's students and society's rising expectations. Many of our children enter school with emotional, physical and interpersonal barriers to learning. Although comprehensive school counseling programs include necessary crisis-oriented responsive services, the emphasis is on the developmental skill building for all students beginning when students enter school and continuing as they progress through the grades.

Effective school counseling programs are a collaborative effort between the counselor and other educators to create an environment promoting school success. Staff and counselors value and respond to the diversity and individual differences in our societies and communities. Comprehensive school counseling programs help ensure equal opportunities for all students to participate fully in the educational process.

This counseling model is compatible with the National Education Goals and the National Standards for School Counseling Programs.

The Professional School Counselor's Role

Within a comprehensive school counseling program, professional school counselors will focus their skills, time and energy on direct service to students, staff and families. ASCA recommends a realistic counselor-student ratio to be 1:250. Professional school counselors will spend 70 percent of their time in direct service to students. Indirect services include counseling program planning, maintenance and evaluation; participation in school site planning and implementation; partnerships and alliances with postsecondary institutions, businesses and community agencies; and other tasks enhancing the program's mission.

The comprehensive school counseling program balances many components. It requires counselors to deliver individual and small-group counseling and large-group guidance; to teach skill development in academic, career and personal/social areas; to provide consultation and case management; and coordinate, manage and evaluate the school counseling program.

As student advocates, professional school counselors participate as members of the educational team. They consult and collaborate with teachers, administrators and families to help students be successful academically, vocationally and personally. Professional school counselors are indispensable partners with the instructional staff in the development of contributing members of society. They ensure, on behalf of students and their families, that all school programs facilitate the educational process and offer the opportunity for school success.

Summary

A written, comprehensive developmental and career K–12 guidance curriculum should be implemented in every school district. It should include a systematic and planned program delivery that productively involves all students and promotes and enhances the learning process. The comprehensive school counseling program facilitates student development in three areas:

- academic development, which includes the acquisition of skills, attitudes and knowledge contributing to effective learning in school throughout the lifespan.

- career development, which includes the foundation for the acquisition of skills, attitudes, and knowledge enabling students to make a successful transition from schools to careers.

- personal/social development, which includes the acquisition of skills, attitudes and knowledge to help students understand and respect self and others, acquire effective interpersonal skills, understand and practice safety and survival skills and develop into contributing members of society.

The comprehensive school counseling program should be supported by appropriate resources and implemented and coordinated by credential professional school counselor.

Source: American School Counselor Association www.schoolcounselor.org

After reading and discussing this chapter, you should be able to

- Identify the essential elements of planning and implementing a successful school counseling program.
- Explain the importance of a strong infrastructure to the development of a comprehensive, developmental school counseling program.
- Identify appropriate methods to collect and use local data from a variety of sources to design, implement, and evaluate a comprehensive, developmental school counseling program.
- Describe the process of formulating program goals and objectives.
- Explain how program goals and objectives are evaluated.

Assume that you are an administrator at KCE. Before you read or react to any presentation, what concerns would you have if someone came to you asking for support for a new or revised counseling program? Assume you are a parent of a student at KCE. What would be your concerns? If possible, imagine you were a student and determine what you would question about a new program. List the likely questions each of these groups may have about a counseling program. As you read the following process determine how your identified questions may or may not be addressed within the program plan.

SCHOOL COUNSELING AS AN INTEGRAL PART OF THE KCE MISSION

Currently, the school counseling program at KCE consists of services delivered on demand bearing little resemblance to the program described in the role statement by ASCA (see Appendix A). Professional school counselors are charged in their ethical standards (see Appendix C, Standard D1c) to notify appropriate people of conditions that limit the counselor in providing effective programs and services (ASCA, 2000). Ms. West recognizes that the situation at KCE restricts the potential of counseling in that setting. To revise the current program into one that is comprehensive and developmental, Ms. West needs to step away from her confusion and take a broader view. That is, she must be able to see how counseling fits into the larger system (KCE). VanZandt and Hayslip (1994) define a system as "a structure whose orderly whole comprises integral parts (subsystems) that function together to accomplish a specific mission" (p. 15). Each school typically has a unique mission statement to guide the development and evaluation of school-related programs. Take a moment to examine the mission statement for KCE. KCE, in this instance, is the "orderly whole" of which the counseling program is an "integral part." This means that the counseling program exists to contribute to, or facilitate the mission of, KCE and is only successful to the extent that it does so. The mission that drives the school's educational enterprise also drives the school counseling program, or as the ethical standards (see Appendix C, Standard D1a) explains, the professional school counselor "supports and protects the educational program against any infringement not in the best interests of counselees" (ASCA, 2000).

Kingston Court Elementary School Mission Statement

The mission of Kingston Court Elementary is to provide a safe, respectful environment where all students have equal access to the human and technological resources needed for academic success. Further, Kingston Court Elementary promotes the development of skills needed to become productive citizens, lifelong learners, and responsible members of a diverse community.

Building any type of program requires determining and describing what is to be achieved as well as what is necessary to produce the desired results, and then checking to see if what was planned has been accomplished. Therefore, planning a comprehensive developmental program involves a number of steps and many people. The planning must take place in the broader system or context in which it is to be implemented and must include careful consideration of local, regional, and national initiatives to reform or improve education. Additionally, all of the school constituents served by the program must be invested in its development and success. The program planners must be able to project into the future and identify what students should be able to do as a result of participating in a school counseling program (Dahir, Sheldon, & Valiga, 1998). Dahir and colleagues articulate a five-phase process of program development: discussion, awareness, design, implementation, and evaluation. In their book, *Vision Into Action* (1998), they develop each phase fully and include planning forms and suggested activities to help school counselors plan and implement programs. However, before we move into a discussion of the five phases, a brief discussion of the process of change is necessary.

Ms. West will probably experience more difficulty in revising a well-established, if incomplete, program than she would if hired to create a program for a new school. Peter Senge (1999) states that most change initiatives fail. Why? The initiatives do not produce the desired results. Additionally, many change initiatives are imposed on educators from powerful external sources (e.g., governors, state education leaders, federal committees) and overlook the need to gain the commitment of all constituent groups necessary for long-term, systemic change. Educators who have been working for 10 to 20 years have seen many change initiatives intended to "fix" the broken educational system in America. Based on their experiences, some educators may have developed a cynical attitude regarding such reforms and are reluctant to encourage other efforts, even those initiated locally.

The school counselor and his or her constituents must be aware that change is ongoing and that every program must grow and change to make a viable contribution to the school's mission (Dahir et al., 1998). To provide leadership for this change, the school counselor must understand the tensions between growth processes, those that enable an organization to change, and limiting processes, those that tend to impede or stop growth (Senge, 1999). In the discussion that follows, consider the counselor's leadership role in facilitating change throughout each of the five phases of program development, including identifying and addressing the limiting processes or barriers to change.

Effective programs are carefully conceptualized, planned, implemented, and evaluated. We will follow Ms. West and her team through this process to illustrate how this can be accomplished. Ms. West will be guided by her ethical understanding (see Appendix C, Standard D1e) that the school counselor "assists in the development of (1) curricular and environmental conditions appropriate for the school and community, (2) educational procedures and programs to meet the counselee's developmental needs and (3) a systematic evaluation process" (ASCA, 2000).

THE PROCESS OF PROGRAM DEVELOPMENT

Phase 1: Discussion

The purpose of this phase is to reach consensus about the purpose of and vision for the school counseling program. Ms. West is entering a well-established system as a new employee at Kingston Court Elementary School. Currently, she is discouraged by the state of the counseling program and overwhelmed by the challenge ahead of her. She needs to recognize that the responsibility for a comprehensive program is not hers alone. She is part of an educational team, of which all members have as their common goal to promote the academic success of students. A basic principle when initiating change is that the rationale for change must be clearly communicated to all those who are involved. People affected in the change process should be involved in designing the changes, thus encouraging their support. Consequently, her first step is to form a leadership team to review and discuss the current program and to provide direction regarding its revision and implementation.

The leadership team should be diverse and represent the total school community. Faculty and student representation should include persons from all grade levels; parent and community members should represent all geographical areas and socioeconomic levels; all social, cultural, and ethnic groups should be represented; and the business community should be represented (Blum, 1998). Ms. Jones should be an integral part of the team, providing valuable information about past efforts, key constituents, and community insights.

The leadership group has two early tasks. Following the suggestions of Blum (1998) the group begins by specifying its purpose, terms of membership, and criteria for appointment to the group, and by adopting an operating procedure with regard to meetings, agendas, and selection of officers. An action plan with time lines for completing the necessary tasks helps the team accomplish its purpose (Basham, Appleton, & Dykeman, 2000). Drawing on her skill as a group facilitator, Ms. West continually encourages the interactions of the group aimed at accomplishing their goals. Once decisions about how the team is to operate have been determined, the group can begin to address the reasons for a counseling program at KCE. As the team identifies the values that are the foundation of the program, the group should draft a brief mission or vision statement for the counseling program that is consistent

Whom do you believe should be represented on Ms. West's leadership team? What process would you use for selection—nominations, volunteers, or invitations? What are the advantages and disadvantages of each type of selection?

What steps could Ms. West take to ensure that Ms. Jones feels included and does not feel personally or professionally diminished by the change initiatives Ms. West wishes to facilitate?

Divide into small groups and assume the roles of persons serving on a school counseling leadership team. Develop a mission statement for the counseling program to serve as a guide for program planning and implementation. Begin with, "As a result of participating in the school counseling program at Kingston Court Elementary School, students will be able to. . . ."

with the mission of the school. Blum suggests that the mission statement contain a clear rationale for including guidance and counseling as an integral part of the instructional program, be reflective of the entire school community, and specify goals and objectives for the counseling and guidance program. Therefore the mission statement will include who is being targeted, what is to be accomplished, and what are the expected outcomes as well as the significance of this mission.

At this stage, Ms. West and Ms. Jones need to identify the potential limiting processes that could impede the work of the team as well as the strengths of the group that will help contribute to success. Some of the common reasons for resistance to a team are previous negative experiences, the activity being perceived as a waste of time, and not accepting the team's purpose (Basham et al., 2000). One of the most frequently cited barriers to change is the time required to plan. How do persons who are extremely busy "doing" incorporate time for "visualizing" into their workdays? Integrating initiatives, scheduling time for focus and concentration, building capabilities for eliminating busywork, and saying "no" to nonessential demands are some ways to respond to the barrier of insufficient time (Senge, 1999). Another potential limiting factor in the discussion phase is relevance. Team members may ask, "How does what we are doing here relate to me and my role in the education and development of students at KCE?" Spending time within the leadership group discussing these barriers and how they compare to the potential positive outcomes of program planning will hopefully lead to greater commitment to the team goals.

Phase 2: Awareness

The purpose of this phase is to reach a mutual understanding of what needs to be done to achieve the vision articulated in phase one. Creating awareness generally involves multiple steps to develop a full understanding of the students, their families, and the social and economic conditions they face. Steps include reviewing existing documents and standards related to school counseling programs as well as examining local data about the community, the school, and the students. The questions that guide the team in this step are: Who are our students? What are their needs? What are the best means of meeting these needs? At this stage the leadership group develops a thorough description of the student body, the school setting, and the community in which it exists.

Information gleaned from student files such as patterns of student placements, academic successes and failures, and course taking, as well as the number and types of discipline referrals will aid in understanding the students' needs. Other important information includes

- Rates of absenteeism for students who may be considered at risk for academic failure.
- Dropout rates for those schools attended by KCE graduates.
- Numbers of children receiving free and reduced-price lunches.
- Standardized test scores for students at KCE.
- Follow-up studies of graduates and dropouts.

In addition to existing documents, other local data may prove helpful in identifying the needs of students at Kingston Court Elementary School. Community demographics provide useful information. Specifically the following local data may be used to identify needs and strengths within the school community:

- Unemployment in the community
- Estimated numbers of children living in poverty
- Juvenile crime rates
- The rate of births to teenagers
- Approximate number of foster families
- Divorce rates in the community
- Racial and ethnic composition of the community
- Major sites of employment for KCE parents

These data need to be reviewed with some regularity as the needs of the school community change in response to employment opportunities, population shifts, and other environmental conditions. Based on the careful and complete review of available information, a report detailing the specific needs of the school community is generated. Careful attention is given to school and community demographic data. These data will be used throughout as a checkpoint to ensure that all plans are inclusive and culturally relevant.

A comprehensive needs assessment strategy forms the foundation for program design and makes it possible to set priorities, establish program goals and objectives, select guidance activities, and schedule the counselor's time (Blum, 1998). According to Anderson and Reiter (1995), the guiding question for this assessment is: How are students different as a result of the guidance program? Therefore, the leadership team might begin by examining existing documents such as school policy and procedure manuals; local, state, and national standards for school counseling programs; and other materials that would help determine the areas to be included in their plan. Even though the local school and school district appear not to have formalized plans for comprehensive developmental school counseling programs, the state department of education may have an approved plan. In fact, Sink and MacDonald (1998) found that 24 states have statewide plans for counseling programs with 17 additional states either developing a state plan or encouraging individual districts to create programs. Consequently, reviewing the minimum standards for school counseling programs established by the state may help Ms. West and Ms. Jones identify components to be included in the local plan and also provide further support for the necessity of articulating a plan. The ASCA *National Standards for School Counseling Programs* (Dahir et al., 1998; Appendix B) specifies student competencies in academic, career, and personal/social development across all grade levels. The leadership team may examine the current program to ascertain the extent to which these competencies are being realized for KCE students.

Once the relevant documents and existing local data have been reviewed, the leadership team can determine what additional information is needed from students, teachers, parents, and administrators to have a comprehensive picture of the current status of students' needs. The information solicited from these groups, usually by survey methods, is intended to help identify the content and priorities of the program, and questions should be directed toward that goal (VanZandt & Hayslip, 2001a). The leadership team must decide whether to administer the survey to all students, parents, and teachers or to do a random sample of each of these groups.

> List the information above for an elementary school you attended. Add any other information you consider relevant for understanding that setting. Compare your description to those of your classmates. By comparing all descriptions, create a matrix of the information that seems to be most important in planning to meet student needs.

Item type and content should be appropriate for the subjects who are asked to respond. Items for a second-grade student will obviously be stated differently from those directed to fifth graders. Additionally, items should be free of educational and counseling-specific vocabulary. Blum (1998) suggests limiting the number of questions to one page and including objective multiple-choice items as well as opened-ended items about the overall school climate for learning. Some surveys are composed entirely of topics to be prioritized by those responding (cf. VanZandt & Hayslip, 1994, 2001a). Items for the survey are generated from a variety of sources, including the information gathered about the school and surrounding community and the school counselor's knowledge about student needs at various developmental stages. For example, if local data indicate that the rates of divorce and remarriage in the community are high, items on the survey related to family disruption are warranted. Based on survey responses to related items, counselors have a better idea about whether to include some program content about family issues such as divorce, single-parent homes, and stepfamilies. The ethical standards from ASCA (2000) state that school counselors are responsible both to the school and to the community in determining and promoting the counselor's role and function in meeting the needs of those served (see Appendix C, Standard D1c). Thus identifying the needs in the ways mentioned previously and using that information to design a counseling program is an ethical imperative.

Much of the data compiled to facilitate awareness also serves to address one of the principal limitations to change, the question of relevance. Establishing the school counseling program as integral to achieving the overall KCE mission and identifying and using data such as those described above can be very influential in demonstrating the relevance of a school counseling program to all persons on the leadership team and to others who will be affected by the school counseling program.

Working in small groups develop a one-page survey instrument suitable for fourth graders to identify types of small groups they feel would be beneficial and in which they would like to participate during the coming academic year. How would the local data already reviewed inform decisions about the types of groups you include on the selection list? How would consideration of the student competencies identified in the National Standards for School Counseling Programs *(ASCA, 2000) influence these decisions?*

Phase 3: Design

Assuming you have gathered and analyzed the various types of data described in the awareness phase, you are now ready to begin designing a school counseling program. Part of the design process involves identifying a model that will enable you to organize and implement the goals of your program. We will provide a brief overview of two popular models. Norman Gysbers and Patricia Henderson (2000) articulate a Comprehensive Guidance Program Model, and Robert Myrick (1997) discusses his "practical approach" to Developmental Guidance and Counseling.

THE COMPREHENSIVE GUIDANCE PROGRAM MODEL

The testing, refinement, and implementation of the Comprehensive Guidance Program Model, also known as the Missouri model, started in 1971 under the direction of Norm Gysbers and his associates at the University of Missouri—Columbia. The majority of the 24 guidance programs identified by Sink and MacDonald (1998) were adapted from the structure of this model. Gysbers and Henderson (2000) describe an organizational schema with well-defined procedures and systems. Life career development is the base of the model, and the three domains of self-knowledge and interpersonal skills; life roles, settings, and events; and life career planning are emphasized. Those are defined as follows:

- **Self-knowledge and interpersonal skills.** Students develop awareness and acceptance of themselves and others, incorporate personal skills for health maintenance, assume responsibility for their decisions, develop and maintain effective relationships, and engage with others.
- **Life roles, settings, and events.** Students develop and incorporate practices that lead to effective learning, responsible daily living, and a purpose in life; they recognize the interactive effects of various life roles.
- **Life career planning.** Students understand and use a decision-making process in determining their life goals.

The Comprehensive Guidance Program Model offers three elements and four components. The elements include the content of the program, the organizational framework, and resources. The content includes student competencies. The organization framework has three structural components (definition, assumptions, and rationale) and four program components (guidance curriculum, individual planning, responsive services, and system support). The resource element incorporates the human, financial, and political requirements for implementing the program. A counseling program, according to this model, has components that incorporate activities and roles and responsibilities of all involved in the counseling program. Some examples are listed and defined below:

- **Guidance curriculum:** classroom activities, school-wide activities
- **Individual planning:** appraisal, advisement, placement follow-up
- **Responsive services:** consultation, personal counseling, crisis counseling, referral
- **System support:** research and development, professional development, staff/community public relations, community outreach, program management

An example from the state of Alabama (Table 3.1) illustrates an adaptation of this model. In conclusion, this model presents a complete framework that can easily be adapted for each school. It has comprehensive lists of procedures and a recommended process for change. It may be considered a template from which to start a discussion of a site- or system-specific model.

DEVELOPMENTAL GUIDANCE AND COUNSELING

Robert D. Myrick's (Myrick, 1997; Gonzalez & Myrick, 2000) program also includes procedures and specific recommendations. Myrick suggests six basic counselor interventions for a counseling program: individual counseling (4 to 6 cases); small-group counseling (4 to 6 groups, seen twice a week); large-group guidance (2 to 4 classrooms, once or twice a week); peer facilitator training (1 to 2 hours a week); consultation with teachers and parents (1 hour a day); and coordination of guidance activities.

A real strength of this model is in a process for including teachers specifically in the counseling curriculum. The teacher advisor program (TAP) is based on the assumption that each student needs a friendly adult in the school (Gonzales & Myrick, 2000). This adult knows and cares about the student in a personal way, helping the student advisee with problems of developing and with maximizing the

TABLE 3.1 State of Alabama: Four Components of a Comprehensive School Counseling and Guidance Program

Guidance Curriculum	Individual Planning	Responsive Services	System Support
Provides guidance content in a systematic way to all students K–12	Assists students in planning, monitoring, and managing their personal and career planning	Addresses the immediate concerns of students	Includes program, staff, and school support activities and services
Purpose			
Student awareness, skill development, and application of skills needed in everyday life	Student educational and occupational planning, decision making, and goal setting	Prevention and intervention	Program delivery and support
Areas Addressed			
Educational	*Educational*	*Educational*	*Educational*
Motivation to achieve Decision making Goal setting Planning Problem-solving skills	Acquisition of study skills Awareness of educational opportunities Appropriate course selection Lifelong learning Utilization of test data	Academic concerns Physical abuse Sexual abuse Emotional abuse Grief, loss, and death Substance abuse Family issues Sexuality issues Coping with stress Relationship concerns School-related concerns: tardiness, absences and truancy, misbehavior, school avoidance, dropout prevention	Guidance program development Parent education Teacher and administrator consultation Staff development for educators School improvement planning Counselor professional development Research and publishing Community outreach Public relations
Career	*Career*		
Awareness of educational opportunities Knowledge of career opportunities Knowledge of vocational and technical training	Knowledge of career opportunities Knowledge of vocational and technical training Need for positive work habits		
Knowledge of self and others	*Knowledge of self and others*		
Self-esteem development Interpersonal effectiveness Communication skills Cross-cultural effectiveness Responsible behavior	Development of healthy self-concepts Development of adaptive and adjustive social behavior		
Counselor Role			
Structured groups Consultation Guidance curriculum implementation	Assessment Planning Placement	Individual counseling Small-group counseling Consultation Referral	Program development and management Consultation Coordination

Alabama State Department of Education (1996). *The revised comprehensive counseling and guidance model for Alabama's public schools.* Bulletin 1966, No. 27. Montgomery, AL: Author. Reprinted by permission.

school experience. The program is designed so that every student in the school belongs to a small group of 15 to 25 peers that meets regularly. Teachers hold these meetings in a homeroom or home base and help students explore their personal interests, goals, and concerns. Teachers thus help deliver the counseling curriculum in these small groups.

To accomplish this, teachers receive training in leading group discussions and in planning guidance units. School counselors not only help teachers in developing the units, but also serve as members of a curriculum team. Counselors may help establish guidance objectives and provide activities that teachers may select or discard according to their needs. This design allows teachers to be more directly involved in the personal development of their students.

Myrick also emphasizes peer helping programs as an intervention. Students who participate in peer programs as helpers and as helpees may gain in productive behavior, attitudes toward school, self-esteem, and report card grades (Campbell, 2000). Other members of the school community also benefit from peer helping programs. Professional school counselors train and coordinate the peer facilitator programs and projects. The focus for peer helper training is in interpersonal and communication skills. According to Campbell systemic training is the most critical variable in the effectiveness of peer programs. Other training needs are determined by the specific skills needed in individual projects, which evolve from the needs of the schools. After the needs are assessed, the projects can be developed to address them. Examples of peer helper projects involve students serving as buddies for newcomers, mediators of disputes, presenters of college preparation seminars, and academic supporters (Campbell, 2000).

Myrick (1997) also provides a reminder for counselors about four approaches to working that need to be incorporated into a developmental program: crisis, remedial, preventive, and developmental. Crisis interventions are inevitable in the counseling office. Counselors may respond to crises by acting as mediators, as listeners, as calm centers, and in other ways to lessen the intensity during the critical time. The remedial approach focuses on identifiable problems with a suggested or applied remedy emphasizing learning or relearning skills that have not developed as expected. Another way to approach problems is attempting to prevent them from happening. These preventive interventions are focused on lessening the possibilities of such problem behaviors as delinquency, absenteeism, substance abuse, and others. Finally, through the developmental approach counselors identify competencies students need to have to be successful and then provide opportunities for those skills to develop. As Ms. West and the leadership team design their school counseling program, these four types of interventions need consideration.

Search the Web for information related to peer helper/facilitator programs currently used in schools. Locate the National Peer Helper Association Web site and review information about training peer helpers at various grade levels.

The leadership team has now deliberated about the mission of the program. The group has carefully considered student and community needs. Different program models have been studied. The team can now begin the task of more specification by integrating the team's vision with the needs of the school to create a responsive and effective counseling program, including the services and activities one might incorporate into the program to support the competencies prioritized by the leadership team (Dahir et al., 1998). Broad student competencies are translated into goals and objectives for students at each grade level.

The school counselor must identify through what strategies or activities the competency will be addressed. Individual and group counseling, classroom guidance activities, peer mediation programs, special events, consultation, and peer facilitation programs are but a few of the mechanisms in the counselor's repertoire for addressing the competencies in academic, career, and personal/social domains. Information from school counseling outcome research helps to determine strategies that have a higher likelihood of success. For instance, interventions on career planning have received positive outcomes with students who have a range of exceptionalities such as being gifted or learning disabled or minority status. Instructing parents in ways to help students with career decisions has also been tested positively. Group interventions, particularly at the elementary level, have also received strong empirical support (Whiston & Sexton, 1998). A well-planned program will delineate these possibilities as well as a monitoring system for deciding which activities are working more effectively.

> Form two work groups. Each group should choose and read more about one of the models presented here. Come to the next class prepared to "sell" your model to the other group. After this discussion, design a model that would incorporate the strengths of both.

Phase 4: Implementation

Once the leadership team is satisfied with the program design, implementation can begin. To fully implement the plan, one needs to answer the questions who will do what, when, and how (Dahir et al., 1998). To complete the implementation plan, the leadership team may proceed by setting and prioritizing goals, assigning responsibilities, and scheduling services. Eventually an annual plan of goals, objectives, and services will be created. Based on the previously identified needs, the leadership team will set priorities that influence the scheduling of activities. That prioritization may occur according to the level of intervention at which the need will be based—crisis, remediation, prevention, and/or developmental. The planning group will also consider time-management concerns, the scope and immediacy of the needs, and the school instructional program. Dahir and colleages propose that one also consider carefully the implementation time line to complement the existing school calendar.

With the priorities agreed upon, the leadership team turns to specifying the content and form of the goals. That specification determines the services and activities identified for accomplishing each goal. As different activities are identified the team needs to recognize the different learning styles and needs of the student population. Therefore strategies should include a variety of possible activities for accomplishing the goal. Providing activities for auditory, visual, and kinesthetic learners is an inclusive way to approach this task. Next the team attempts to establish who will be responsible for addressing each goal. Finally a schedule is designed for the implementation of the program. The following has been modified from Schmidt (1999) and illustrates these steps.

> Brainstorm ways the KCE school counseling program may address the student competency of applying decision-making skills to career planning. Follow the steps of setting and prioritizing goals and objectives, determining activities, assigning responsibilities, and scheduling services. Then, using a school calendar, chart multiple interventions for addressing elementary school students learning about career decision making.

Competency: Students will acquire the attitudes, knowledge, and skills that contribute to effective learning in school across the lifespan.
Goal: Students will apply effective study skills.
Objective: Kindergarten students will:
   1. Describe the tools they need to do their work in school.

Strategies	Person Responsible	Student Outcome
Sing-a-song of school; complete a puzzle of school tools	Classroom teacher	By Oct. 1, each kindergartner will be able to name paper, pencil, ruler, books, crayons, and scissors as tools one needs to use in school.
Choices during classroom sessions, counselor-led game	Classroom teacher/ Counselor	By Nov. 1, each kindergartner will demonstrate appropriate use of the classroom tools identified above.

Source: From Schmidt, John J., Counseling in schools: Essential services and comprehensive programs, 3e; © 1999. Adapted by permission by Allyn & Bacon.

Phase 5: Evaluation

Although evaluation is discussed as the fifth and final phase of program development, in actuality it must be considered from the very beginning. Ethical standards (see Appendix C, Standard D1e) state that evaluation is a component of the school counselor's responsibility to the school and to the community. The evaluation guides in planning programs and services (ASCA, 2000). The purpose of the evaluation is to determine the extent to which program goals are being met and provide information that will lead to program improvement. Goals that are not clearly articulated in measurable, observable terms are difficult to monitor. However, if the program design incorporates student competencies, evaluation will be a fairly straightforward activity.

Evaluation can be used to assess the counseling program; to determine the effects of the program on students, teachers, and parents; to monitor the use of time; and to provide evidence of the value of the counseling program. In other words evaluation helps determine effectiveness, efficiency, and worth. Just as the other parts of the counseling program, this assessment needs to be integrated into the total school program. Questions to be answered through the evaluation include "What have our students achieved?" and "What did we do to help our students achieve?" Blum (1998) lists the following steps for the evaluation process:

- Assess the needs of students, parents, and teachers each year.
- Identify program goals and student competencies.
- Design the program to achieve the goals and learning objectives.
- Implement the program.
- Measure ongoing activities and assess progress toward goals.
- Maintain, modify, or discard program strategies and activities based on the results of these evaluation activities.

Two types of evaluation need to occur. Product or summative evaluation focuses on the effects of the program; specifically, what were the outcomes of our activities? This type of evaluation is concerned with identifying the new skills and attitudes that were learned as a result of the students' participation in this program. The types of information that can be collected for summative evaluation include the work

For five of the actions you listed to address the competency regarding career decision making, explain ways to evaluate the progress of the student. Use multiple sources (teachers, parents, administrators, peers) and multiple means (self-reports, case study, a product).

products of students resulting from participation in program activities; observations of student progress, skill development, and behavior by teachers, parents, administrators, and others in the school community; records of student achievement; student self-reports; needs assessment; and case studies.

Process or formative evaluation is used to estimate progress toward achieving goals during the implementation of the program rather than at the end. Process data is not necessary for every activity but should be focused on those in which intermediary feedback is needed (Baker, 2000). Counselors and teachers may survey participants at the end of each activity. They may also identify changes of participants along a continuum that leads to the overall goal. Having participants review the past session and/or activity can also be used to evaluate the progress being made. Another method would be to solicit feedback from teachers or parents about changes in behaviors or attitudes of student participants.

SUMMARY

Effective school counseling programs are comprehensive, purposeful, and focused on student competencies. These programs support the school mission, are designed to help all students, and are based on developmental theory. Professional school counselors lead program development by recognizing growth processes as well as limiting processes and by working with others in a five-phase process of discussion, awareness, design, implementation, and evaluation.

PORTFOLIO COMPONENTS

1. Reflect on an experience when you participated in an effort to effect change in an organization or system. How did you react emotionally? Behaviorally? Did your response lead to facilitation or blocking of change efforts? How might you use this experience to identify skills and behaviors you need to develop to become an agent of change?

2. Select one of the ASCA national standards in the career development area. For middle school students, develop a statement of competency, goal, and objective. Specify the activity, person responsible, and student outcome measure that you would use to determine whether the competency has been mastered.

3. Select one of the ASCA national standards in the personal/social development area. For high school students, develop a statement of competency, goal, and objective. Specify the activity, person responsible, and student outcome measure that you would use to determine whether the competency has been mastered.

C H A P T E R   4

The School Counselor as Program Coordinator

COORDINATING A SCHOOL COUNSELING PROGRAM: TURNING THE VISION INTO A REALITY

Mr. Larson and Ms. Fairley have been working together for 3 years at North Oneonta High School (NOHS) in central Alabama. Last year a new principal was hired who instructed them to transform their existing services-oriented program into a comprehensive developmental school counseling program that conformed to all state guidelines. They met with their school counseling leadership team throughout the academic year and completed phases one through three of the program planning process. Consequently, they have identified program priorities, adopted the Alabama state model as their program model, and incorporated the national standards into their program objectives.

They are eager to begin the transition and implement their new program in the fall. However, they are uncertain about how to manage the new program. They have decided to collaborate over the summer months to develop a management strategy for program coordination. They are especially interested in increasing their ability to manage time effectively, use more organizational strategies, and work more efficiently with volunteers and supervisees. They want to reduce or eliminate duplication of effort in program coordination. Finally, they want to streamline the administrative responsibilities associated with each program element, so that they can spend more time focused on implementing the priority goals and activities.

As we have already discussed, creating a comprehensive development program requires careful planning and design, involves the entire school community, and is based on identified student needs. Although, as we have emphasized, the integration of such a program into the total school curriculum requires the commitment of all program constituencies, responsibility for coordinating the program is that of the school counselor. According to the American School Counselors Association (1999a),

> Coordination is a leadership process in which the counselor helps organize, manage and evaluate the school counseling program. The counselor assists parents in obtaining needed services for their children through a referral and follow-up process and serves as liaison between the school and community agencies so that they may collaborate in efforts to help students. (p. 15)

The extent to which the counselor is an effective program coordinator or manager will determine, at least in some measure, the success of the program he or she coordinates. In this chapter, we will review the requirements for successful program coordination and provide practical strategies for managing the responsibilities associated with the school guidance and counseling program by assisting Mr. Larson and Ms. Fairley in their efforts to adopt a management strategy. Although these counselors are working in a secondary school, the principles of program coordination will be the same even though the specific tasks and allocation of time to each may vary.

After reading and discussing this chapter, you should be able to

- Develop a school counselor job description.
- Use an organizing framework to identify coordination responsibilities and time commitment.
- Identify the human, financial, and technological resources/skills needed to plan, implement, and evaluate a program.
- Establish procedures for prioritizing activities and managing a counseling office.
- Identify committees and programs that may be appropriately coordinated by school counselors.

For over three decades, coordination has been characterized as one of the three major counselor roles along with consultation and counseling (Myrick, 1997). Coordination is an indirect intervention. Coordination is not a service delivered to students; rather it is an intervention that makes the delivery of other services possible. Myrick (1997) defines coordination as managing the many services offered in a comprehensive developmental program. Coordination encompasses all the functions and activities used to ensure the scheduled, delivered, and evaluated service, event, or project that is part of the school counseling program. Coordination is an organizational procedure that helps counselors attend to the meaning and purpose of the activities undertaken and to avoid duplication unless they are purposefully planning multiple interventions. Kameen, Robinson, and Rotter (1985) suggest that a counselor interprets the role of coordination on such factors as the size of the school, the availability of specialists, and the needs of the community. Previously, Mr. Larson and Ms. Fairley each coordinated the program components directly associated with the grades for which they were responsible. They wish to move to a model of more diversified or differential staffing (Blum, 1998). This means that each of them would assume responsibility for specific coordinating activities for the entire school. Eliminating duplication of effort should allow each of them more time to address the high-priority program items identified by their leadership team. For example, only one of them would need to attend in-service training activities related to peer-facilitation programs. To begin, they agree to review the model job description for a high school counselor published by the state of Alabama (as follows) as well as the desired allocation of time spent in each type of program component (Alabama State Department of Education, 1996).

School Counselor Job Description: North Oneonta High School

Position: High School Counselor

Primary Function: As a member of the system's counseling and guidance staff, the high school counselor provides a comprehensive counseling and guidance program for high school students; consults and collaborates with teachers, parents, and staff to enhance their effectiveness in helping students; and provides support to other high school educational programs.

Major Job Responsibilities:
- Implement the high school counseling and guidance curriculum.
- Guide and counsel groups and individual students through the development of educational and career plans.
- Consult with small groups and individual students.
- Consult and collaborate with teachers, staff, and parents in understanding and meeting the needs of students.
- Refer students with problems and their parents to appropriate specialists, special programs, or outside agencies.
- Plan, evaluate, and revise the counseling and guidance program.
- Pursue professional growth.

Desired Allocation of Time

Guidance Curriculum	15–30%
Individual Planning	20–40%
Responsive Services	20–40%
System Support	10–20%

School systems may already have job descriptions in place, or as with NOHS, they may adopt a description endorsed by their states or by professional organizations such as ASCA (see preceding example). The job description establishes an agreed-on set of expectations for the counselors. It also serves as a template for Mr. Larson and Ms. Fairley against which they can compare the coordinating responsibilities traditionally identified with their program. They will use three guides as they plan. The national standards serve as a primary reference. They realize that every activity should have a student objective that is related to a specific grade-level competency in the national standards. Activities that cannot be so linked will be eliminated. Additionally, the job description and the accompanying time allocations provide them with direction about the desired outcome of their revision efforts. Coordination is a feature of each of the four curriculum components identified by the Alabama State Department of Education (1996). We will now discuss coordination in the context of these four organizing components.

COORDINATING GUIDANCE CURRICULUM (15–30%)

The guidance curriculum includes the student competencies identified for all students at each grade level in academic, career, and personal/social development. The focus is on the students gaining a cognitive understanding of the material and having opportunities to practice that understanding. The curriculum provides the scope and sequence of student learning and is implemented by many of the educators in the school setting through classroom guidance and schoolwide activities (Gysbers & Henderson, 2000). However, responsibility for coordinating the development of the curriculum and its implementation falls to the school counselor. Recall that the counselor efforts in the guidance curriculum for a high school should take up between 15 and 30 percent of the available time. For Mr. Larson and Ms. Fairley coordination includes making certain that the curriculum for high school students is developmentally appropriate, theoretically sound, and relevant to the needs of students in their school. They work with the school counseling leadership team and others in the school to collect the data they need to make such decisions. Additionally, they participate on interdisciplinary curriculum development teams to develop and refine curriculum in content areas (Alabama State Department of Education, 1996). They believe that spending 2 hours per week in activities related to the development, implementation, and evaluation of the curriculum, including those interactions with the leadership team, is the minimum time needed to do an adequate job. Additionally, they plan to deliver some of the curriculum themselves through classroom guidance activities. They have determined that they need to spend 4 hours per week in classes. Several other schoolwide programs are coordinated out of the counseling and guidance office, specifically, the schoolwide honors program that occurs each spring and activities related to high school graduation. They determined that they could accomplish these tasks in an additional 1 hour per week. The total amount of time they plan to spend on coordinating and implementing the guidance curriculum is 7 hours, or approximately 17.5 percent of their total time allocation.

COORDINATING INDIVIDUAL PLANNING (20–40%)

Individual planning involves activities to plan, monitor, and evaluate student learning as well as the development of their career and educational plans (Gysbers & Henderson, 2000). These activities help students understand and monitor their development and take actions toward their future. At NOHS, the counselors coordinate a teacher advisor program (TAP). Each student is assigned an advisor upon entering ninth grade who remains with the student, barring unusual circumstances, through graduation. Much of the career and educational planning of the high school students occurs in this program. The advisor also functions as the homeroom teacher in most circumstances. If the number of students in a homeroom exceeds 20, some of the students are reassigned to educators who do not have responsibility for homerooms, such as special resource and gifted education teachers, media specialists, and administrators. Advisement occurs monthly for 1 hour immediately preceding lunch. The school counselors are responsible for meeting with grade-level advisors to plan the agenda for one session per month (see Table 4.1), identify the materials and resources needed to conduct the advisement session, and make certain that all necessary resources are distributed well in advance of each session. Additionally, the counselors provide the staff development training for advisors in the basic skills necessary for successful advising (listening skills, problem-solving skills, effective communication strategies) (Gysbers, & Henderson, 2000).

Students at NOHS complete a career and educational plan during the spring of their 8th-grade year. The plan is reviewed and revised each fall from 9th through 12th grades during advisement time to ensure that students are making the appropriate academic choices to meet their career and educational goals. The TAP

TABLE 4.1 NOHS Teacher Advisement Schedule

DATE	9th Grade	10th Grade	11th Grade	12th Grade
8/30	Set goals Review plans	Set goals Review plans	Set goals Review plans	Set goals Review plans
9/30	Interest inventory results/analyze interests	Administration of aptitude test	Postsecondary planning calendar	Postsecondary planning review
10/30	Career/educational planning review	Career/educational planning review	Career day	Career day
11/30	Registration	Registration	Registration	Registration
1/6	Study skills	Decision-making skills/analyzing abilities	Postsecondary goals	Postsecondary planning day for students and parents
2/6	Test-taking skills	Time management for effective learning	Relationship between school success and time allocated to studying	Learning over the lifetime
3/10	High school graduation exam	Developing positive attitudes	Job opportunities/job-seeking skills	Discrimination and sexual harassment in workplace
4/10	Identifying and using commmunity resources	Combating career stereotypes	Respecting others	Future goals and appreciation for cultural differences
5/10	Registration	Registration	Registration	Graduation celebrations

Divide into small groups of 3 to 4 students. Each group chooses one of the scheduled advisement times from Table 4.1 and identifies a possible agenda, activities, and resources/materials that may be needed to complete the activities.

ensures that a significant adult (advisor) is available to help each student develop and monitor a plan for the future. The regular, ongoing program also provides ample opportunity for students to incorporate new data into their plans as information becomes available. Coordinating all aspects of the TAP requires approximately 2 hours per week or 5 percent of the total time allocated.

Placement and follow-up activities are aspects of individual planning as well. The focus here is on helping students with the natural transitions between grades as well as those that occur between graduation and work, college, or other postsecondary training. Those activities at NOHS for which the counselors are responsible include a career day where local employers representing the major occupational categories listed in the Dictionary of Occupational Titles (U.S. Department of Labor, 1991) are invited to campus to provide interested students with information about the requirements, benefits, and opportunities available in their respective fields. Participants represent a wide range of employment opportunities, including those that require no postsecondary training. The counselors also coordinate a college night where students and their parents can come to speak with representatives from the most frequently attended colleges and universities. In the past, they have held separate college, financial aid, and military careers days. As the counselors discussed these activities, they determined that they could have one postsecondary planning day that would include college, technical schools, and military recruiters; and they could offer rotating minisessions on financial aid, college applications, and writing college essays during the program. They estimate that these activities will take another 4 hours per week for coordination, and implementation, and evaluation. Additionally, they spend approximately 4 hours per week in activities such as reviewing college applications and essays, writing reference letters, and identifying scholarship and other funding opportunities for which their students may be eligible (20%).

The counselors are also responsible for coordinating the appraisal activities in their school. Entering ninth graders take a career interest inventory as part of their preregistration for high school activities, and all tenth graders are administered an aptitude test and the high school graduation test. All high school students are administered standardized achievement tests, and some juniors and seniors take college admissions tests. Some students also take more specialized tests to receive credit for some college courses and advanced placement in others. The counselors coordinate the scheduling, administration (often conducted in advisory groups), submission of test materials for scoring, and in some cases the identification of appropriate students for specialized tests. Once the school has received results, the counselors arrange small-group interpretations for all students and some evening interpretations for parents. These activities require approximately 3 hours per week (7.5%). The total amount of time Mr. Larson and Ms. Fairley allocate to individual planning is 32.5 percent.

> Identify transition activities to meet the needs of fifth-grade students, who will be moving to middle school next academic year, and their parents. Also, identify activities to address the transitional concerns related to middle school students entering high school. Based on the previous suggestions for high school students, how might you meet the needs of each of these other two groups? Keep in mind the developmental differences between these two groups.

COORDINATING RESPONSIVE SERVICES (20–40%)

Counselors use responsive services to provide help for students who face difficulties that hinder their healthy development. These services meet the immediate needs and concerns of students, especially those with critical problems. Counselors balance these responses and work in prevention as well as remediation efforts. Professional school counselors design programs that focus on encouraging children and adolescents to make healthy and appropriate choices and to employ effective coping strategies. Counselors use remedial interventions with students who have not developed or demonstrated the skills to make healthy choices and for those who need assistance in coping with difficult situations. The processes involved in responsive services include individual and small-group counseling, consultation, and referrals.

Historically at NOHS counselors have allowed many other responsibilities to interfere with the consistency of having a schedule of either individual or small-group counseling. They have talked to students as they appeared. The counselors know that to implement this program component, they need to block out the necessary time required to deliver services. They want to streamline the process of students referring themselves for counseling and to be more solution focused with those adolescents. The counselors also want to refine a process for referrals of students for counseling from teachers and other adults. They are going to formalize a once-weekly meeting in which they discuss case management and build plans for responsive services accordingly.

Mr. Larson and Ms. Fairley have decided to begin by identifying four students each for individual counseling. They will meet with each of those four students once a week for a 6-week grading period. That time commitment of 4 hours each week involves 10 percent of their time. They also decide to post an hour each day (2.5%) for drop-in services, so that students will know when one of them will be available on an as-needed basis. Both counselors also know that they must guard against anything infringing on these commitments to meeting with students and are determined to honor these appointments.

Additionally they each will begin four small groups that will meet for a grading period, a commitment of 10 percent of their time. After studying the needs assessment they completed during the awareness phase of planning, as well as the previous year's program evaluation, they have decided on topics they see as priorities for two groups each will conduct. Mr. Larson will lead the groups on substance abuse prevention and managing anger. Ms. Fairley has decided she will begin with some groups for teenage mothers and for students who are grieving. During this first year they will repeat the groups with different students invited to participate for each grading period. At the end of the semester they will consider whether to switch topics.

They will use the rest of their time devoted to groups focused on their theme of the year, "Learning through Service to Others." During this academic year these groups will be more task oriented and will integrate some social skills with a social interest project. The counselors will carefully select these group participants to build coalitions among students who have few opportunities to contribute to larger school or community projects and those who are more active in the school. Those groups will meet once each week for a semester.

Some needs of the students will exceed what the counselors can provide. Having known this, they already have in place a system of referrals for off-campus help such as social agencies, mental health services, and the legal system. For help within the school and school system they have procedures for referring to educational placement and programs, student assistance teams, child study teams, and crisis response teams. Their office manual includes contact information and scheduling responsibilities as well as letters and forms to make referrals and follow up a smooth, timely, and appropriate process. With this well-established system, the school counselors spend about an hour per week on referrals.

Working with teachers and parents as a consultant helps school counselors share their skills. They see different teachers on a daily basis and find they spend about an hour each day working with them. Mr. Larson and Ms. Fairley want to increase the parent group meetings they offer and be more available to teachers. They decide to discuss with their principal some flexible scheduling for one day every week for each of them so they can offer two series of parent groups on two nights of the week at a location other than the school. They have some data from their yearly needs assessment on topics and have ideas about using an empty store at the mall so that public transportation would be available for some parents who need it. Initially they know the planning and set up of this scheme will take around 3 hours a week. If they succeed in providing these parent groups and continue their current consultation with teachers, they will be devoting another 10 percent of their time to responsive services, for a total of 32.5 percent to this area.

COORDINATING SYSTEM SUPPORT (10–20%)

System support includes two types of activities: those that sustain the counseling program and those that support other educational programs. Listing sample activities in each of these categories may help counselors better manage counseling programs.

To support the counseling program, some of the crucial systems of support include

- Building and maintaining a strong leadership team to guide the program.
- Collecting and analyzing data to plan, implement, and evaluate the program and services.
- Assessing needs as well as the effectiveness and efficiency of the program.
- Building public awareness of the school counseling program.
- Participating in professional development.
- Managing a productive environment.

To support other school programs, counselors may contribute their time to

- Providing orientation for students, parents, and teachers.
- Doing follow-up studies of graduates and dropouts.
- Coordinating parent volunteers and paraprofessionals.
- Delivering staff and community development opportunities.
- Serving as a member or advisor on committees.

The counselors at NOHS have some priorities that will guide their time spent in system support also. First they are going to plan monthly meetings for their leadership team and work with a parent volunteer to make the counseling area more accessible and the information in it easier to retrieve. They will also ask another parent volunteer to design an updated brochure for them. They have been diligent about collecting needs assessment data and now want to devise a better method of monitoring whether the activities they have chosen to meet those needs are effective. They will be talking with a professor from a local university to help them develop some ways to determine whether they are accomplishing what they want to accomplish. Most of these activities can be spread across the month, so they estimate that scheduling 2 hours (5%) per week will provide enough time to generate the procedures to support their counseling program.

The other process they want to formalize involves a study of the graduation records, so they can begin to identify patterns of adolescents who are not completing a challenging high school curriculum. This and other assessment data will help them support school personnel in identifying barriers to all students' achievement and in eliminating those things that hinder success. Once again they will devote 2 hours (5%) each week to this task.

Mr. Larson serves on the curriculum committee at NOHS and on the school district counseling advisory board. Ms. Fairley is a member of the school climate team and of the safe community initiative board. Those meetings require an hour (2.5%) each week.

What additional coordinating responsibilities would you add to this discussion? How would the lists differ for a middle school counselor? Elementary school?

As they consider these new strategies for managing their program, the school counselors recognize that they need to update some of their skills and knowledge. They have decided to take an online course in cultures and counseling as a first step in a renewed effort to be more attuned to the diversity and multicultural teaching and learning. They will help lead some in-service training for the campus faculty next year on that topic. That learning commitment will involve another 2 hours of their time, for a total of 17.5 percent of their time in system support.

DIVIDE AND CONQUER

Identifying the various activities is, believe it or not, the easy part! Many factors will influence the decisions of Mr. Larson and Ms. Fairley about how to share their work responsibilities. Work preferences, interest, skills and abilities, personality, special knowledge, past experience, and managerial style are some of the considerations. In addition to their personal skills and traits, a discussion of some of the essential skills for effective program management may be helpful to the counselors as they attempt to divide their coordinating responsibilities in an equitable manner.

PROGRAM MANAGEMENT SKILLS

Leadership

Pounder and Ogawa (1995) studied school leadership as an organizational quality. They wanted to link the relationship of leadership, effective organizations, and measures of school effectiveness. Their research supported the impact of school leadership on school performance; however, they overlooked the leadership of school counselors in their study. Professional school counselors are educational leaders. Their roles can be constructed within the same framework of effective CEOs that has been explained by Bennis (1995). School counselors are concerned with the program's basic purpose, the reason(s) it exists, and its general direction. They are committed to doing the right things and have the following competencies:

- **Vision.** An ability to see what is needed or what is possible and to move toward it; for school counselors this involves some iteration of being an integral part of an educational enterprise that makes it possible for students to learn and thrive.
- **Communication.** The capacity to share their vision to gain the support of others; for school counselors this propels them to build teams and to inform students, parents, teachers, other school personnel, and the community about the school counseling program.
- **Persistence, consistency, focus.** The ability to maintain direction in spite of difficulties; for school counselors this means commitment to the students and attention to continual monitoring and revision of activities to provide excellent programs.

- **Empowerment.** The capacity to create environments that identify and use people's energies and abilities.

McFarland, Senn, and Childress (1995) state that leaders in the 21st century recognize the importance of bringing out excellence in others and being interpersonally sensitive. Leaders adopt a holistic approach and use a variety of qualities, skills, and capabilities in achieving their goals. Finally leaders master change rather than merely react to it. Counselors will recognize these attributes as dimensions of their everyday practice.

Clark and Stone (2000) discuss opportunities for school counselors to exhibit advocacy and leadership in staff development, school reform, multicultural awareness, mentoring programs, and political involvement. They describe this shift as a natural alignment for counselors who have special leadership skills and opportunities. We concur and encourage school counselors to focus on identifying their unique leadership abilities. Building teams such as the leadership team allows this to happen. Johnson and Johnson (1997) describe a team as a group whose interpersonal interactions are structured to accomplish established goals. Team members develop cooperative working relationships to achieve a shared objective to which they are committed. Effective teams have healthy, constructive relationships; established goals, procedures, and methods; and a focus on improvement in their relationships and in their task (Basham, Appleton, & Dykeman, 2000). Professional school counselors build teams by helping the group gain a common understanding of team effectiveness. They present the mission of the team to build commitment to the team's activities. They help create high levels of expectation for quality and personal commitment to the team process, and they make team meetings safe and enjoyable. They also match their leadership style and intervention strategies to developmental stages of the team process (Kormanski, 1999).

Counselors who provide direction and maintain commitment foster change. They also employ strategic planning to balance attention both on present, operational concerns and on future, strategic issues. This type of planning allows counselors and teams to determine and manage multiple change issues and to think and act more decisively about the program's future. Strategic thinking provides multiple solutions and a variety of perspectives, allowing a "stacking" effect with actions based on needs and resources (Kormanski, 1999). Professional school counselors use their leadership skills and effective teams to influence and propel change that leads to student success.

Administration

When counselors come together for informal discussions, an oft-repeated comment is "I want to do less administration." They are often referring to the time spent in coordinating the school counseling program. Myrick (1997) points out that the coordination responsibilities associated with a comprehensive developmental program will take as much time as counselors will commit. Time management, organization, and supervision skills are not going to add more time to any counselor's day, nor are they intended to increase the amount of administrative detail that can be covered in the allotted time. Rather, careful consideration of how one manages time, office, people, and tasks, coupled with a serious review of currently assigned nonguidance tasks for possible displacement or streamlining (Gysbers & Henderson, 2000) is intended to decrease the amount of time spent in administrative activities with the "gain" being spent on high-priority items (Silver, 1995).

Organization

Silver (1995) defines an organizing system as "a combination of appropriate tools and habits to get a job done or reach a goal" (p. 7). One of the first steps to achieving a highly organized counseling office is to clearly articulate program goals and priorities (as described in chapter 3). Once this is done, organizers know what they are trying to achieve and commit to directing most of their energies to the goals. Second, one needs to decide how one's office and workload are going to be handled. Let's start with the office. One of the central features of an office is the workspace/desk. Most organizational specialists will tell you that a messy desk with lots of piles on it is not part of a productive work environment. How many times have you watched people go through every pile on their desk to retrieve something they are absolutely sure is there, only to find that the object of the search is not there? Even if the activity only takes 2 minutes, making the same search three times each day, five days each week adds up to 30 minutes per week. Multiply that weekly half hour by four and you can add 2 extra hours each month to your high-priority items!

Some suggestions for keeping a clear work space include having only one open file on your desk at any given time, keeping only items used daily (planner, telephone, clock) as permanent desk fixtures, keeping items you use daily or several times each week most accessible to your work space, and sorting or grouping together similar items or those requiring action (Silver, 1995). Setting up a daily paperwork system to routinely address active files and incoming paperwork is essential for avoiding a massive pile up. Silver suggests developing categories based on the types of papers that come your way each day. For Mr. Larson and Ms. Fairley, that includes mountains of information related to postsecondary planning (military, colleges and universities, financial aid, scholarship opportunities, college testing information); requests for information about specific students; requests from students for appointments, references, and applications; correspondence; reading material; messages from parents and teachers; phone calls; priority items on which they are working; things to be filed; and items pending action, but not requiring immediate attention.

Color coding is one strategy used to increase accessibility of objects without having them out on your desk. For example, say you decide to use the color red to code all things related to parents. You keep parent programs and information for parents in a red binder divided by grade level; all correspondence to parents, including permission letters for group participation, is stored on a red diskette; a red folder is in your vertical file to receive requests from parents.

Additionally, preprinted notes (e.g., referral forms for teachers, students, parents), computerized forms, storage bins, in and out boxes, three-ring binders, cabinets and boxes for long-term storage (e.g., bulletin board materials announcing Honors Day are used once annually), and magazine and literature storage containers may be helpful.

Develop a categorization scheme for these counselors that includes no more than four daily organizing categories. Generate ideas about effective ways to "contain" the papers and empty the containers each day.

How could this example be applied to one of the categories in your list?

Filing systems, long and short term, need to be easily understood by others in your workplace. The following five-point filing system is suggested by Silver (1995):

1. Categorize existing files as active or inactive. Pull inactive files from your existing system.
2. Write out your filing system on a piece of paper and get input from others in the workplace who will be using the files.
3. Physically set up the system purging and consolidating files as you go.
4. Label drawers and prepare a file index.
5. Maintain your system by sticking to a routine. (p. 152)

Finally, the physical layout of your office needs to be conducive to the work that you do. Try to avoid working in one space and having materials/resources in another space. Think about the activities that you conduct in your workspace and lay out your office to maximize privacy, convenience, and comfort.

Generate a list of the activities you believe will be carried out in your office. Assume you have been assigned a workspace that is 10' by 12', identify the furniture and accessories you need, and then plan physical placement in the room. Evaluate the space you have designed according to the activities you identified.

Time Management

According to Silver (1995), time management is essential to good organization. School counselors who have already established and prioritized program goals are laying a foundation for good time management. Bliss (cited in Silver, 1995) suggests dividing goals into three priority levels. A-level priorities are important and urgent (e.g., student in crisis). B-level priorities are important but not urgent (e.g., a program that is planned for several months away). C-level priorities are urgent but not important (e.g., request for non-school-related information with a deadline of tomorrow). Program balance is achieved when the counselor spends most of his or her time on A and B priorities and very little time on C-level priorities. As Silver points out, most of us are competent handlers of A-level priorities, but do not do as well in making time for B-level priorities. To achieve one's goals, some time each day must be spent on B-level priorities.

Seven time management tools to consider are calendars, to-do lists, master lists, tickler systems, planners/organizers, computerized systems, and electronic organizers (Silver, 1995). A calendar is a basic tool that allows one to track events over time. Counselors should maintain only one calendar for both personal and professional information. The size should be adequate, but not burdensome. Important information should be photocopied in case of loss. The calendar should be accessible to you both in and out of the office. Some calendar systems include to-do lists where one can enter items to be completed on a given day. Try to list only those items that must be done today and commit to finishing the list. At the end of each day, one might prepare the next day's to-do list. Big projects are not so easily managed on a calendar or to-do list and might best be viewed on a master list or project management sheet.

A tickler system is a reminder system. For example, one might use an accordion file to keep cards to be mailed during a certain month, or notes about items to do (e.g., call speakers in October to schedule them for the January 6 postsecondary planning workshop). Or, one might develop an annual list of things that must be done each month. Organizers, both paper and electronic, can be effective time management tools as well. There is a wide range available and one can actually customize an organizer to meet very specific needs.

Sabella (1996) identifies several timesaving methods for school counselors using their desktop computers. Consistent with our previous statements, computer usage is not intended to increase the amount of paperwork tasks completed by the counselor. The time saved by automating some of the more routine functions can be applied to other areas of importance. Specifically, Sabella recommends using various word processing, merging, data management, and e-mail functions to perform repetitive tasks such as generating forms and letters, managing student data, accounting for time spent on various tasks, keeping records and logs, and communicating with others.

Supervision

In their role as program managers, Mr. Larson and Ms. Fairley are responsible for the administrative supervision of a secretary assigned to the guidance and counseling office, student office assistants, a group of parent volunteers, peer facilitators, and school counseling practicum and internship students. The counselors want to manage themselves and the people with whom they work in such a way that NOHS and its students profit (Blanchard & Johnson, 1983). They have identified three keys to effectively working with people: communication, involvement, and training (Silver, 1995).

COMMUNICATION

The preparation for school counselors often emphasizes communication. The relationship skills we develop to relate positively and effectively with our "clients" also serve us well in our efforts to keep informed and exchange ideas with the persons whose work we direct. Silver identifies the following as important aspects of communicating:

- Keep people informed.
- Keep communications clear, precise, and positive.
- Use multiple channels of communication.
- Ask people what they think and listen to their answers.
- Standardize communication when possible.
- Personalize communication.

Keeping these points in mind, Mr. Larson and Ms. Fairley have decided to have a daily 15-minute meeting with each other, their secretary, and the parent volunteer of the day to discuss their goals, plans, and availability. On the days that student counselor interns or practicum students are in the school, they will also be asked to attend. The meeting is scheduled during the 15 minutes set aside at the beginning of each day for teachers to take attendance and disseminate information of which students should be aware. During this time, they will exchange schedules and review the daily to-do lists, making sure everyone present understands what is expected of him or her during the day. They will be sure that they ask for feedback from all present regarding their daily tasks and how the work might be most efficiently managed. Each person in the meeting will be responsible for writing his or her goals and keeping them posted in a place that is visible, so they will be reminded of their top priorities for the day. The secretary is also responsible for the direct oversight of student assistants and will meet with them for 2 to 3 minutes at the beginning of each class period to review the tasks they are expected to accomplish. During their next regularly scheduled meeting, each attendee will briefly review progress made toward the goals and discuss any items that need to be carried over. Such meetings provide Mr. Larson and Ms. Fairley an opportunity to provide ongoing feedback to the persons they are supervising. Similar meetings will be scheduled once each week with the peer facilitators who are supervised by the counselors. The counselors also arrange two half-hour sessions each week with practicum and intern students to discuss their progress, address any administrative concerns or issues related to the placement, and provide supervision/consultation about students' development and the interventions they are providing for NOHS students.

INVOLVEMENT

Silver (1995) cites research that indicates a positive correlation between employee involvement and motivation, quality, and productivity. By establishing regularly scheduled meetings with each of their teams of supervisees, Mr. Larson and Ms. Fairley have established a mechanism for both communication with and involvement of those persons who will be carrying out many of the tasks associated with coordinating the school counseling program. They have increased the likelihood of an integrated effort directed toward the program goals they and their leadership team have established. Additionally, people who feel supported in solving their own problems are less likely to depend on the counselors for daily oversight of routine matters such as transcript preparation, maintenance of records, and preparation of reports, letters, and forms. They are also more able to respond to A-level (urgent and important) and C-level priorities (urgent but not important) without interruption of the counselors' schedules.

> Identify a work experience that you found particularly satisfying. What were the communication skills/style exhibited by your supervisor? How might you use these skills to work effectively with those you supervise in the future?

Effective Management of A-level Priority

Jason had a motorcycle accident on the way home from school yesterday. He is hospitalized and will not return to school for at least 4 weeks. His parents called the counseling office to explore the options for keeping Jason up to date with his schoolwork. Mr. Larson and Ms. Fairley's secretary has called the program coordinator for homebound students and provided him the information needed to contact Jason's parents. Additionally, she has secured a copy of Jason's schedule from the school schedules database and has given it to the parent volunteer for the day. The parent will clean out Jason's locker and contact his teachers during each class period to get assignments for the rest of the week. During the last period of the day, the student assistant will take all materials for Jason to the front office where his parents will pick them up. The secretary will notify the counselors via e-mail of the actions she has taken on Jason's behalf. When the coordinator calls her back with more information, she will let teachers know how long Jason will be out of school and arrange to have his weekly assignments e-mailed to the teacher who will be working with him during his period of confinement.

> The secretary easily and efficiently handled this A-level priority because she had the authority and responsibility to do so. With teamwork, each person had a small part of their work time redirected toward solving the problem, but no one person had to carve out time during the day to carry out all of the necessary steps.

TRAINING

To be successful, employees and volunteers must know what they are expected to do and have the skills and knowledge to carry out their assigned tasks. The importance of continuous training and staff development cannot be overemphasized. Friend and Cook (2000) state that the many strategies considered essential for 21st-century schools cannot be implemented without staff development and support. Training is linked to program goals and is intended to increase job performance through skill enhancement. What skills and knowledge do professional, administrative, and volunteer staffs need to meet the established program goals? Some training may be group oriented, such as that provided to teachers in preparation for their role as advisor or to peer facilitators who will serve as tutors or mediators. Other training needs may be individually oriented such as a course in computer-based presentations for counselors to deliver the guidance curriculum or make presentations to community groups. The secretary may need a course in using data management software in order to secure information about student achievement and scheduling that counselors need for more effective educational planning. Cross training (Silver, 1995) may be provided by persons in the school system who work in other departments. Experts outside the system may also be used to provide specialized training (Friend & Cook, 2000).

The developmental needs of children and adolescents are an integral part of school counselor preparation programs. However, for counselors who are leading or planning training activities for staff, developmental characteristics of adult learners must be considered. Friend and Cook (2000) identify the following characteristics of adult learners:

* They learn better when their knowledge and experience is validated.
* They learn better when they are involved in their learning activities.
* They perceive that what they are going to learn will meet their objectives.

Divide into pairs and assume the roles of Mr. Larson and Ms. Fairley. Considering your own skills, personality, interests, and abilities, negotiate the coordinating responsibilities of the counselor whose role you have assumed. Based on the information provided in this chapter, develop an organizational chart depicting an equitable distribution of the coordinating tasks for each of you, including those that are assigned to each as well as those you decide to share.

SUMMARY

In this chapter, we have provided information about the coordination activities required to manage a comprehensive developmental program employing the structure articulated by Gysbers and Henderson (2000), the model most widely adopted by state departments of education in this country. Examples of coordinating activities within each of the four program components have been provided along with estimates of the time required for each. The skills needed to effectively coordinate a program have also been presented.

PORTFOLIO COMPONENTS

1. Describe a time that you participated in a team or group project that had a successful outcome. What did the leader do to promote cohesion and commitment to the team and its goals? How did members respond? Use this experience and others to develop a one-page description of how you would approach building a team to achieve one or more goals of your school counseling program.

2. Identify your managerial strengths and weaknesses as a potential program coordinator. Articulate a plan of professional development, including goals and activities, to become more competent in this area. Focus on specific strategies and skills you need to develop prior to your graduation.

The School Counselor's Responsibility as an Educational Leader

CASE STUDY

FACILITATING CHANGE IN SCHOOLS: IDENTIFYING LEADERS

Mr. Terman, the system-level coordinator of school counseling programs for Washington County schools, is meeting with the administrative team (central office professional staff, school principals) for a final debriefing at the close of the school year. Several changes in the system are expected to be made over the next 2 years to be consistent with the most recent reform initiatives linked to *No Child Left Behind* (U.S. Department of Education, 2001). Specifically, to increase the effectiveness of schools, the plan calls for increased focus on accountability and student outcomes, more students placed in academically challenging classes, more parent involvement, and higher levels of English proficiency among students. The superintendent, Dr. Pickens, expects planning and implementing the reforms to be challenging because teachers and staff have been asked to respond to several different initiatives during the past decade with little input from them prior to implementation. These repeated efforts have drained energy from all and fed the cynicism of some of the veteran teachers.

One principal commented that these new emphases were consistent with the concerns of their school system. Namely, student attendance declined during the previous 3 years, and participation in extracurricular events had a corresponding decline. The number of students entering ninth grade who remained in school through graduation dropped from 89 percent in 1990 to 78 percent in 2000. There has been an increase in enrollment of immigrants from the war-torn regions of central Europe, many of whom speak little English and are living in extreme poverty. The general educational and vocationally oriented courses are beyond capacity, whereas enrollments decline each year in the college preparatory and advanced placement courses.

Dr. Pickens asked for ideas from the staff about who might provide positive leadership for planning and implementing some reforms that would address these local concerns as well as those stemming from the national initiative. Mr. Terman identified one of the elementary school counselors, Ms. Schroeder, as a strong positive force in the school and community. He referred to her as a "natural" leader. Further discussion of leadership led to the identification of at least one potential leader from each school in the system.

Dr. Pickens will speak with Ms. Schroeder about chairing a system-level steering committee comprised of key members from each school. The members will in turn be asked to chair transition teams at each school. Dr. Pickens will ask that each member of the steering committee participate in five staff development days with a change consultant learning as much as they can about the characteristics of school systems and gaining a better understanding of systemic change. Dr. Pickens believes that the group facilitation and planning skills demonstrated by the counselors will be especially helpful to the transition efforts and appoints one to each building-based transition team.

The statistics and reports released for public information about the effectiveness of schools are confusing and often distorted, with some groups claiming that public education is abysmal and others that public education is effective (Bracey, 2000). Numerous studies of effective schools have identified common characteristics, but simply adopting those characteristics has not proven an effective strategy for those schools wishing to become effective (DeBlois, 2000). A common denominator among those schools that work well is that all school personnel help with planning, implementing, evaluating, and revising the institutions' programs and policies. To be successful in these four areas, school administrators must identify, support, and encourage a number of school leaders and rely on the professional expertise of all those who contribute to the educational mission of the school (DeBlois, 2000). DeBlois points out that successful leadership depends on the ability of the leader to establish relationships in the day-to-day work environment.

Professional school counselors spend most of each workday developing and maintaining relationships with students, teachers, parents, administrators, and community resource persons. School counselors have unique skills, abilities, and knowledge that enable them to provide leadership in some instances and to support the emergence of leadership in others.

After reading and discussing this chapter, you should be able to

- Identify the skills and styles of effective leadership.
- Explain systems and systemic change.
- Describe collaboration and team building.
- Understand how to lead efforts in advocacy.

LEADERSHIP

Ms. Schroeder was surprised to hear that Mr. Terman described her as a leader. Like many counselors, she views herself more as a support for the administrators who provide leadership and as a collaborator with teachers in their efforts to identify and respond to the needs of the student body rather than as someone who initiates change efforts. She had always assumed that the principal was the only person in the school who served in the leadership capacity. Ms. Schroeder shares that belief with many others who equate leadership with titles rather than behaviors.

Ms. Schroeder feels confident in her ability to manage the school counseling program and wonders if it is those skills and abilities that Mr. Terman refers to as leadership. To better understand his perceptions, Ms. Schroeder seeks to distinguish between management and leadership. Lewis, Lewis, Packard, and Souflee (2001) identify these components of management:

- **Planning**—developing visions, strategies, setting goals and selecting models
- **Designing**—structuring and coordinating the work to be done to accomplish the plans
- **Developing human resources**—enabling the people needed to make things work and enhancing their potential
- **Supervising**—monitoring and supporting the skills of personnel
- **Managing finances**—planning the use of resources to reach goals and control expenses
- **Monitoring**—tracking progress on objectives and activities
- **Evaluating**—comparing accomplishments with standards set at the planning stages and using the results as a base for change (pp. 10–11)

> Identify a person you have observed providing leadership to a group of others committed to a common goal. Was this person the official leader or did the person emerge as a leader as the work continued? Make a list of the skills and behaviors you observed this leader use that seemed to be effective in moving the work forward.

Ms. Schroeder realizes that her work as a school counselor involves these management activities. Additionally, as she continues to explore the organizational and school literature about leadership, she begins to understand what Lewis and colleagues mean when they say that what unifies these processes is leadership. Rauch and Behling (1984) define leadership as "the process of influencing an organized group toward accomplishing its goals" (quoted from Hughes, Ginnet, & Curphy, 1995, p. 42). The idea of leadership being a process of social influence directed toward a goal expands the possibilities for leadership in schools. Leadership enables an organization to work as an integrated system, the way schools need to operate. Leadership involves moving beyond the individual's concern (managing the school counseling program in Ms. Schroeder's case) and assuming more responsibility for the collective concerns of the organization (DeBlois, 2000).

In schools a person, usually the principal, occupies a position of authority and is charged with managing the school, or with duties such as having buses run on time, keeping order in schools, monitoring budget and facilities, and handling other operating responsibilities. Some authors (Neuman & Simmons, 2000; Lambert, 1998; Hibert, 2000; Bemak, 2000) separate management from leadership based on the idea of shared responsibility. Neuman and Simmons (2000) use the phrase *distributed leadership* to explain a concept of leading in which every person associated with schools—principals, students, teachers, all school staff, district personnel, parents, and community members—takes responsibility for the academic achievement of students, with particular individuals assuming leadership in areas of their competence and skill. Essentially, all who are involved adhere to shared values and adopt roles that are determined by the current tasks exhibiting what Jackson (2000) refers to as skills of "followership."

Katzenbach, Beckett, Dichter, Feigen, Gagnon, Hope, and Ling (1995) characterize people who contribute to growth and high performance in organizations as having the following attributes:

- Dedication to making things better
- Courage to challenge the status quo
- Initiative to question current definitions
- Motivation of themselves and for others
- Caring about how people are treated and are supported
- Willingness to keep attention on the process and goal rather than on self
- A sense of humor

These are the skills and attributes that led Mr. Terman to label Ms. Schroeder a "natural" leader. Further, based on these attributes, the administrative team identified others in the schools who are potential leaders. According to Rosener (1995), leadership efforts include encouraging participation, sharing power and information, enhancing other people's sense of self-worth, and energizing followers. Ms. Schroeder recognizes that to have a successful transition effort, she will need to provide leadership in the following ways:

1. Helping all participants develop the shared vision of the school community's values by including staff and community in a dialogue that permits them to

reflect on their values, listen to the values of others, and merge the personal and community values into a shared vision statement.

2. Organizing, focusing, and maintaining direction in the conversations about student learning.
3. Interpreting and protecting school community values such as parent involvement while ensuring a focus and commitment to learning.
4. Working with everyone to carry out decisions.

Ms. Schroeder found some specific leadership behaviors that will help her accomplish these four objectives (Lambert, 1998):

- Asking questions that challenge underlying assumptions.
- Remaining silent so that other voices are heard.
- Promoting conversations.
- Generating a range of possibilities and avoiding simplistic answers.
- Focusing on the shared values.
- Using data to inform decisions.
- Turning concerns into questions.
- Publicizing strategies in a way that models, demonstrates, and teaches others to use them. (p. 27)

A professional community provides a place in which adults contribute to the decision making, have a stated and shared sense of purpose, work together, and accept joint responsibility for the outcomes of their work (Lambert, 1998). To meet the challenges facing their school system, Ms. Schroeder will focus on building such a community. According to Newmann and Wehlage (1995),

> The most successful schools were those that used restructuring tools to help them function as professional communities. That is, they found a way to channel staff and student efforts toward a clear, commonly shared purpose for student learning; they created opportunities for teachers to collaborate and help one another achieve the purpose; and teachers in these schools took collective—not just individual—responsibility for student learning. Schools with strong professional communities were better able to offer authentic pedagogy and were more effective in promoting student achievement. (p. 3)

Based on the attributes and skills discussed so far, as well as your own experiences as a follower or leader, work in a group to develop an inventory of leadership qualities. Rate your self on the inventory and identify your strengths as well as skills and qualities you need to develop to be an effective leader.

SYSTEMS

In contemporary management and leadership theories, the "professional community" is often referred to as a "system." Because of their staff development training on systems and systemic change, Ms. Schroeder and the other steering committee members learned that a system refers to interactions and interdependencies of subsystems or units committed to a common goal. Scholtes (1998) identifies the following as characteristic of a system:

- A system is the whole comprised of many parts.
- A systemic unit has a purpose.
- Each part of the unit contributes to the systems purpose, but no part can achieve that purpose by itself.

- We can understand a part of a system by seeing how it fits into the system, but we cannot understand the system by identifying each part.
- Looking at the interaction between parts in a system might help us understand how the system works, but to understand why the system exists we must look outside the system.
- To understand a system we must understand its purposes, its interactions, and its interdependencies (when you take a system apart it loses its essential characteristics).
- When we look at an organization such as the school we're looking at a complex social system. (p. 21)

The steering committee members agreed that they had previously considered their roles in the context of their academic assignment, but rarely if ever thought of themselves as a subsystem (such as counseling and guidance) interacting with other subsystems (such as instructional, extracurricular, administrative) to achieve the common goals of the larger system in which they all worked, the school. Counselors often talk about supporting the academic mission, for example, but spend little time interacting with the teachers (instructional unit) about sharing this responsibility. Similarly, teachers frequently refer to the counselors students who seem to have poor social skills, low self-esteem, or difficulty making relationships, but spend little time interacting with counselors about sharing responsibility for improving conditions for those students. Schools can be viewed as places with three nested systems of connected activity, as illustrated in Figure 5.1 (Senge, Cambron-McCabe, Lucas, Smith, Dutton, & Kleiner, 2000).

Senge and colleagues recognize that viewing schools as systems necessitates a continuous exploration of the theories of everyone in the professional community. The shift from an individual, program focus to systems thinking requires practice and commitment. The steering committee proposes to Dr. Pickens that a model articulated by Demming (cited in Scholtes, 1998) be followed to help the professional community make a shift from individual to systems thinking. According to this model, members of the school community need to consider their mutual purpose (mission statement); identify the beneficiaries of their services (the school and greater community); design a process or method to meet the needs of their beneficiaries; identify the policies, plans, specific needs, and the environment needed to achieve the purpose of their system; and develop a mechanism for informing those working within the system as to how the system is functioning in order to identify improvements or changes needed to meet the purposes of the system (Scholtes, 1998). Such a model requires everyone to examine his or her current, individual practices in the light of the new, systemically oriented vision.

> Within the school, what are the interacting interdependent parts, what are their purposes, and how may each affect the school's ability to achieve its purpose? If one looks outside the school to society at large to understand the purpose of schools, what might that purpose be?

> As a member of this professional community, you have been asked to facilitate a faculty/staff discussion regarding the shared values of the school and community related to educating youth. Develop a list of open-ended questions you would use to lead such a discussion. Describe how the answers to these questions relate to the development of a mission statement for the school.

SYSTEMIC CHANGE

One of the constants in any organization or system is that the system will either change or stagnate (Lewis et al., 2001; Scholtes, 1998). The challenge for the school community is to determine how that change will occur. Lewis and colleagues

FIGURE 5.1   The Interacting, Interdependent Parts Within a School

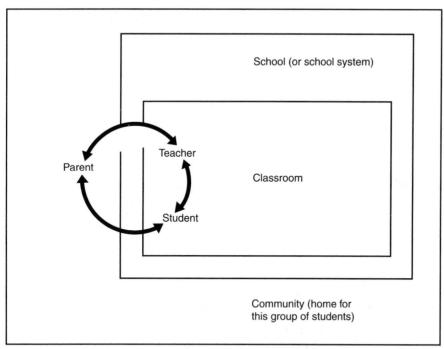

Source: From *THE FIFTH DISCIPLINE FIELDBOOK* by Peter M. Senge, Charlotte Roberts et. al, copyright © 1994 by Peter M. Senge, Charlotte Roberts, Richard B. Ross, Bryan J. Smith, and Art Kleiner. Used by permission of Doubleday, a division of Random House, Inc.

(2001) explain three methods of organizational change. One involves leaders as change agents who guide as well as empower their staff. This is the method embraced by Ms. Schroeder and her committee described earlier as distributed leadership (Neuman & Simmons, 2000).

The second method is change that is initiated and driven by the staff. Although Ms. Schroeder is clearly both a manager and a leader, this will not always be the case. Principals, for example, will evidence many different styles of leadership and may or may not be leaders of change or systems thinkers. Some may be excellent managers and strong leaders in some situations but not in all situations. In such cases, the skills of the counselor or others in the school may lead to the building of a professional community. Under this organizational change method, counselors and other leaders may facilitate systemic change by focusing on student learning, making appropriate suggestions about quality, posing stimulating questions, volunteering to take responsibility for tasks, and giving constructive feedback.

TABLE 5.1   Approaches to Organizational Change

Critical Intervention Variables	Administrative Change	Consultation	Staff-Initiated Organizational Change
Change agent/ action system	Administrators with officially prescribed authority to initiate change	Outside consultant retained by agency administration to facilitate change	Employees with no prescribed authority or responsibility to initiate change
Primary sources of legitimacy	Legislative order, formal roles and authority, policy	Contract with administration	Professional ethics and values, employee or professional associations
Primary sources of power	Formal authority, control over resources and information	Expertise (knowledge and skill regarding change processes)	Other workers, knowledge of the problem, professional expertise
Common tactics	Directives, fiduciary control, personnel changes, visionary leadership, restructuring, consensus building through staff participation	Data feedback and problem solving, team building, strategic planning, employee empowerment, Total Quality Management (TQM), reengineering, analysis of processes	Participation on agency committees, fact finding, building internal support through education and persuasion
Major constraints and sources of resistance	Subordinate inertia stemming from fear or skepticism, entrenched interests, scarce resources, lack of external support, limited control of implementation	Limited time involvement, lack of administrative support, employee distrust of outsider, employees' prior negative experiences with consultants	Superiors' disagreement, insufficient time or energy, uncertain legitimacy, fear of reprisal and disapproval, job insecurity

Source: From *Management of Human Service Programs, 3rd edition,* by J. A. Lewis, M. D. Lewis, T. Packard, F. Souflee, Jr. © 2001. Reprinted with permission of Brooks/Cole, an imprint of the Wadsworth Group, a division of Thomson Learning. Fax 800-730-2215.

When have you been involved in some type of organizational change? List as many instances as you can remember. Using the descriptions above, identify the method of change you believe was operating in those instances. You may realize that more than one approach was being used. Also identify your reactions to those changes.

Finally, these authors discuss consultation models of change in which a person outside the organization leads the process. School systems often hire experts to consult with school personnel to effect change in particular areas such as curriculum revision, program development or evaluation, increased sensitivity to diversity, and so forth. The differences and similarities in these methods are depicted in Table 5.1. Senge and colleagues (2000) acknowledge that other methods to compel change such as rational empirical arguments and coercion are also sometimes used in schools.

Senge and colleagues (2000) have identified the following keys to successful change in schools:

1. Change is only sustainable if it involves learning.
2. Change starts small and grows.
3. Significant change initiatives raise two questions about strategy and purpose: "Where are we going?" and "What are we here for?"

4. Successful change takes place through multiple layers of leadership.
5. Challenges are a natural part of organizational change.

Ms. Schroeder decides to make posters of these keys to change and keep them available for review when the steering committee feels impatient with the process they are about to initiate. The school has not arrived at its current condition in a short time and change will not be instantaneous. Also, not all personnel in the school will embrace change. The challenges are a necessary and natural part of the process.

IDENTIFY THE PURPOSE

One of the committee's first recommendations to Dr. Pickens was for each school to begin the new year by bringing staff members together to review the school mission statement and to either affirm its relevance or revise it to more accurately reflect the consensus view of the faculty and staff. The mission statement is an expression of the shared values of the faculty and staff and provides the direction needed to develop goals that are consistent with the school's mission. Lewis and colleagues (2001) state that a good mission statement is current, relevant, and useful and answers the questions: Who are we? What basic needs do we address? What do we do? What makes us unique? What is our niche? Because people who have participated in the formulation of goals are much more likely to feel accountable for the achievement of those goals, the committee believes the first step to success is to develop a mission statement on which most can agree (See following.).

> With a team of four others develop what you would consider a mission statement for an urban high school. Besides answering the five questions proposed by Lewis and colleagues, include four core values that will form the way the mission will be approached (for example, compassion, dignity, empathy, and so forth)

Sample Mission Statement

The entire school community of Washington County is committed to providing a high-quality, challenging, and culturally appropriate curriculum for all students in a safe and respectful school environment. We intend that all graduates be prepared to exercise a wide variety of postsecondary options and take full advantage of opportunities ranging from immediate entry into the workforce to admission to the college or university of their choice and to persist in their chosen educational and vocational placements. Additionally, we fully expect our graduates to demonstrate the skills necessary for successful relationships with peers, family, and a culturally diverse community.

IDENTIFY THE NEEDS OF BENEFICIARIES

The primary beneficiaries of schooling will be students. However, as can be inferred from the sample mission statement others in the school community benefit as well. Future employers benefit from a well-educated workforce composed of persons respectful of individual differences. Families and future family members, peers, and colleagues benefit by being associated with persons who understand what is required to build and maintain strong positive relationships. Additionally, the immediate community and society at large benefit by the addition of young adults who are interested in participating in and supporting community activities.

Are the beneficiaries of your services clear from the mission statement you developed? If not, take time now to revise the statement such that persons reading it could ascertain who would benefit if the purposes you stated were achieved.

With a clear purpose, we turn our attention to addressing the needs of our students. How do we identify those needs and other constituencies? Kretzmann and McKnight (1993) explain that traditional needs assessments convey part of the truth but not all of it. There are multiple sources of school, state, and national data. Ms. Schroeder and her committee decide to conduct the basic type of analysis suggested by the Education Trust (n.d.) called the education pipeline. Through this analysis, educators create a portrait of what happens to children as they journey through school. They will begin with entering ninth-grade students in 1990 and for each identifiable racial or ethnic group enrolled will gather the following pieces of information:

- How many graduated from high school with their class?
- How many graduated college-ready?
- How many entered 2-year colleges?
- How many entered 4-year colleges?
- How many were still enrolled 2 years later?

This analysis is an excellent beginning for identifying possible equity issues that need to be changed. The committee will also examine disaggregated data for students who are retained or overaged by 2 or more years; dropout patterns; persistence in college; the completion of homework; relationships among rates in test performance, excessive absenteeism, and special student placements; enrollment in college preparation courses by socioeconomic status as well as racial and ethnic group; achievement test scores at selected grade levels; grades distribution and SAT scores by race and parental education; number of graduates held for remedial coursework in college; student and parent expectations; and quality of teacher preparation.

Reflecting on your own school experiences, what were the assets or strengths of your school and community? How did these assets affect your educational experience? In what ways might the assets have been used more effectively to address some of the needs you can identify from your own school?

As well as identifying student needs through the analysis of these data, the committee will identify some of the assets of the individual schools. Eventually, a review of the skills, talents, and specialties of all the school personnel will need to be undertaken. Community strengths such as residents' skills, talents, and willingness to volunteer; civic organizations; families' contributions; goods and services; and other resources are identified as assets. Identifying the school and community assets highlights the strengths that may be useful to this professional community as it begins to explore the resources available to address identified needs.

PROCESSES OR METHODS

With a purpose clearly articulated and the needs and assets of students identified (data gathered), the next step for the steering committee is to identify the process or processes most likely to result in the desired change for the system. Kurpius and Rozecki (1992) note that school counselors are inclined to spend more time implementing individual and small-group interventions and often spend less time focusing on specific populations of students in need. Given the characteristics of a system, changing the individuals in a system does not change the system itself (Scholtes, 1998). Therefore, if the examination of school data highlights a group or groups of students who encounter institutional barriers to success, individual interventions may not be the most appropriate. This realization has been somewhat startling for Ms. Schroeder and the other steering committee members and points out the need to work more collaboratively with others in their system to effect change leading to better learning conditions for future students.

COLLABORATION

In the early stages of the change process, Dr. Pickens and the administrative team recognized the need to create an environment in which people felt encouraged to work together rather than continue to work in isolation. In other words, they wanted to establish an environment where collaboration was possible. Friend and Cook (2000) define collaboration as a "style for direct interaction between at least two coequal parties voluntarily engaged in shared decision making as they work toward a common goal" (p. 6). Collaboration is not an intervention with well-defined steps. As the term implies, collaboration is a process that involves two or more people working together to achieve a common goal. O'Looney (1996) discusses the informal process or spirit of collaboration as sharing goals, values, ideas of fairness, and the experience of joint activity. Abramson and Rosenthal (1995) propose stages of collaboration that require key tasks. At the formation stage, collaborators establish a common mission, a shared view of tasks, and clear operating ground rules. At the implementation stage, collaborators deal with communication difficulties, group dynamics, and interpersonal problems that interfere with completing the work. At the maintenance stage, more issues or tensions may arise about power, leadership, goals, strategies, and follow-through.

> Share with the class a time when you have worked together with someone else to achieve a common goal. Read on to discover the defining characteristics of collaboration and then describe how the circumstance you recalled either was or was not a collaborative process.

The terms *collaboration, consultation,* and *teamwork* are often used interchangeably and do, in fact, share some common characteristics. Dettmer, Dyck, and Thurston (1996) state that in schools, all three approaches involve

- Addressing problems within the school context.
- Engaging in interactive processes.
- Using specialized content for the purpose of achieving goals.
- Sharing resources.
- Serving as catalyst for change or improvements.

Expanding on their definition of collaboration, Friend and Cook identify some of the defining characteristics of collaboration:

- Collaboration is voluntary.
- Collaboration requires equal value and equal power in decision making of all participants (parity).
- Collaboration is based on mutual goals.
- Collaboration depends on shared responsibility of participants.
- Collaborators share resources.

• Collaborators share accountability for outcomes.

During prior reform initiatives, each person worked on different parts of a puzzle without any sense of how the pieces were supposed to fit together to lead to better educational outcomes for students. For this new effort, the steering committee recommended to Dr. Pickens that staff and faculty in each school get together in a day-long retreat. The retreats took place off school grounds, and everyone was asked to bring their favorite picnic dish to contribute to lunch and invited to dress casually. The goal of these retreats was to establish an inviting atmosphere in which employees might get to know each other beyond the impressions associated with their individual roles at the school.

At each retreat, participants were asked to divide themselves into four groups, each facilitated by a school counselor, to take an inventory of the activities in which they were currently engaged that directly related to the school mission. During this process, the participants discovered that there was a great deal of similarity, overlap, and sometimes redundancy reflected in their individual efforts. They spontaneously, and voluntarily, began to identify ways to share their tasks, resources, and responsibility for the achievement of their goals. One outcome of the activity was that the employees expressed the desire to establish more formal opportunities for collaboration and wanted to learn about ways to organize themselves to collaborate on issues of mutual interest and concern (shared goals). An evaluation of the retreat indicated that the individual participants felt less isolated and more connected with each other than they had prior to their day together. In fact, they requested that Dr. Pickens arrange for a similar planning retreat during the next professional development day to establish formal structures for collaboration. One such structure that all agreed would be helpful was more extensive use of grade-level teams in the middle and high schools and subject-area teams in the elementary schools.

Teaming

The commitment to continue talking and working together provided a momentum to build their teams. The counselors at each school were recruited to help the team development effort. They began by asking a local counselor educator to lead some professional development sessions for them to refresh their knowledge about groups and to teach them more about team building. Those sessions included definitions and characteristics of effective teams, as well as leadership functions and team development patterns. After their study and practice of these concepts, the counselors agreed they had the skills and knowledge to help the teams organize and structure themselves.

Johnson and Johnson (1997) define a team as a group of people whose interactions are focused on accomplishing a shared goal. The team "is more than the sum of its parts" (p. 508). To function effectively teams incorporate the following components. First the members commit to developing and maintaining constructive relationships among themselves. Furthermore helpful teams have established goals, roles, and ways of functioning. All individuals know the focus of the group, responsibilities of each member, and how the team will go about accomplishing their task. A final component of effective teams is continual work on improving their relationships and their work (Basham, Appleton, & Lambarth, 1998).

Henderson and Gysbers (1998) identify the advantages of teams. They recognize that when all members help in an effort, the level of support for the work and for each other increases. A team provides a forum for its members to be challenged to take risks, to be creative, and to contribute. Another advantage noted by these authors is the team accepting responsibility for its work.

Developing productive teams requires attention to fostering

- The team—members trust and depend on each other and grant each other mutual respect.
- Problem-solving skills, conflict resolution, and building relationships.
- Accountability for accomplishing the task and for influencing the work process.
- Encouragement and help in promoting everyone's efforts to achieve.

The counselors learned that a group becomes a team as members move into sharing goals and commitment. As small-group counselors, they have helped a group focus on the growth of the individual members. As a facilitator of a team, they will help the group focus on the task. The counselors bring their understanding of group dynamics, relationship patterns, personality characteristics, and the educational process as they facilitate the team-building process. Besides their knowledge about the different focus of small groups and team building, the counselors needed to investigate the phases of becoming a working group. They studied a team-building model described by Kormanski (1999). Based on group development theory, this model emphasizes the work and outcome of each stage of team development. Table 5.2 summarizes those components.

In the beginning members become oriented to the team concept. They learn what behaviors are acceptable to the group and transition from an individual to a member status. The members may exhibit testing behavior and may depend on the leader to

TABLE 5.2 The Work and Outcome of Each Stage of Team Development

Team Stage	Member Behavior	General Theme	Task Outcome	Relationship Outcome	Facilitator Behavior
Beginning	Cautious Observing	Awareness	Commitment	Acceptance	Linking Modeling
Transition	Resistant Exploring Careful	Conflict to cooperation	Clarification Involvement	Belonging Support	Modeling Challenging differences
Working	Participating Dealing with issues Listening, understanding other points of view	Productivity	Achievement	Pride	Focus on work, solutions, negotiations Collaboration
Ending	Learning put in perspective Discussion of lessons learned	Separation	Recognition	Satisfaction	Summarizing

Source: Adapted from Kormanski, C. L. & Mozenter, A. (1987). A new model of team building. In J. W. Pfeiffer (Ed.). *The 1987 annual: Developing human resources* (pp. 255–268). San Diego, CA: University Associates; and from Shoffner, M. F., & Williamson, R. D. Engaging preservice school counselors and principals in dialogue and collaboration. In *Counselor Education and Supervision, 40* (2) (pp. 128–140). © 2000 American Counseling Association. Reprinted with permission.

provide structure. Members will attempt to identify tasks, parameters, and methods of accomplishing the goal as well as decisions about what information is needed and how it will be used. During this early stage members may be reluctant to participate. As facilitators of the team-building process, the counselors will help each grade-level group in this early stage to begin to identify its philosophy and rules. In Washington County, counselors will lead the teams in determining the common assumptions they hold about teaching and learning as well as the areas on which they disagree. The team will need to discuss good team communication strategies, the steps they will use to reach their goals, and how they will go about making decisions. Counselors will also lead a discussion on confidentiality about sensitive matters and on loyalty to the team and its work. Early work on these basic concepts will prepare the team members for building their competence and accomplishing their work to improve the educational climate of the school for the students in each grade level—each team's overarching goal.

During the transition stage members look for more clarification and explore the trustworthiness of other members and of the process itself. This will hopefully lead to a better sense of the team's direction. The counselors will work to help the team members learn to listen and understand each person. Counselors may use their mediation skills to help resolve any defensiveness that could sabotage the team's effectiveness. As members demonstrate a respectful regard for each other, they will move to a greater sense of belonging and purpose, setting the stage for an acceptance of the team, team norms, their own roles, and each other. At this point team boundaries are well established and easier to maintain and more work is accomplished. Counselors would expect more open communication and cooperation among team members.

The working group will move into effective problem solving in an interdependent way. During this productive phase of the team, the counselors' facilitating job will become less difficult as they help the group focus on the work, solutions, and negotiations necessary for agreements. Members will be participating more fully and openly about dealing with issues as they emerge. During the working stage the team members will be listening carefully to each other and understanding other viewpoints.

For each team the end will be determined by the school term. As a preparation for the next year's work as well as a culmination for the previous team, the counselors will help team members summarize their progress and discuss future collaborations. Team members will be encouraged to discuss the lessons they have learned and to reflect on the perspectives they have gained. The team will also review outcomes they have accomplished as they end this team's term until the next year.

Johnson and Johnson (1997) provide more specifics for structuring and nurturing teams:

1. Encourage the team to define their compelling purpose and their goals specific to their team.

2. Have frequent and regular meetings for opportunities to interact personally and to promote each other's success.

3. Pay particular attention to the first meeting.

4. Establish clear rules of conduct at the outset especially some pertaining to attendance, discussion topics, confidentiality, confrontation, and contributions.

5. Measure the progress of the team toward its goals.

6. Show progress.

7. Expose the team to new facts and information.

8. Provide training to contribute to the work on the task and to team skills.

9. Celebrate team and member success.

10. Ensure frequent team-processing sessions. (pp. 521–523)

As the counselors reviewed these suggestions and integrated them with their skills with groups, they felt better prepared to help extend the collaboration begun in the retreat by helping build teams of grade-level teachers focused on talking and working together to help students succeed.

Advocacy

Collaboration and teaming make possible the use of another process for systemic change: social advocacy. D'Andrea and Daniels (1999) state that literally millions of people in society lack the opportunity to participate fully in establishing those rules and policies that affect their lives. As D'Andrea and Daniels note, young people are often disempowered by the policies and practices in the institutions that purport to serve them. The primary role of school counselors as advocates is to create opportunities for all students to define, nurture, and accomplish high aspirations (House & Martin, 1998). This goal is highly consistent with the motivation for change in the Washington County school system.

House and Martin (1998) suggest that school counselors work as change agents and advocates for the elimination of systemic barriers that impede academic success for all students. For example, based on the initial review of data analyzed by Ms. Schroeder and the steering committee, students whose first language was not English were placed in lower level, unchallenging classes at all grade levels. Ms. Schroeder speculates that these students may need relief from what Kurpius and Rozecki (1992) describe as social, psychological, or educational inequities limiting their opportunities for success. Some of these students, if receiving instruction in their native language, would most certainly be placed in advanced academic courses. The challenge for Ms. Schroeder and others is to address the real problem—language skills—so that these students can achieve to their full academic potential. To that end, Ms. Schroeder and the committee have decided to lobby the school board for a teacher for students with English as a second language (ESOL). They will also ask for placement tests to be given in the students' native language to achieve a more accurate understanding of each students' ability. Additionally, they will reach out to parents of these students and assist them in making the community contacts they need to access resources.

Advocates in schools focus on reducing institutional barriers leading to achievement gaps between poor and minority youth and their more advantaged peers. According to House and Martin (1998), school counselors have a broader view of the academic achievements and failures in their schools than perhaps any other single professional, because they routinely receive information from multiple sources about student successes and failures, test scores, course-taking patterns, and student placements. Although the activities described here are in the context of advocating for a systemwide change initiative, school counselors are in a position to identify issues such as these at the building level and to advocate for needed change.

The social advocacy position is based on the belief that individual or collective action must be taken to improve conditions for the benefit of an individual or group (House & Martin, 1998). Therefore, school counselors who believe that all students can achieve at high levels work to create conditions that promote achievement and reduce systemic barriers that do not. Sears (1999) states that school counselors accomplish these goals by using data to help the whole school look at student outcomes; using data to effect change; advocating for student experiences to broaden career awareness; and placing students in challenging courses. House and Martin (1998) suggest that school counselors do the following to become successful advocates who empower students to achieve at the highest level:

- Actively work to remove barriers to learning.
- Teach students how to help themselves (e.g., organizational skills, study skills, test-taking skills).
- Teach students and their families to successfully manage the bureaucracy of the system (teach parents how to enroll their children in academic courses that will lead to college).
- Teach students how to access support systems for academic success.
- Use local, regional, and national data to promote system change.
- Collaborate with all school personnel to promote change.
- Offer staff development training for school personnel promoting high expectations for all students.
- Challenge the existence of low-level and unchallenging courses.
- Highlight information that negates the myths about who can and cannot achieve in rigorous courses.
- Organize community activities to promote a supportive structure for high standards for all students.
- Help parents and community organize efforts to work with local schools to institute higher standards.
- Work as a resource broker within the community to identify available resources to help all students achieve.

Review the behaviors identified by House and Martin and identify specific actions that might be taken on behalf of the students for whom Ms. Schroeder is currently attempting to advocate.

The educators in Washington County believe that the grade-level and subject-area teams they have established will enable them to more effectively advocate for all students. The counselors in each school have agreed to serve as the data managers, systematically reviewing and reporting to the team all "pipeline" information on the students for whom they are responsible. The counselors will also review the data to detect patterns of possible inequities that extend beyond a particular grade level to the entire school experience of groups of students. Systematic, regular reviews of data, as well as serving on grade-level teams where more anecdotal data are also plentiful, will be integral to the success of the change initiative in Washington County.

SUMMARY

In this chapter, we have described leadership, systems thinking and change, and processes that lead to systemic change. School counselors possess the most important leadership skills—the ability to establish relationships and create conditions where collaboration is possible. Collaboration is an essential process for promoting systemic change. School-based teams, such as grade-level teams, are examples of collaborative efforts where the team members are all working toward a common, agreed-upon purpose. Finally, advocacy was discussed as a process for achieving desired systemic change on behalf of specific groups of students who encounter institutional barriers to academic success.

PORTFOLIO COMPONENTS

1. Based on the outcome of the inventory of leadership qualities you completed earlier, identify specific learning activities in which you will participate to develop the skills and behaviors you currently do not display. Include a description of the method of evaluation you will use to determine whether these activities have been successful.
2. In no more than one page, describe a team-building activity you might use if asked to facilitate an initial team meeting such as the one Ms. Schroeder has been asked to chair.
3. Based on an examination of the ACES technology standards (http://filebox.vt.edu/users/thohen/competencies.htm) what skills might you need to conduct a "pipeline" data analysis such as the one described in this chapter? Of those competencies you identified but have not mastered, specify learning activities you will use to develop competence.

The Guidance Curriculum

================= **CASE STUDY** =================

COORDINATED, SYSTEMWIDE PLANNING: DEVELOPING A K–12 GUIDANCE CURRICULUM

Mr. Terman and the counselors in Washington County are revising their existing curriculum to a standards-based guidance curriculum. The standards with which the counselors will be working are those developed by the American School Counselors Association. In addition, a systemwide needs assessment has been conducted to determine what unique needs exist among the students. Information from both of these sources will serve as the basis for the new K–12 curriculum.

The school system includes four elementary schools with one counselor each, two middle schools with two counselors each, and one secondary school with four counselors. These counselors are working to develop a curriculum that addresses the priorities identified by leadership teams and endorsed by each individual school. Mr. Terman has developed the following agenda for the counselors' first meeting:

1. Develop a statement of purpose for the group.

2. Identify the steps necessary to achieve the purpose and develop a time line for achievement.

3. Identify the resources available to achieve the purpose.

4. Identify the potential barriers to success and plan ways to overcome them.

5. Organize for the work.

Through team-building exercises, group members learned more about each other and their experiences on similar tasks. Each of them then explained their understanding of the task they were undertaking and agreed on some ground rules to help make their meeting smooth as well as productive. As this initial meeting progressed they began feeling more like a team with a serious yet achievable mission. To celebrate their resolve and their partnership, the counselors proclaimed themselves TK12 for "Think K–12" and began their work.

Students of all ages attend schools to learn. Most Americans agree that a good education is associated with success in life, so the learning enterprise prepares pupils for a better future. Ideally, students throughout their schooling acquire the knowledge, skills, values, and attitudes they need to become contributing members of society (Ballantine, 1997). In addition to the verbal and analytical skills and competencies essential to academic success, students learn the prevailing cultural norms and values about what behavior is acceptable and not acceptable. Students learn about careers, the requirements for a particular type of work, and ways to obtain the skills and knowledge they need for entering a particular profession. In short, what one learns during the first 13 years of schooling provides a foundation on which one builds for the rest of one's life. "The purpose of a counseling program in a school is to promote and enhance the learning process. The goal of the program is to enable all students to achieve success in school and to develop into contributing members of society" (ASCAa, 1999, p. 30).

The guidance curriculum is a central feature of any school counseling program. The curriculum is designed to provide for the delivery of systematic, age-appropriate concepts to all students in the school (Wittmer, Thompson, & Loesch, 1997). The curriculum is sequential, with concepts at one level building on those learned at the previous level. Consequently, the planning of the curriculum needs to include persons working at all developmental levels in any given school system. The purpose of the guidance curriculum is to promote optimal development of all students in educational, career, and personal/social domains.

After reading and discussing this chapter, you should be able to

- Define guidance curriculum.
- Identify desired student competencies in each of the three areas of development with which school counselors are concerned.
- Develop guidance units and lessons.
- Articulate the skills and competencies necessary for conducting classroom guidance lessons (implementing the guidance curriculum).

DEFINITION

As noted in chapter 1, the earliest school counseling programs consisted of guidance "lessons" delivered by high school teachers to prepare young people to make vocational choices. These lessons were the forerunners of what we identify today as the guidance curriculum. As the profession of school counseling has evolved to its current status, so have the various program components for which the counselor is responsible. Currently, the guidance curriculum is intended to deliver the guidance content identified as essential to all students, K–12, in a systematic and sequential way (Gysbers & Henderson, 2000). According to Gysbers and Henderson, the curriculum generally includes the student competencies or outcomes to be achieved in each of three developmental domains (academic, career, and personal/social) across all grade levels.

Counselors and/or teachers most typically deliver the guidance curriculum through planned activities in which entire classes of students participate. For example, in career development in a middle school, all seventh-grade math classes might participate in a six-session unit designed to explore careers in mathematics. All eighth graders in the same school might learn about careers in journalism during their regularly scheduled language arts class. The seventh and eighth graders might all learn about the variety of career opportunities in their community through a schoolwide career fair. All these activities are examples of methods for delivering that part of the guidance curriculum concerned with the career development standards.

Considering the information provided above and the case at the beginning of this chapter, work as a group to refine a project plan for preparing the K–12 curriculum. The first task is to develop a statement of purpose for Mr. Terman and his group of planners. Based on this statement, develop goals with clear outcomes, determine responsibilities for the tasks, and set time lines for achieving your purpose.

CURRICULUM DEVELOPMENT: SCOPE AND SEQUENCE

An initial structuring task for the TK12 team is to determine how they are going to organize themselves to work most efficiently. On the surface, it seems that cooperative work groups based on level (elementary, middle, secondary) might be the most expedient way to proceed. However, after further discussion, the group decides to work by domain (academic, career, personal/social). Consequently, there is someone representing each developmental level on each of the three subgroups for each domain. Ms. Serita Jones is the team leader for the academic subgroup; Mr. Tony Harris is team leader for the career subgroup; and Ms. Emmy Lou Rice is team leader for the personal/social subgroup. Each subgroup will meet throughout the school year to plan curriculum in their particular domain, with at least one full team meeting every 3 months.

Before they break into their subgroups for planning, the TK12 team members agree to identify the shared values on which their work will be based. Their primary concern is that their curriculum be sufficient in scope and sequence. They have also agreed that the curriculum will be standards based (Dahir, Sheldon, & Valiga, 1998; see Appendix B). Additionally, in a recent school- and communitywide needs assessment concern was expressed about an increase in bias-motivated incidents (vandalism and harassment) directed toward both people and property. The leadership team from each school identified the elimination of these incidents as a priority. With these guidelines in mind, the counselors believe they have identified the "scope" of the curriculum. The "sequence" will be based on general principles of cognitive, physical, socioemotional, and racial identity development from which the academic, career, and persona/social needs (and capabilities) of students at the elementary, middle, and high school levels are derived.

> What are the advantages of the decision to organize by domain for the planning team? What are the disadvantages?

Basic developmental principles provide guidance for school counselors so that the classroom guidance activities at each grade level are appropriate to students' ability to learn. Schoolwide activities that are part of the guidance curriculum also need to be planned according to the ranges of developmental levels in one's school. For example, a schoolwide career fair for grades 9–12 might include activities that encourage identification of career interests and exploration of broad career areas consistent with students' interests and abilities. For the seniors in the school, more emphasis might be placed on identifying and contacting prospective employers, preparing the resumé, gaining interviewing skills, and practicing successful work behaviors. A schoolwide career fair at the middle school might focus on the dissemination of information about careers. At the elementary level, a career fair may focus on careers in students' communities and the work their own and their classmates' parents perform (see Table 6.1).

According to Ormrod (2000), certain principles of development hold true for almost all children. Although development is somewhat orderly and predictable, it occurs at different rates for different children and is influenced by both heredity and environment. According to Pai and Adler (1997) development may proceed either continuously or discontinuously and is influenced by the developing person's social relationships and cultural environment. Culture refers to the knowledge, skills, behaviors, attitudes, and beliefs developed by a group and passed from one generation to the next (Pai & Adler, 1997). According to Pai and Adler, "The culture to which one belongs, then, becomes the root of the individual's identity because culture gives us a sense of power and confidence by giving us the basis of achieving our goals, determining what is desirable and undesirable, and developing the purpose of

TABLE 6.1 Sample Developmental Guidance Needs

	Academic Development	Career Development	Personal/Social Development
Elementary School The formation of basic attitudes and information about self and life opportunities begins	K–2: Students need help developing the following: • Essential skills they need to be successful in school (read, write, and do basic computations) • Descriptions for how they learn something, how they recall information, and how they plan to complete an assignment • Ability to identify situations in which learning is easy or hard • Ability to identify the benefits of learning	Students need help developing the following: • Ability to describe workers in various settings, type of work of family members, type of work children do • Ability to describe what they like to do and how they change from year to year • Awareness of differences among peers and themselves • Awareness of the skills they have	Students need help developing the following: • Self-awareness, confidence, and competence • Skills to describe relationships and the process of making and keeping friends • Positive description of attributes and unique qualities of self and others • Responsibility for tasks at home, school, and regarding care of self and belongings
	3–5: Students need help developing the following: • Strategies that help them learn such as note taking, practicing memory skills, goal setting, and preparing for tests • Understanding of how learning occurs differently for different people and how it occurs both in and out of school • Ability to apply different skills to different school subjects and settings • Ability to describe things they learned about themselves from taking tests	Students need help developing the following: • Recognition of choices people make about work and their many other life roles • Ability to describe work of men and women, and relationship of interests and abilities to work • Ability to define "future" and describe what their lives may be like in the future	Students need help developing the following: • Description of themselves, their strengths • Recognition of the impact their actions have on others and that their choices have consequences • Understanding of how traits develop • Ability to express appreciation to others for their own unique qualities • Ability to know when change is and is not possible • Recognition and acceptance of cultural differences • Ability to identify and express feelings in an acceptable manner

Source: Alabama State Department of Education (1996). *The revised comprehensive counseling and guidance model for Alabama's public schools.* Bulletin 1966, No. 27. Montgomery, AL: Author. ERIC/CAPS (1990) *Building Comprehensive School Counseling Programs.* Greensboro, NC: Author. Reprinted with permission.

TABLE 6.1 *continued*

	Academic Development	Career Development	Personal/Social Development
Middle School Exploring and reality testing attitudes and information about self, others, and opportunities	6–8: Students need help developing the following: • Ability to assert themselves by asking questions, both at home and at school • Plans for their own study areas, study schedule, and study style • Ability to achieve balance between school and other activities • A tentative 4-year education plan and portfolio based on high school graduation requirements	Students need help developing the following: • Understanding how stereotypes and experiences influence their career choices • Ability to discuss career planning process and identify and use career resources • Projections for how some careers may be different in the future • Descriptions of their existing skills and how those relate to current workforce demands • Explanations for how needs can be met in work and leisure	Students need help developing the following: • Positive health habits • Good communication skills • Understanding peer pressure • Ability to apply problem-solving models to real-world problems • Ability to identify and use personal strengths • Understand how past choices influence present and future actions • Descriptions of unique qualities of self, positive self-concept, and understanding of one's uniqueness as well as similarities with others • Ability to deal with pressure • Understanding of relationship between personal responsibility and life management
High School Specific planning related to imminence of making the transition from school to work or college	9–12: Students need help developing the following: • Ability to identify and use community resources • Understanding when and why 4-year plan may need to be revised • Ability to analyze test results and use to plan for improvement • Effective work habits • Describe relationship between student behavior and academic success • A plan for collecting postsecondary information, making contacts and plans for graduation • Plan for future education or training • Ability to evaluate and revise future goals based on performance, interest, and range of available options	Students need help developing the following: • Description of skills, abilities, interests, needs, and understanding of how those factors influence career choice • Understanding nontraditional careers open to them • Congruence between educational plan and career goals • Assessment of ability to achieve goals and integrate learning into planning • Descriptions of skills and qualifications to obtain and keep specific jobs of interest • Strategies for coping with sexual harassment, sexual discrimination, and other potential difficulties in the workplace	Students need help developing the following: • Skills to respond to pressure • Recognition of qualities of people who are different from self and identification of own biases and stereotypes that interfere with establishing relationships • Development of strategies for overcoming stereotypes and biases • Ability to generate alternatives and assessing consequences before acting • Ability to direct and control feelings • Understanding of all that goes into making choices

life" (p. 26). A curriculum that is developmentally appropriate builds on the skills and abilities students have at any given grade, provides enough challenge to lead to the acquisition of new skills and knowledge, and is flexible enough to accommodate individual differences within the student body, including those differences associated with students' cultural identities.

CURRICULUM DESIGN

Review the topics in Table 6.1 under academic development. Identify those topics that could be addressed by the classroom teacher in the context of the regular school day.

All class members visit the Web site for Orange County Public Schools (http://www.ocps.k12.fl.us /framework/subject.php? subject = 18). Assign each person a strand (developmental domain) and a standard to work on as you read through the rest of this chapter.

As with most effective planning, the counselors begin to design curriculum by considering the desired student outcomes. In this case, the goal is to implement the ASCA *National Standards* (see Appendix B) and achieve associated student outcomes reflective of student needs in this particular school district. Instructional goals planning considers the needs of the students, the societies (cultures) in which the students now live and will live as adults, and the requirements of the subject matter being taught (Gunter, Estes, & Schwab, 1995). Based on these multiple perspectives, counselors develop the purposes and a description of desired student outcomes, or curriculum. Based on the curriculum, the essential topics to be covered at each grade level emerge. These topics lead to the development of units and lessons to be delivered in the classroom or through schoolwide activities. Sometimes counselors will help teachers find ways to incorporate these themes into their presentation of subject matter. At other times counselors themselves will be in classrooms teaching the lessons.

GUIDANCE UNIT CONTENT

All well-designed guidance units have the following characteristics:

- A clear purpose
- Age-appropriate activities
- Coordinated and sequential lessons
- Opportunities for students to apply, reflect, and evaluate their learning
- Summary and evaluation (Blum, 1998)

Clearly articulated goals provide the foundation for the curriculum planning process. Planning involves determining what the students will learn, through what activities (experiences), and with what materials. Planning a guidance curriculum requires considering each grade and breaking the material into segments by the year, term, unit, week, and day. These plans work best as flexible frameworks that help instructors start and maintain their lessons in the right direction rather than as scripts with no opportunities for elaboration.

Tomlinson (1999) explains levels of learning previously articulated by Hilda Taba. People can learn facts, discrete bits of information. They can develop concepts, or categories of things with common elements to help organize, retain, and use information. Humans can also understand principles, rules that govern concepts. Students develop attitudes, or degrees of commitment to ideas. Finally individuals can acquire skills, the ability to put to work the understandings gained. Many of the specific outcomes of a counseling curriculum are generic and therefore easily linked to other subjects. Skills such as listening, interacting, and forming goals are examples of generic skills in the counseling curriculum that could easily weave into many subjects. The ASCA *National Standards* presents a list of facts, concepts, principles, attitudes, or skills. The TK12 team discusses each standard and labels it at its level of learning. Consequently, they are able to generate specific lists of what students should know (facts), understand (concepts and principles), and be able to do (skills). For example, to develop curriculum around a career development standard, decisions might include the following possibilities:

Facts: appropriate definitions of careers
Concepts: classifications of careers
Principles: economic supply and demand for specific careers
Attitudes: value of work to student and society
Skills: gathering information about specific careers

> Based on the standard you were assigned previously, choose one grade from each of the three levels (elementary, middle, and high school) and identify facts, concepts, principles, attitudes, and skills students need to learn.

Figure 6.1 illustrates this sequence for a particular topic of importance in the development of the Washington County students.

Instructional content must be organized into manageable parts and sequenced for effective presentation. A unit of instruction centers on a broad concept or a cluster of related concepts. The elements of a unit include the scope (the range of content), focus (what will be emphasized), and sequence (the order in which the content is arranged). The processes (activities that help the students learn) and the product (ways the students will demonstrate their new knowledge) are also identified. These considerations, as well as the age of students, will lead logically to decisions about how many lessons will be contained in each unit.

> Look at the product statement in Figure 6.1. Transform this statement into a three-part learning objective. Now, do the same with the product statements in the three grade-level examples you developed earlier.

According to Gunter, Estes, and Schwab (1995) a learning objective is "a statement of the measurable learning that is intended to take place as a result of instruction" (p. 25). Mager's (1975) three-part system for establishing objectives includes the intended student behavior, the conditions under which the behavior will occur, and the criteria for an acceptable performance.

Another approach presented by Gronlund (1995) begins with general outcomes and then clarifies those by listing a few of the sample behaviors that provide evidence that the student has learned. Here are some examples from a conflict resolution lesson:

General objective: Students will apply problem-solving skills to peer interactions that involve conflict.
Specific examples:

1. Explains each side of the conflict.
2. States possible responses of each side.
3. Identifies potential outcomes for each response.

FIGURE 6.1   Sequence for Skill Development

Strand: Personal/Social Development (2nd Grade)

Standard: The student acquires the knowledge, attitudes, and interpersonal skills to help understand and respond to self and others

A Topic of Study Consists of: Valuing Diversity

Key Facts:
Information about diverse groups of people

Organizing Concepts:
Similarities and differences exist among all people

Guiding Principles:
We live in a pluralistic society

Associated Attitudes:
Self-awareness; acceptance of self and others

Essential Skills:
Demonstrate respect for others

Content:
Student will be able to recognize and appreciate individual differences among classmates.

Process:
Circle of Hands Activity. Each student draws his/her hands on a large piece of paper so that when drawn side by side the hands form a circle or square with blank space in the center. Inside his or her own hands, each student identifies and writes individual strengths or accomplishments. Throughout the year, significant events or accomplishments of individual students are added to the center opening of the drawing.

Product:
Students are able to discuss the collective strengths of the group and identify goals that could be accomplished by the group, but not by the individual.

Sources: Adapted from *The Differentiated Classroom: Responding to the Needs of All Learners* by Carol Ann Tomlinson. Alexandria, VA: Association for Supervision and Curriculum Development. Copyright © 1999 ASCD. Reprinted by permission. All rights reserved. Kottman, T., Ashby, J., & DeGraaf, D. (2001). *Adventures in guidance: How to put fun into your guidance program.* Alexandria, VA: American Counseling Association. Copyright © ACA. Reprinted with permission.

4. Discriminates between helpful and nonhelpful responses.
5. Demonstrates peaceful, nonviolent resolution to situation.

Many counselors use taxonomies to plan units and lessons. Benjamin Bloom and his colleagues (1956) presented a way to identify educational outcomes and to classify those outcomes by categories in a hierarchical pattern. In their taxonomy they list the three domains of education: cognitive, affective, and psychomotor. Table 6.2 includes the general and more specific categories for the three domains of educa-

TABLE 6.2   Educational Taxonomies

Sample of Verbs in the Cognitive Domain

Knowledge	to recall, to repeat, to recollect, to memorize, to list
Comprehension	to identify, to recognize, to select
Application	to use, to solve, to practice, to reproduce, to compare, to contrast
Analysis	to investigate, to separate, to study, to research, to describe
Synthesis	to combine, to formulate, to deduce, to unite, to assemble
Evaluation	to appraise, to judge, to assess, to assign value to, to accept

Sample of Verbs in the Affective Domain

Receiving	to take in, to listen, to encounter, to be aware
Responding	to react, to reply, to answer, to comply
Valuing	to accept, to reject, to esteem, to regard, to desire
Organization	to compare, to order, to prioritize
Characterization	to internalize, to personalize, to demonstrate

Sample of Verbs in the Psychomotor Domain

Readiness	willing, prepared, watches
Observation	attends, is interested
Perception	senses, has a feel for, is able
Response	practices, imitates, replicates
Adaptation	masters, develops, changes

Source: Adapted from Gunter, M. A., Estes, T. H., & Schwab, J. (1999). *Instruction: A models approach* (3nd ed.). Published by Allyn and Bacon, Boston, MA. Copyright © 1999 by Pearson Education. Reprinted by permission of the publisher.

tional taxonomies. Cognitive objectives focus on the intellectual outcomes, facts, concepts, and principles mentioned earlier. In the cognitive domain the categories are knowledge (recalling information and facts), comprehension (understanding, translating the information), application (using information to solve problems), analysis (breaking down information into parts and revealing organization), synthesis (creating a new idea, product, or solution), and evaluation (assessing something against a standard).

The affective domain describes the attitudes, feelings, and dispositions that students are expected to acquire (Krathwohl, Bloom, & Masia, 1964). Those objectives are receiving (being aware or attending to something), responding (showing some new behavior as a result of an experience), valuing (showing definite involvement or commitment), organization (integrating a new value), and characterization (acting consistently with the new value).

The psychomotor domain involves ability and coordination objectives. Gunter, Estes, and Schwab (1995) explain that taxonomy in the psychomotor domain identifies these levels: readiness (being willing to participate), observation (watching the behavior), perception (recognizing the behavior), response (performing the behavior), and adaptation (incorporating the behavior into one's repertoire). Gronlund (1995) suggests using the domains to get ideas for objectives, to help in writing clear statements about expectations, and to provide a check on completeness.

The framework developed by the Orange County Public Schools identifies the following statement as a benchmark (educational objective) in the career development standards for an eighth-grade student: "The student locates community resources for exploration related to personal interest, aptitudes, and skills." At what level of the cognitive domain is that written? Identify four other cognitive objectives from the Web site and determine their level.

The framework developed by the Orange County Public Schools identifies the following statement as a benchmark (educational objective) in the career development standards for a first-grade student: "The student recognizes all careers are acceptable to any gender." At what level of the affective domain is that written? Identify two others from the Web site and determine their level.

The framework developed by the Orange County Public Schools identifies the following statement as a benchmark (educational objective) in the career development standards for an eleventh-grade student: "The student applies job readiness skills to seek educational and employment opportunities." Which parts of the psychomotor domain might this objective include?

Write an objective based on this career development standard: "The student employs strategies to achieve future career success and satisfaction" for a seventh-grade student using cognitive, affective, and psychomotor domains. Compare your objectives to those written by your classmates.

Working on the strand you were originally assigned, develop a lesson plan using the outline presented in Figure 6.3 for one grade in elementary, middle, and high school.

Another approach to planning uses a constructivist perspective in which an overarching goal guides the instructor's planning. Educators focus on creating an environment for students to discover the depth of an idea and a variety of perspectives. To begin the instructor determines a topic, such as careers. The counselor may map the concept as a way of thinking about how learning and understanding may emerge from the theme. Figure 6.2 provides an example of a map for a counselor planning a career development unit. The counselor and students may then work together to identify activities, materials, projects, and behaviors that will help students learn and apply the goal. The students "construct" knowledge that is meaningful to them at this particular time.

Counselors may find the following questions helpful in their planning processes:

- What overarching understandings are desired? (What will students understand as a result of this unit?)
- What are the overarching "essential" questions? (What "essential" and "unit" questions will focus this unit?)
- What evidence will show that students understand?
- Given the targeted understandings, other unit goals, and the assessment evidence identified, what knowledge and skill are needed?
- What teaching and learning experiences will equip students to demonstrate the targeted understanding? (Wiggins & McTighe, 1998)

The lesson plan outline in Figure 6.3 provides a way for instructors to check on whether they have fully addressed these questions.

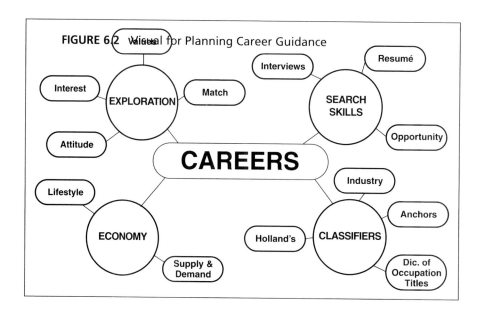

FIGURE 6.2   Visual for Planning Career Guidance

FIGURE 6.3 Sample Lesson Plan Format

Lesson Plan

Topic:
Class:
Date:

Learner Outcomes: Lesson objectives
    The Learner Will

Introduction: Engaging the learner in the topic, connecting the topic to something already known
    Identify focus:

    Create anticipation:

    Encourage learning:

Learning Activities: Teaching procedures and student activities
    Teacher:

    Student:

Assessment/Evaluation: Checking for understanding

Closing: Summary and extended practice

Follow-up: Independent practice and homework

Resources: Equipment, materials, other teaching aids

IMPLEMENTING THE CURRICULUM

The overarching goal of the guidance curriculum is for students to learn specific skills, behaviors, and attitudes that lead to school achievement and success in life. Learning is (1) the relatively permanent changes in behavior that occur due to experiences and (2) the relatively permanent changes in mental associations that occur as a result of experiences (Ormrod, 1999). These two definitions agree that learning is relatively permanent and is a result of experience (Ormrod, 2000). They differ in that the first definition specifies that changes associated with learning are behavioral, which implies that the changes are immediately observable. The second definition describes changes in mental associations, which may or may not result in immediate, observable behavioral change.

For example, consider the goal of teaching 18 fifth-grade students to resolve conflicts in a peaceful, nonviolent way through a series of lessons presented in their classroom by the school counselor (Personal/Social Development Standard C: Students will understand safety and survival skills). Assume that the subject has been introduced and the necessary skills both explained and demonstrated by the counselor. The counselor asks for five students to volunteer to role-play a conflict that they attempt to resolve using the skills previously introduced. If these five students successfully resolve the conflict using the new skills (or behaviors), we can assume that learning has occurred for them, but what about the other 13 students in the classroom? Are we to assume that no learning has occurred because they have not demonstrated the skills or behaviors to which they have been exposed? From a cognitive (mental association) point of view, students who have experienced the lessons related to conflict resolution strategies may also learn the skills through their observations of the counselor and the subsequent student role play. The behaviors, however, may not be evident until such time as they need to use the skills to resolve a conflict. The key to learning, from either perspective, is experience. The challenge for instructors is to create situations that become meaningful learning experiences for a diverse student population.

Instructional Approaches

Counselors facilitate learning by using many methods of instruction (Woolfolk, 1998). Using a counselor-centered approach, they may choose to lecture and explain as a method for communicating material to the learners. Another approach to teaching is through recitation and questioning. Thought-provoking and varied questions increase the effectiveness of this teaching method, where students learn how to ask and how to explain. Counselors may also use supervised practice activities of seatwork and homework as follow up to a lesson. These teaching practices are centered on the teacher who presents, questions, reacts, and corrects. These approaches might be used when explaining to high school juniors and their parents the process of applying to college.

Student-centered practices require more active participation from the learner. Group discussions allow students to ask questions, answer each other's questions, and respond to each other's answers. Brainstorming allows students to generate lists and to evaluate and prioritize the possibilities. Simulations and role playing encourage

Working in small discussion groups, identify classroom guidance topics and grade levels where counselor-centered strategies may be appropriate. Also discuss the cultural values and norms that may be transmitted by this approach and identify cultural groups whose values may be in conflict with those values on which this approach is based.

students to explore many dimensions of a situation. Simulations involve the creation of an experience, perhaps a dilemma, problem, or crisis, within the classroom. Students may then propose, debate, and evaluate courses of action. Role playing involves a student accepting a role in a scenario and acting out that person in that situation. Brookfield (1990) provides guidelines for instructors to create and guide simulations and role plays. Computers, videodiscs, and other technology provide valuable tools for encouraging learning and problem solving. For example, computer simulations introduce simplified versions of real-life situations with which the student can interact. Problem-based learning is a strategy that promotes varied learning strategies. Other student-centered learning practices are cooperative learning groups. These groups create positive interdependence enhanced by interactions, social skills, group processing, and individual accountability (Johnson & Johnson, 1999).

> Discuss the cultural values and norms that may be transmitted by the cooperative work group approach and identify cultural contexts in which those values may be in conflict with students' values.

Along with the selection of strategies, counselors select materials and resources to use in their classes. Evaluating materials for suitability for the topic, age of students, and bias all are the responsibility of the counselor. Counselors should review all materials they plan to use with students to ensure that the standards for success in life, including work and family roles, are not based on traditional roles, stereotypes, or biases.

Classroom Management

Some of the activities counselors use will be similar to those used by the classroom teacher and others will be different. Students may be asked to talk to each other and to move about the classroom in ways that are not typical of their standard classroom conduct. Most schools and classrooms have rules of conduct established with which students are familiar. Counselors also need to be familiar with these rules, apply them consistently, and if one intends to deviate from the norm, clearly explain to students the new rules. Some other strategies for managing classroom behavior suggested by Blum (1998) include establishing positive relationships with students, maintaining an awareness of special needs of students in the group, and incorporating a system for recognizing appropriate behavior. To deliver lessons effectively in a large group, counselors must be able manage classroom behavior.

> In your small groups discuss the special needs that might be exhibited by a student or students for whom English is a second language. How might you respond to these needs? What about a student who has a physical disability such as a severe visual impairment?

Evaluation

Tomlinson (1999) explains that content is the substance of what a student learns (facts), understands (concepts and principles), and can do (skills) that results from a segment of study such as a lesson or unit. Activities and materials enhance the student's interaction with the content. Process involves the different ways students make sense of the content and work with it. Activities are more likely to be effective if they have a clearly defined purpose, focus students on one key understanding, and cause students to use a skill to work with the ideas. Instructors who ensure that students will have to understand rather than just repeat the idea, who help students relate new ideas to previous ones, and who match the student's level of readiness to the material also increase the likelihood of activities being effective. The other component of the equation is the product, the way that students show what they have come to know and to be able to do.

Counselors establish their expectations during the planning stage with goals and objectives. Evaluation methods may have been written into those statements. Instructors recognize different ways students can demonstrate they have mastered the topic and realize that strategies for checking students' learning should match their learning objective. Consequently, objectives in the three domains of cognitive, affective, and psychomotor require appropriate types of evaluation processes. Gunter, Estes, and Schwab (1995) present a variety of evaluation procedures for the three domains. Ways of checking cognitive learning may involve oral questions, classroom interviews, journals, logs, and participation in activities and projects as well as tests. Simulated situations in which students demonstrate their learning may be particularly effective. Students could also create, either verbally or orally, a before and after summary of their understanding of the topic. Measuring attitudes, feelings, and beliefs—the substance of the affective domain—requires different strategies. Using pre- and postunit questionnaires and checklists; making observations; tape recording class discussions; and monitoring the frequency of using materials such as occupational information are different ways to assess attitudes and beliefs. Psychomotor skills are presented in measurable parts with a degree of acceptable performance stated. In this domain, evaluation would be a careful record of the student's progress on those steps. Students may keep their own record in this skill development, in cognitive learning, or in the affective domain. Some assignments may be designed to capture learning in all domains. In a career unit, for instance, building a career portfolio may require that students apply information by identifying the different categories of careers of all school personnel and presenting that in a graphic display; then presenting a rationale for one of those jobs they believe to be most important; and finally, recording an interview with one person

> Use one of the objectives you wrote earlier and plan a lesson.

who works in the school. Counselors and teachers can generate other ideas for projects, problem solutions, summary descriptions, writing a script, and numerous other possibilities for students and instructors to evaluate and confirm learning.

EFFECTIVENESS

In their review of the school counseling literature, Borders and Drury (1992) note that school counselors are the primary sources of content, plans, strategies, and materials for classroom delivery of the guidance curriculum. They also cite the effectiveness of this intervention on the academic achievement and school adjustment behaviors of children. As we have discussed, counselors may be primarily planners of the curriculum and they may also be the instructor that works in the classroom helping students master this content. Therefore knowing what makes teachers effective will prepare them to use classroom time most constructively.

Cotton (n.d.) reviewed educational research to describe characteristics and practices that improve student learning. Counselors prepare students for lessons by attending to the following practices: explain objectives in simple language and continue to refer to those purposes to maintain focus; check periodically to be sure students understand the objectives; and connect the current topic to previous studies and help students recognize how the concepts or skills build on each other. Students' curiosity is aroused about the content by relating it to things that have personal relevance to them. Counselors let students know in advance the expectations such as participation and they gauge students' readiness to learn. Advance organizers, study questions, and predictions help prepare students for learning.

Besides these methods of preparing students for learning, counselors engage the students by providing clear and focused instruction. They review activities, give clear directions, emphasize key points, and check students' understanding. Lecture and demonstrations are clear. When possible, they use learning strategies and materials that are appropriate to different learning styles. Counselors provide opportunities for guided and independent practice with new concepts by giving instruction in studying, remembering, and applying what is learned. Counselors choose problems and academic tasks that are varied, challenging, and well matched to the lesson so that success is high. Computer-assisted activities supplement and are integrated with teacher-directed learning.

Next teachers and counselors give students feedback on their learning progress. They respond to comments and assignments, acknowledge correct answers, and help students understand and correct errors. Specific feedback is related to unit or lesson goals. Outcomes are measured and disaggregated to determine whether one or more racial or ethnic groups fail, disproportionately, to master the objectives. If so, culturally competent instructors do not attribute lack of achievement to cultural or familial deprivation, but instead examine the curricular experiences to insure relevance to all students in the class (Hollins, 1999). Based on this review, counselors and teachers revise and reteach lessons as necessary. They teach strategies for problem solving, decision making, and other study skills. They incorporate probing, redirection, and reinforcement to improve the quality of student responses.

Effective instructors create a positive classroom environment that encourages participation and promotes curiosity. They are in charge of their classrooms and they manage human relations well. Counselors who master the strategies described will be effective classroom instructors. Besides the teaching skills summarized above, Blum (1998) reminds counselors they need to expand their knowledge of the expectations and needs of teachers with whom they work. Effective counselors will consider teachers' time, schedules, and requirements as classroom guidance schedules are developed. Blum further suggests posting counseling schedules on doors to provide ongoing notification of the lessons, grade levels, and dates of the counselor's presentations.

SUMMARY

School counselors affect students by planning and implementing a guidance curriculum. Indeed counselors have been urged to use their skills in the classroom as a parsimonious and visible way of helping students (Myrick, 1987; Fall, 1994). This chapter has provided information necessary for understanding the meaning, scope, and sequence of a guidance curriculum. A review of some developmental milestones that affect student learning has also been provided. Finally an overview of the specifics of planning, implementing, and evaluating units and lessons has been given. Applying these concepts will allow school counselors to engage the school in increasing students' competencies in academic, career, and personal/social content areas.

PORTFOLIO COMPONENTS

1. Reflect on the effective teachers you have observed and from whom you have learned. Develop a composite of these teachers reflecting your own ideal of how you would like to plan and deliver instruction, manage classroom behavior, and relate to your students. What skills or behaviors do you need to develop to meet your ideal? How will you go about developing the requisite abilities? Are there any natural styles of interaction you now use that need to be altered to meet your ideal? What are they?

2. Develop a description of your current stage of development in the following areas: personal/social, academic, career, and racial identity. How might your own stage or process of development in these areas be reflected in curriculum planning? How will you address any developmental needs arising from your consideration of these questions?

3. Develop a set of questions and interview a school counselor about the system used in his/her school to manage classroom behavior. Determine whether any adaptations during classroom guidance lessons are made, why, and how students are apprised of the differences in standards of behavior. Prepare a one-page reflective statement describing what you learned about classroom management and how you will use the information in your own practice.

CHAPTER 7

Individual Planning

CASE STUDY

PLANNING FOR THE FUTURE

Mr. Terman and the Washington County Schools team are meeting for the final time in May to discuss the status of the school counseling program. Mr. Terman begins the meeting, "Congratulations to everyone involved in developing our guidance curriculum. Both the system administration and school board have approved the adoption of the curriculum, and we are set to implement in August. Please submit a request for materials needed for implementation to me no later than June 1. Today I would like for us to discuss the program element we wish to review and revise during the next school year, articulate our goals, and develop our time line. Is that an agreeable agenda?" With the team's approval, the meeting continues.

Ms. Ina Lerner and Mr. Igor Grund observe that the highest priority identified in their most recent needs assessment—helping students and families plan for the future—does not seem to be fully addressed in the approved guidance curriculum. Therefore, the group agrees that the individual planning program element will be the focus of their planning activities during the coming school year. Ms. Amelia Farmer suggests that the skills and knowledge necessary to plan for one's career and educational future are acquired and/or developed during the elementary school years through participation in the classroom guidance curriculum. The elementary counselors agree that this is the case and remind the group that approximately 50 percent of their time will be spent in classroom guidance with only 10 percent or less spent in activities related to individual planning. Middle school and high school counselors will spend far less time on the guidance curriculum, approximately 20 percent, with 30 percent of their time devoted to individual planning.

Following an extended discussion, the group agreed on the following goals:

1. Review the skills and knowledge related to future career and educational planning supported by the elementary school guidance curriculum and supplement with individual planning activities (e.g., appraisal, placement) as needed.

2. Identify the relevant national standards associated with career and educational planning and determine the extent to which the standards are met in the current program.

3. Identify ways to strengthen the current individual planning program element, particularly in grades 7 through 12.

4. Identify the means for delivering the program element at each grade level.

Individual planning provides students the support, skills, and knowledge they need to set goals for themselves and to systematically monitor their progress toward those goals (Gysbers & Henderson, 2000). The activities associated with individual planning are designed to be preventive. The interventions assist students in planning their futures as well as managing their personal and career development.

Career and educational planning are intertwined. The successful preparation for careers is predicated on appropriate academic preparation. As Graham (1993) points out, the needs of the American workforce in 21st-century American society dictate that all children must become academically proficient. For much of the 20th century the emphasis in U.S. schools was on increasing participation in and access to the educational enterprise. Graham reports that we have been successful in meeting both goals. Students from all settings, all types of families, and with widely varying abilities participate at the greatest rate in our history in education. However, as a result of the changing economy and occupational opportunities students must graduate from high school with more than basic literacy skills if they are to the successful in the 21st-century workforce. Consequently, individual planning has an increased importance in today's society.

After reading and discussing this chapter, you should be able to

- Define individual planning and identify the relevant professional standards most appropriately met through this program element.
- Identify the goals most often associated with this program element at each grade level.
- Identify the counselor skills and functions associated with this program element.

INDIVIDUAL PLANNING

The term *individual planning* is sometimes confusing for those learning about school counseling programs. One might logically assume that because the word *individual* appears in the title that the associated services are delivered to students on individual basis. As related to this program element, the word *individual* actually means that the counselor uses whatever methods are most appropriate for helping individuals make plans about their future (VanZandt & Hayslip, 2001). School counselors want to help young people make careful decisions by exploring all their options, using many sources of information and identifying probable outcomes. That goal guides this program element. Some examples of the approaches counselors can take to accomplish this include individual counseling and group counseling with students, consultation with parents and teachers, coordination of community resources, classroom guidance focused on career education, and development and maintenance of career information centers. In these ways counselors and others assist all students in the development of career life plans consistent with their personal/social, academic, and career goals (Gysbers & Henderson, 2000). Gysbers and Henderson categorize these interventions as individual appraisal, advisement, and placement and follow-up.

Appraisal

Student appraisal takes many forms in a school counselor's job. Schmidt (1999) identifies appraisal as an essential element in school counseling. Through appraisal activities, counselors collect and interpret data about students' achievement, aptitudes, attitudes, interests, skills, and behaviors.

Appraisal in schools often refers to the administration of tests or assessment instruments. Counselors may serve as the administrator of testing. In that role they may be responsible for coordinating test selection, ordering the tests, making arrangements for scoring, implementing the testing process, and disseminating the results. Counselors may work as interpreters of tests, providing information directly to students, parents, and teachers. Counselors may also be consultants in the appraisal process, helping teachers understand the meaning of test results and ways they can present that data to others. Table 7.1 contains a list of some assessment instruments used by school counselors. Baker (2000) highlights the competencies needed by school counselors as they work with assessment:

- Knowledge about measurement principles such as scales, scoring systems, reliability, and validity
- Knowledge about standardized tests such as intelligence, aptitude, achievement, interests, and personality instruments
- Knowledge about nonstandardized assessment strategies such as card sorts, work samples, and observations
- Knowledge about managing a school testing program
- Knowledge about assessment issues such as invasion of privacy, test bias, and test anxiety
- Knowledge about selecting and administering assessment instruments
- Knowledge about communicating assessment information accurately

Throughout the K–12 experience students use the information they gain from appraisal activities to identify their interests, their strengths, areas in which they want to improve, areas they want to explore, and things that are important to them. Standardized instruments can help in the individual planning process in the following ways:

- Intelligence tests may be given in groups or individually. Group intelligence tests have often been used to measure academic promise. Individually administered intelligence tests may be part of a battery for determining neurological functioning, learning disabilities, and the ability of nonreaders.
- Another way academic promise may be identified is through aptitude tests, used to predict a student's ability to achieve in a certain area. Aptitude tests may be used to help distinguish patterns of traits—useful information in career decision making. Tests such as the Differential Aptitude Test (DAT) and the Armed Services Vocational Aptitude Battery (ASVAB) provide a range of aptitude scores. Counselors and students can use those tests to consider a student's abilities that may be further developed for educational or career potential.
- Achievement tests are used to assess academic progress, a popular form of testing in schools. These tests may be used as part of the individual planning process to predict future learning, to identify students' strengths and weaknesses in certain areas of learning, to estimate students' amount and/or rate of learning, and to compare students' achievement (Gibson & Mitchell, 1995).
- Personality tests describe traits and characteristics of an individual's personality. Two examples used by school counselors are the Mooney Problem Checklist and the Myers-Briggs Type Indicator (MBTI). The MBTI may be used with high school students for career planning.

Student appraisal includes other forms of assessment. Interest and other types of career inventories may be used to help identify interests related to career areas, lev-

TABLE 7.1 Career Development Assessment Tools

Instrument	Grade Level	Description
Wide Range Interest Opinion Test	5	Perceptions of ability, level of aspiration, and social conformity
Career Maturity Inventory Attitude Scale & Competency Test	6	Students' attitude and competencies about career decisions
COPSystem Interest Inventory Form/R COPSystem Intermediate Inventory	6	Interests related to occupational clusters
Explore the World of Work	4–6	Vocational interests
Hall Occupational Orientation Inventory (Intermediate)	3–7	Psychological needs as related to worker's traits and job characteristics
Individual Career Exploration	3–12	General career areas of interest
Safran Students Interest Inventory Level 1	5–9	Occupational interests and school subject interests
Career Awareness Inventory Attitudes	3–12	Student knowledge about careers and about their own career choices
Marlin-Hills Attitude Surveys	K–12	Attitudes toward teachers, learning, language, and arithmetic
Survey of School Attitudes	1–8	Attitudes toward reading and language arts, social studies, science and math
Values Inventory for Children	1–4	Values of children and their relations to other children, parents, authority figures
The Affective Perception Inventory	1–12	Students attitude toward self and school and specific subject areas
Martinek-Zaichkowsky Self-Concept Scale for Children	1–8	Global self-concept and physical, emotional, and behavioral aspects of self-confidence
SCAMIN: A Self-Concept & Motivation Inventory	Preschool–K	Early elementary forms
Motivation Inventory	1–3 3–6	Achievement investment, role expectations, achievement needs, and self-adequacy
Coopersmith Self-Esteem	3–12	Attitudes toward self, school, family, and peers
Culture Free Self-Esteem Inventory	3 +	General self-esteem, school, peer, parent, self
Piers-Harris Children's Self-Concept Scale	4–12	Student self-concept in areas: behavior, intellectual and school status, physical appearance and attributes, anxiety, popularity, happiness and satisfaction

Career counseling: A developmental approach by Drummond, R. J. & Ryan, C. W., © 1995. Reprinted by permission of Pearson Education, Inc., Upper Saddle River, NJ.

As described by Campbell and Dahir (1997) the Career Development, Standard C, is: Students will understand the relationship between personal qualities, education, and training and the world of work. Students will demonstrate how personal qualities relate to achieving personal, social, education, and career goals. Design a sequence of appraisal activities for the elementary, middle, and high school level that would assist students in identifying their qualities.

els of career development, and career maturity. Counselors and students can use those results along with achievement and aptitude scores to assist with individual planning. Schmidt (1999) suggests the data can verify choices, uncover other areas of interests, and stimulate exploration of opportunities. The Self-Directed Search (SDS), the Kuder General Interest Survey, the Kuder Occupational Interest Survey, and the Ohio Vocational Interest Survey (OVIS) are a few of the many interests inventories used in schools. Other methods of gathering data include interviews, rating scales, observations, and consultations.

Standardized testing and other forms of appraisal may help accomplish several goals in schools. For the individual planning program element, appraisal activities help students gather information about themselves that they may then use to make informed decisions about their futures. For example, students who consider their results on achievement and aptitude tests have information for identifying their skills, proficiencies, and abilities as well as their academic achievement. Students who know their interests, abilities, and personality preferences have more valuable data and can associate their preferences with careers. Students create a successful educational and career experience using all this information.

Ms. Farmer and the other elementary counselors involved in the Washington County Schools team are meeting to review the types of appraisal activities conducted in the elementary school and to try to determine whether any changes need to be made. As part of the statewide testing initiative, the elementary students take tests that measure reading, social studies, and math achievement. Currently, the results of these tests are used to help parents, students, and teachers understand students' strengths and weaknesses in particular subject areas. The counselors' goal is to identify ways that these achievement test batteries might be more fully used to inform the development of activities in individual planning. One counselor suggests that the results be reviewed, along with student grades, to identify those who might benefit from training in study skills with the goal of increasing achievement in one or more subject areas.

Identify three other individual planning activities at the elementary school that may result from a review of achievement test scores and student grades. How would these activities be modified for the middle school level? For high school?

Another counselor questions whether explanations of the test results to parents have been effective. The counselors have followed a procedure to help parents understand test results and implications described by Holmgren (1996). He recommends an evening presentation that includes illustrations and a profile of test results at various levels. Parents with their own child's profile can compare and question results. Some typical questions are "Does this test count very much?" "Who sees these test scores?" "What does standardized test mean?" and "What does it mean in relation to my child's grades?" The counselors have had good attendance and excellent feedback for their interpretive sessions and have used a similar procedure to help teachers understand test results.

One of the counselors now wants to consider some follow-up activities to determine how the children and their parents relate the assessment results to future planning. She will also be responsible for creating a checklist for counselors to follow in preparing for sessions devoted to test interpretation.

With your classmates, create that checklist.

Ms. Farmer notes that appraisal activities are also conducted when students are referred to school-based student assistance or support teams. Multiple professionals who interact with the student come together to share data gathered through testing;

classroom work and behavior; observations by school personnel, parents, and community persons; and sometimes a student's self-assessment. Using all the data available to them, the members of this team develop a plan for helping the student reach his or her full academic potential.

The process that guides decisions related to providing services to students who have special needs appears in Figure 7.1. The nation's special education law—the Individuals with Disabilities Act, or IDEA (http://www.ed.gov/offices/OSERS/OSEP/)—details the requirements. First the child is identified as potentially needing special education or related services. An evaluation of all related areas follows. The group of professionals and the child's parents then determine whether the student needs services. If the child is found eligible for special education and related services, a meeting is held in which an individual education plan (IEP) is written. An IEP includes information about current performance, annual goals that the child can reasonably accomplish, and the program that has been designed to meet that child's unique needs. After the parents consent, the services are provided and progress is measured and reported. Every year the IEP is reviewed, and the child is reevaluated every 3 years. School counselors participate in this process by being involved in the meetings to determine appropriate services and helping develop the IEP. They may also provide counseling for the students and consulting for parents. Counselors may work with the classroom and special education teachers also.

> Examine a school system's procedure for the special education process. In the procedure you reviewed, what is the role of the school counselor? Compare your findings with those of your classmates.

The counselors also identified areas where they were not assessing student progress or competence, primarily in career development. They have numerous program activities associated with career development, including a systemwide career day, field trips to local employers, job shadowing opportunities, and classroom guidance units focused on the career development standards articulated by Campbell and Dahir for ASCA (see Appendix B). However, they have no idea about the helpfulness of these activities in terms of student development. They decide to investigate some inventories of career maturity, interests, and personality to use as tools in monitoring students' progress throughout their K–12 years. That information will help them check for the effectiveness of their activities and can also be included in the career portfolio students develop.

Finally, the counselors wish to use the assessment information available to them to ascertain whether particular groups of students (low income, racially and ethnically diverse students, and those with disabilities) are developing the skills needed to plan for their futures and to reach their fullest potential in their career and educational goals. As you will recall from chapter 2, much evidence suggests that access does not necessarily equal opportunity. Counselors will help disaggregate or break down the school testing data by gender, ethnic group, and socioeconomic group to study whether inequities need to be addressed.

> In dyads, state at least one student outcome expected for those who participate in each of the career development activities (career day, field trip, job shadowing). For each of the three outcome statements you state, identify how the counselors would assess whether the outcomes are achieved (assessment strategy) and how the assessment information would be used by the counselors for future decisions regarding the individual planning program element.

They will also examine the appropriateness of the tests for all groups. The counselors recently participated in a state workshop on the multicultural counseling competencies. Those competencies state that counselors know about potential bias in assessment instruments. Herring (1997) cites criteria for culture-free tests:

1. Are items relevant for the culture being tested?
2. Is the meaning of each item the same in each culture?

FIGURE 7.1 The Basic Special Education Process under IDEA

Step 1	Child is identified as possibly needing special education and related services by parent, teachers, or other school personnel.
Step 2	Child is evaluated in all areas related to the suspected disability; results will determine child's eligibility for special education.
Step 3	Eligibility for services is decided by a group of qualified professionals by looking at the child's evaluation results.
Step 4	If child is found eligible for services, an IEP meeting must take place within 30 days.
Step 5	The school schedules an IEP meeting with the parents and others attending who may have special knowledge or expertise about the child.
Step 6	An IEP meeting is held, the IEP is written by the IEP team, and the child begins to receive services as soon as possible after the meeting.
Step 7	Services agreed on by the IEP team are provided to the child, and the school makes sure the child's IEP is being carried out as it was written.
Step 8	The child's progress toward the annual goals is measured and reported to the child's parents.
Step 9	The child's IEP is reviewed by the IEP team at least once a year or more often if the parents or school ask for a review.
Step 10	At least every 3 years, the child must be evaluated to assess whether the child continues to be a child with a disability and what his or her specific needs are.

Source: Adapted from http://www.ed.gov/offices/OSERS/OSEP/Products/IEPGuide/
#TheBasicSpecialEducationProcessUnderIDEA

3. Is the method of assessment comparable across cultures?
4. Would the interpretation of variables remain the same when compared with the norm for each culture studied?
5. Is the test measuring the same theoretical construct across cultures? (p. 226)

As well as checking tests for cultural bias, the counselors will interpret findings in culturally appropriate ways. They decide to identify and practice test interpretations among themselves not only to streamline their process but also to demonstrate their abilities at culturally appropriate results. After the review of appraisal activities, the counselors decide to consider another component of individual planning—advisement.

Reflecting on the types of data identified in chapter 2 that are available to school counselors, how might one determine whether the academic and career goals are being met by students in groups that are most often underserved?

Advisement

One advisement intervention is providing information that focuses on students increasing their career awareness, self-knowledge, and skills at making decisions. Optimally all school personnel are involved and community resources are incorporated. These informational programs designed for individual educational and career planning incorporate three components:

1. **Student component.** This part focuses on exploring careers, developing career options and areas of interests, participating in career experiences, being exposed to role models, and connecting values to careers possibilities.
2. **Parent component.** This section familiarizes parents with educational and career decision making and teaches ways they can facilitate the processes in their children.
3. **School personnel component.** This element provides the principles of career education and ways to incorporate them into the classroom and other school programs. All schools in Washington County have some type of teachers-as-advisor program. Counselors are involved by providing information to help teachers help students.

These components serve as general guidelines for the processes involved in planning for the future. Counselors also work in other ways to help students gather and use data specific to the individual for more focused exploration.

To be useful, the information students obtain from the appraisal activities conducted during their middle and high school years must be understood by them and their parents. Advisement activities are intended to help students use the data gathered to increase their self understanding and awareness and to use that information to achieve their personal/social, academic, and career goals (Gysbers & Henderson, 2000). All school personnel, students, and parents typically share responsibility for advisement. Much of the advisement takes place in homogeneous groups organized by grade level, interest area, career objective, or postsecondary plans. Depending on the desired outcome, advisement may include individual or group exploration and discussion; information dissemination by counselor, teacher, or other expert; and, whole school activities such as career fairs.

Middle and high schools in the Washington County School system have begun using a teacher-as-advisor program. In these programs, teachers are assigned a group of 15 to 20 students as advisees. In the high school programs a teacher advisor has the same advisees throughout their high school experience, creating a base for the students as well as an adult who closely monitors their educational planning and school progress. Teachers develop strong relationships with their advisees during the 4-year period. The advisee groups meet regularly in a home-base period 3 days a week in the middle schools and 2 days a week in the high schools. Those advisement periods last about 30 minutes. During that period the group participates in a guidance lesson as well as in individual planning activities. Gonzalez and Myrick (2000) report some units offered in a Florida middle school: orientation to school, time management, self-assessment, communication, decision making, relationships, career development, and education planning. The home-base period includes time for the teacher advisor to meet individually with the student. When teachers find students need additional help, they refer the pupils to the school counselor.

Counselors may coordinate the teacher-as-advisor program, provide resources and topics for the home-base periods, and help teachers refine the skills they need to build an advising relationship with students. Schmidt (1999) states that teachers who have good communication and facilitation skills and who understand effective helping skills can provide excellent advisement to students. In the Washington County middle and high schools 80 percent of the teachers were involved in this program, and their commitment to it was high.

As a result of advisement, students have an opportunity to consider their own abilities and interests in conjunction with information about the labor market, postsecondary options, and current secondary school offerings. Based on this information along with opportunities for discussion and exploration with peers, teachers, parents, counselors, admissions counselors, and future employers, students plan for their futures. Ms. Lerner asks the group to review the academic/educational goals for students K–12 identified by Blum (1998) to see whether they are being adequately addressed through individual advisement or elsewhere in the school counseling program.

1. Achieve goals commensurate with individual potential:
   a. Plan and pursue a balanced educational program.
   b. Be prepared for postsecondary education or a full-time job.

2. Become an independent learner:
   a. Maintain a positive attitude toward learning.
   b. Become aware of own abilities, interests, and educational needs.
   c. Acquire knowledge of educational opportunities.
   d. Prepare for next level of education.

3. Apply effective skills for life-long learning:
   a. Develop goal-setting skills.
   b. Develop study skills.
   c. Develop test-taking skills.
   d. Develop time-management skills.
   e. Develop problem-solving skills.

4. Accept personal responsibility for self-direction. (Blum, 1998, p. 113)]

The counselors agree that the foundation of skills listed under goals 3 and 4 is being addressed fully in grades K–6. Building on these skills, the middle and high school counselors need to review the attention currently given in their programs to goals 1 and 2 as well as on reinforcing goals 3 and 4.

The other major emphasis, career planning, also needs to be reviewed by the Washington County School team. As with educational planning, they begin with a review of the career goals for all students articulated by the National Occupational Information Coordinating Committee (NOICC) (1992) that appear in Table 7.2. The process begins with children becoming aware, then exploring and expanding to preparation for a meaningful life.

> Work in small groups to develop inventory forms that, when completed, would identify what interventions are currently being delivered to assist students in meeting the goals.

Obviously, a good number of the student skills important for educational planning are also necessary for career planning. In addition to those skills identified by the elementary counselors as goals of their programs, elementary students need to acquire knowledge about technology, understand the value of work, and learn to work cooperatively in teams (Blum, 1998). Further, elementary students must begin to relate what they are learning in school to what they will be doing in life after school. Such a connection is necessary if students are to set and pursue educational goals that are congruent with their interests, abilities, and values. Magnuson (1997) explains a method for documenting components of elementary students' personal and career development. Counselors collect materials related to preferences, interest, personal descriptions, and goals at each grade level. The counselor discusses the portfolio process and gives the collection to each child in the fourth grade. Students continue to add to the materials related to their career and educational planning. Sixth-grade parents contribute a letter that discusses the parents' perceptions of the students' qualities that will be assets in a career. The portfolio goes with the children as they move to a middle school.

Currently, students develop a 4-year plan at the beginning of ninth grade that includes coursework to support their future plans. They complete individualized career plans designed by the National Center for Research in Vocational Education (see Figure 7.2). Mr. Grund and Ms. Lerner propose that the planning begin in the seventh grade with a 6-year, flexible plan. They are also concerned about the evaluation of outcomes with regard to educational and career planning. Consequently, they propose that at the time the 6-year plan is developed students also begin a career portfolio that will serve as a qualitative assessment of students' development when they graduate from high school. The specifics of these plans will be more fully discussed in the next section.

> Working in small groups, identify the types of artifacts and reflections students might include to demonstrate that the career goals identified in Table 7.2 have been achieved.

Placement and Follow-up

Counselors and others who have been responsible for appraisal and advisement of students continue to assist them as they move from the school into the workforce or other postsecondary educational or vocational settings (Gysbers & Henderson, 2000). Some of the placement activities currently in place include opportunities for structured work experiences that are consistent with student interests; preparation for employment and college interviews; seminars and an informative Web page for students and parents about college admissions, financial aid, and applications;

TABLE 7.2   National Occupational Information Coordinating Committee: Career Development

	Elementary	Middle	High School
Self-Knowledge	Knowledge of importance of self-concept	Knowledge of influence of a positive self-concept	Understanding the influence of a positive self-concept
	Skills to interact with others	Skills to interact with others	Skills to interact positively with others
	Awareness of importance of growth and change	Knowledge of the importance of growth and change	Understanding the impact of growth and development
Educational and Occupational Exploration	Awareness of the benefits of educational achievement	Knowledge of the benefits of educational achievement to career opportunities	Understanding the relationship between educational achievement and career planning
	Awareness of the relationship between work and learning	Knowledge of relationship between work and learning	Understanding the need for positive attitudes toward work and learning
	Skills to understand and use career information	Skills to locate, understand, and use career information	Skills to locate, evaluate, and interpret career information
	Awareness of importance of personal responsibility & good work habits	Knowledge of skills necessary to seek and obtain jobs	Skills to prepare to seek, obtain, maintain, and change jobs
	Awareness of how work relates to needs and functions of society	Understanding of how work relates to the needs and functions of economy and society	Understanding of how societal needs and functions influence the nature and structure of work
Career Planning	Understanding of how to make decisions	Skills to make decisions	Skills to make decisions
	Awareness of interrelationship of life roles	Knowledge of the interrelationships of life roles	Understanding of the interrelationships of life roles
	Awareness of different occupations and changing male/female roles	Knowledge of different occupations and changing male/female roles	Understanding of the continuous changes in male/female roles
	Awareness of career planning process	Understanding of the process of career planning	Skills in career planning

National Occupational Information Coordinating Committee (NOICC), U.S. Department of Labor (1992). *The national career development guidelines project.* Washington, DC: U.S. Department of Labor.

My Education and Career Plan

Name: _____ School: _____ Grade: _____

Beyond High School

Post-Secondary Education Goals:

_____

_____

_____

Possible Careers:

_____

_____

_____

	Student _____
	Date _____
	Parent _____
	Date _____
	Counselor _____
	Date _____

Course of Study**:

☐ Career Prep
☐ College/University Prep
☐ College Tech Prep
☐ Occupational Prep

8	9	10	11	12	Graduation Requirements	
English I	English II	English III	English IV		4	4
Math	Math	Math	Math		4*	4*
Science	Biology	Science	Science		4*	4*
Economic, Legal & Political Systems	World Studies	U.S. History	Elective		3	3
PE or Dance	PE or Dance	Elective	Elective		1	1
Life Mgmt. Skills	Health & Safety				1	1
Elective	Elective	Elective	Elective			
Elective	Elective	Elective	Elective			
	- - - 4 PERIOD DAY ONLY - - -					
Total: 7 or 8	7 or 8	7 or 8	7 or 8		23	26

English	☐ ☐ ☐ ☐ ☐ ☐ Art
Math	☐ ☐ ☐ ☐ ☐ ☐ Foreign Language
Science	☐ ☐ ☐ ☐ ☐ ☐ Military Science
Social Studies	☐ ☐ ☐ ☐ ☐ ☐ Music
Life Skills/Health	☐ ☐ ☐ ☐ ☐ ☐ Vocational Ed.
Physical Education	☐ ☐ ☐ ☐ ☐ ☐ Other

*Four units or math must include Algebra 1; Science must include biology, environmental or Earth Science, a physical science and one additional science.
Graduation course requirements shown are for the class of 2002 and later.

☐ = Required Courses; ▓ = Elective Courses

**Begining with the Class of 2004, students who do not complete a course of study will not receive a high school diploma.

Source: Winston-Salem/Forsyth County Schools (n. d.) My education and career plan. Winston-Salem, NC: Author

scheduled sessions with military and local employment recruiters; and student advisement sessions that reinforce these activities, as well as others related to career and educational placement.

Additionally, school personnel collect follow-up data from graduates and their employers/supervisors to assist with school counseling program evaluation and improvement. Counselors wish to learn how well students were prepared to set and achieve their postsecondary goals from the perspectives of the students themselves, their parents, and their employers or supervisors.

Schwallie-Giddis and Kobylarz (2000) include and expand on the interventions identified by Gysbers and Henderson (2000) to help students gather, analyze, synthesize, and organize information related to their futures. These interventions can be modified for different age levels.

> Reflect on your own school experiences and describe how your experiences in middle and high school influenced your educational and career planning both during and after high school graduation. Compare these experiences with those of your classmates. Identify the classmates who experienced the most comprehensive implementation of the individual planning program component during their middle and high school years. What were the long-term benefits to them?

- **Outreach.** An approach used to alert all students to the information and services available.
- **Classroom Instruction.** Curriculum activities delivered by teachers and counselors in large group activities. Integrating career concepts into academic instruction makes material meaningful to students.
- **Counseling.** In an individual or small group forum focusing on helping students explore personal issues that are related to their plans for the future. Students examine ways to apply information and skills they have learned to their personal plans and to the development of their individualized educational and career plans.
- **Assessment.** Assessment includes the administration and interpretation of both formal and informal measures that give students a clearer understanding of their skills, abilities, interests, achievements, and needs.
- **Career Information.** Resources are provided that present current and unbiased information to students about occupations, educational programs, postsecondary training, the military, and employment opportunities.
- **Career Information Delivery System.** In some states, a computer-based career information delivery system includes comprehensive, accurate, and current information about occupations and education/training opportunities.
- **Work Experience.** Students have chances to participate in actual work settings.
- **Placement.** Resources and assistance are given to help students make a successful transition from high school to employment, postsecondary education, military service, or other options.
- **Consultation.** Counselors give direct assistance to teachers, administrators, parents, and others who interact with students that will help the adults better understand career development and strategies for supporting it.
- **Referral.** For students who have barriers that may inhibit career development, school counselors recognize the problems and make appropriate referrals.
- **Follow-up.** Counselors maintain long-term contact with students as they move through their school years and beyond. (pp. 214–215).

Counselors may also coordinate programs that incorporate volunteering and/or service learning opportunities to introduce students to the world of work.

CAREER AND EDUCATIONAL DEVELOPMENT

Drummond and Ryan (1995) summarize the specific responsibilities of counselors as

1. Helping teachers implement career education in classrooms.
2. Serving as a liaison between the school and the business community.
3. Helping incorporate career education concepts within the family system.
4. Facilitating students with their educational and career development planning.
5. At the high school level participating in job placement programs and follow-up studies of former students.

Counselors incorporate individual planning into a counseling program using standards from organizations, such as the ASCA National Standards for School Counseling Programs (Campbell & Dahir, 1997; see Appendix B). In addition to the ASCA standards for academic and career development, the National Career Development Guidelines (VanZandt & Hayslip, 2001) and those from the National Occupational Information Coordinating Committee (NOICC) (1992) offer counselors sets of skills and knowledge in three areas—self-knowledge, educational and occupational exploration, and career planning—across the three levels typically associated with K–12 schooling. The documents include additional guidelines for adults.

The following steps are one state's (Schwallie-Giddis & Kobylarz, 2000) sequence for accomplishing an integration of career and academic training.

1. **Grades K–5:** Students develop an awareness of self and the value of work. They are exposed to careers and to technology.
2. **Grade 6:** Counselors, teachers, and parents help students assess their personal aptitudes, abilities, and interests and then relate those qualities to careers. Students also learn the role of technology in work.
3. **Grades 7–8:** Students set career-oriented goals and develop a 4-year program of study for high school that supports their goals. Students, parents, and educators review plans each year.
4. **Grades 9–12:** During high school an "applied curriculum" relates academic concepts to the workplace.

Teachers and parents contribute to career education and planning in many ways. Teachers help by creating or locating materials that help students understand and appreciate the career implications of their subject area. They use career-oriented activities in their instruction and help students learn and use good work habits. Teachers also help students develop, clarify, and assimilate meaningful work values. Parents also play a part by helping their children gain and practice good work habits. Parents who emphasize positive attitudes toward work and who work toward maximum career development options and opportunities for their children aid the career development process (Drummond & Ryan, 1995). Seligman (1994) states that people—particularly parents and teachers—have great influence on the career choices of children. Counselors can help parents by conducting study groups that focus on their roles in children's career development. Counselors can also coordinate resources for parents and organize career activities for families (Herbert, 1986).

Blum (1998) provides more specific ways to accomplish this sequence at different grade levels. In elementary school students develop personal and career attributes. They acquire an appreciation of learning and of following directions and rules. They begin to acquire decision-making and goal-setting skills and the action necessary to achieve their purposes. They learn about technology and the value of work and have opportunities to work in groups and on teams. Students in elementary settings relate school to work by acknowledging the relationships of good work habits, personal responsibility, and behavior and consequences in school and at work. By attaining career information they learn about careers and jobs and about workers in the community. Students increase their understanding of self by recognizing personal strengths, interests, and abilities and relating them to careers. They learn about a career portfolio and prepare a 6-year plan for their education. In K–6 schools counselors help children with career preparation by increasing children's self-awareness, promoting skills needed later in life, and presenting general information about occupations and work.

Children in elementary schools learn through concrete experiences and observations. Successful educational and career development programs will incorporate concrete experiences for students as well as observational learning opportunities. Elementary students begin to learn their "self-concept systems," which are sets of their individual traits. The stage-related development of self-image as it relates to occupational aspirations has been discussed by Gottfredson (1996) as a movement that begins with children recognizing adult occupational roles and exhibiting same-sex preferences for adult activities. In the second stage children focus on what is appropriate for one's sex, recognizing that adult activities are sex-typed. Children tend to disregard careers that they perceive as appropriate for the other sex. The third stage involves children dismissing occupations they regard as low-status careers. Adults who work with elementary children acknowledge the changes in children's understandings as they progress through these stages and help broaden their concept of possible careers.

In their responses to the most recent needs assessment, community employers indicated that prospective employees tend to seek jobs that are consistent with gender stereotypes. Consequently, counselors are interested in examining their programs for activities and information about careers that may reinforce stereotypes and biases about gender and work. Seligman (1994) highlights influences on career development for counselors to consider. Family factors such parents' roles and early childhood experiences relate strongly to a person's occupational expectations. Students who are exposed to a variety of occupations and lifestyles and have access to role models with differing occupational status expand their exploration of the world of work. Boys and girls need to see a broad range of career opportunities to reduce gender stereotyping that may inhibit choices. Counselors need to monitor materials and assessments for any notions that may imply limitations. Counselors need to find models of both genders in familiar occupations. Those models may be provided in speakers, photographs, films, stories, field trips, and games.

The counselors also follow Blum's (1998) recommendations about career counseling female and minority students. First, counselors explore their own hidden biases by taking the hidden bias inventory located on the Teaching Tolerance

(2001) (http://www.tolerance.org) Web site. Then, they examine the materials they use in classrooms and in parent and teacher training for evidence of hidden and more overt bias. Finally, they replace current materials that reflect stereotypes with those that reflect gender and equity fairness, a culturally diverse workforce, and persons working in nontraditional occupations.

Materials and activities that encourage a wide view of the world of work enhance this ongoing process of developing a work identity. However, elementary children are also influenced by the values of their communities, especially families, and may experience expectations that are different from those expressed in school. Ms. Lerner states, "I am working with a large community of refugee children from middle European countries. Their native countries do not have mandatory attendance laws. Their families expect them to work as soon as they are physically able, and girls in these families are often married before age 16. School attendance is not an expressed value, and these students are achieving at very low levels due to erratic attendance patterns. As the students become more 'Americanized' there are conflicts emerging in these families. How can I provide career and educational development activities that are both based in the American values of equity education and are culturally sensitive to these children and their families?" Such students may need special encouragement to consider a variety of career fields. Additionally, school personnel succeed by involving parents, relatives, and role models in emphasizing individual potential (Zunker, 1998).

In middle school, students develop their personal and career attributes by increasing their appreciation of learning and expressing positive attitudes toward their studies (Blum, 1998). They increase their self-direction as well as accept responsibility for their own behavior. They develop an appreciation for quality in their work and enhance their positive interpersonal and social skills leading to cooperative work skills. They grow in their ability to make good decisions and in self-confidence. In relating education and career learning, students in the middle grades acknowledge the relationship of educational achievement and career opportunities. They locate and use information when making academic and career plans, and they select courses related to their career plans.

Mr. Grund and the others agree that middle school is a place for exploration and identity development. They are happy with the career resources they have and the way that teachers integrate career development activities into the academic curriculum. Specifically, teachers encourage students to research and report on careers of interest to them, including everything from how one prepares to enter the profession or occupation to the benefits of employment, likely trends in the particular segment of the labor market, and what personal interests and personalities may be most satisfied in the occupation. They also integrate career and educational planning activities into the time periods immediately preceding and following the school's annual career exploration fair. Before the fair, they help students use the results of their career inventories to identify areas about which they wish to learn more, develop lists of questions students might ask career fair participants, and provide opportunities for discussion with peers about career options. After the fair, they spend time discussing students' experiences and identifying additional questions to be researched. They also help students learn about job searching, interviewing, and

In small groups, identify at least six ways counselors and other educators might expand elementary school students' conception of the career choices available to them. Think in terms of everyday behavior (e.g., modeling equity- and gender-fair language and behavior) as well as specific individual planning interventions (e.g., schoolwide career fairs with representation of persons in nontraditional occupations).

Working in small groups, identify ways that you might work with the parents of these children, in a culturally sensitive manner, to increase their view of opportunities available to their children.

completing applications in anticipation of the job-shadowing experiences students have in the eighth grade.

Ms. Farmer points out that the career interest inventory currently used in the middle school needs to be reviewed for applicability to all of the students in the schools, and specifically for fairness. Additionally, screenings of the most recent participants in the career exploration fair reveal that women represent all of the occupations stereotypically associated with females. Mr. Grund, who coordinates the career fair, commits to finding more diverse representatives in these areas.

Academically, students use the decision-making and goal-setting skills developed in elementary school to begin their 6-year educational plans and their career-life planning portfolios (Blum, 1998).

The portfolio projects help students plan their education and set goals. Drummond and Ryan (1995) outline the objectives of a portfolio program as follows:

1. Students collect information about their learning styles, abilities, interests, and expectations.

2. Students evaluate the information they have compiled and form their choices after learning about the decision-making process.

3. Students design and create a collection that reflects their personal strengths and challenges, their academic and vocational interests, social interests, immediate and future goals, and plans for completing their goals. (p. 103)

Through these planning tools, students, parents, teachers, and counselors can see whether students are using the assessment data available to them to achieve an understanding of themselves, including their interests and abilities, in order to plan effectively for their futures. At this level, the plans are flexible enough to allow students to make changes based on new information about themselves, the ever-changing world of work, and academic developments.

In small groups discuss and develop a list of ways that the influence of peers, predominant among middle school students, may both positively and negatively influence career and academic decisions of students. Identify ways that educators might respond to your list to increase the chances of positive outcomes for students.

Peterson, Long, and Billups (1999) studied the effects of three types of interventions on the educational choices of eighth graders. As a result of their research, they suggest that counselors include a well-designed set of print materials, individual monitoring, and support from counselors and teachers in helping prepare middle school students for educational choices. Bergmann (1991) suggests that middle school counselors help the career development process by conducting needs assessments of the students, establishing peer groups for discussion and exploration, involving students in community service, encouraging age-appropriate social activities for at-risk students, and serving as a good role model and caring adult.

Students in high school refine their educational and career goals and demonstrate achievement of them by successfully completing their educational plans and career-life planning portfolios. Drummond and Ryan (1995) suggest that career portfolios include

- School activities
- Hobbies and leisure activities
- Abilities, skills and special talents; test profiles
- Work experience
- Activities log
- Educational courses completed

- Career plans and information
- Resumé (p. 118)

During these final years of schooling, students have increased opportunities to make decisions that have long-term consequences for their professional and personal lives. In addition to gaining occupational information and making choices based on interest, aptitude, and attitude, high school students are also considering the kind of lifestyle and family life they wish to have in the future. These personal and social concerns influence the types of postsecondary opportunities pursued by high school graduates.

Two studies support the impact of counseling programs on student success. Lapan, Gysbers, and Sun (1997) studied the statewide guidance program in Missouri. Students in schools with more complete counseling programs were more likely to report higher grades, more satisfaction with their preparation for the future, availability of career and college information, and a more positive school climate. Similar positive results were fund in a study of Utah's counseling program (Nelson & Gardner, 1998). Another summary reviews the benefits of career education. In a meta-analysis of 67 studies about career education, Evans and Burck (1992) concluded that the interventions had a positive impact on students' academic achievement.

Ms. Farmer expresses concern about the lack of success of students of color and those with disabilities in obtaining their goals. Local data suggests that both groups of students are overrepresented in unchallenging courses and select postsecondary options such as immediate entry into the workforce and military service at much higher rates than the white students in this particular district regardless of other indicators of academic success such as grades and achievement scores. Again, the counselors turn to Blum (1998) to identify factors that they might emphasize in program development for the students of concern. Activities designed to increase self-confidence, provide role models, present accurate and specific information about options, explore cultural expectations, and encourage participation in a rigorous and varied curriculum are a few of the areas she suggests to increase the likelihood of success for these students.

In small groups choose one of the two groups about whom Ms. Farmer is concerned as the focus for your discussion. For your group of interest, identify at least one individual planning intervention that might be used to increase self-confidence and explore cultural expectations with the goal of expanding the range of options students believe to be available to them.

Career Centers

Counselors need to be familiar with career information to accomplish the tasks related to individual planning. They also need to make this material accessible to the students and adults. A career center that incorporates a wide variety of resources allows others to investigate materials related to occupational planning.

Zunker (1998) suggests the following categories of information be included: occupational descriptions, occupational outlook projections, postsecondary education and training information, military information, apprenticeship and internship information, information for special populations, a resource-persons file, and financial aid information. Further, career planning resources may include career decision making, vocational assessment, job search skills, and job simulation. These materials may include print materials, audiovisual resources, videotapes, and Internet files.

Computer-assisted career guidance systems such as DISCOVER (American College Testing Program, 2000) System for Interactive Guidance Information (SIGI)

Plus, and Career Information Delivery System (CIDS) provide interactive informational systems. People who use them have immediate access to large databases of occupational and educational information as well as interest inventories and decision-making skills. Those systems can be purchased for career centers. Many other resources on career information can be found on the Internet. The web site of the U.S. Department of Labor (http://www.acinet.org/acinet) helps link people to helpful career-related information. When considering computerized guidance systems, counselors use the following suggestions from Baker (2000), Brown and Srebalus (1988), and McDaniels (1982):

1. Consider the characteristics of the people who will be using the system, their needs, and their limitations.
2. Determine how the system fits into the goals of the program and how the counseling staff will expect to interact with the system and its users.
3. Study the system for theory, consistency, validity and reliability, skills needed, and outcomes.
4. Investigate practical considerations such as cost, response time, attractiveness to users, and customer service.

Creating a career resource center helps counselors provide individual planning interventions for students who are investigating and planning for their future.

TABLE 7.3   Primary Focus of Individual Planning Activities

	Appraisal	**Advisement**	**Placement**	**Career**
K–3	Special needs	As needed for special concerns	Special needs	Awareness of work/self; exposure to concepts
4–5	Special needs Achievement Intelligence	Educational planning; middle school curriculum	Middle school choices	Awareness of work/self, choices; exposure
6–8	Special needs Achievement Aptitude Intelligence Interests	Educational planning; high school curriculum	High school choices; work experience/service learning possibilities	Exploration of self/careers; set preliminary goals
9–12	Special needs Achievement Aptitude Intelligence Interests Personality Entrance exams	Educational planning/ career planning; entry postsecondary preparations	Continuing high school choices; work experience/service learning possibilities/ postsecondary options	Continuing and deeper exploration of self/careers; set goals; implement plans

SUMMARY

We have described the program element of individual planning and offered some examples of the goals of this element at elementary, middle, and high school. A summary of the focus of the individual planning activities at different levels appears in Table 7.3. The principal focus of this chapter has been the interplay between educational and career planning, and equipping students with the skills they need to set and reach educational and career goals. Numerous factors influence students' progress in these two areas including but not limited to stage of individual development, worldview of the student and family, socioeconomic status, gender, race, ethnicity, and ability status. Additionally, we described several experts' views of ways to implement this program element.

PORTFOLIO COMPONENTS

1. Complete the hidden bias inventory at http://www.tolerance.org and write a reflection about how you will use your findings to guard against unintended bias in career and educational programming when you become a school counselor.
2. Consider your own K–12 school experiences and write a reflection about how these experiences relate to your decision to pursue a career in school counseling. Be sure to consider the development of self-understanding in your discussion.
3. Using one of the NOICC career development goals, create a matrix that describes inadequate, marginal, adequate, and exemplary examples of student outcomes related to the goal for each grade level. An example follows:

		Inadequate	Marginal	Adequate	Exemplary
Skill to understand, use career information	1st grade	No ability to identify a career	Can sometimes identify a career	Identifies careers consistently	Identifies careers and information sources

Responsive Services

CASE STUDY

MEETING THE REMEDIAL NEEDS OF STUDENTS

Mr. Terman and his team are meeting at the close of the school year to discuss their school counseling program. They have worked diligently during this school year to fine-tune the individual planning program element. A thorough examination of both the new guidance curriculum and individual planning elements reveals that they are adequately addressing the developmental and preventive goals for their systemwide program. For this coming school year they will turn their attention to the responsive services program element. The counselors agree that they will be able to spend more time in the responsive services area than they have in the past because the developmental and preventive services covered under guidance curriculum and individual planning are now more efficiently meeting the typical developmental needs of students.

To facilitate their planning in the responsive services area, the counselors reorganize themselves into grade-level teams. This organizational schema will allow counselors to focus on the interventions uniquely appropriate for students at their grade levels. Their goals for the summer are to

1. Examine existing needs assessment and other local data to identify the immediate concerns of students, parents, and teachers.

2. Develop a survey to be used with students at the beginning of the next school year to identify those whose personal circumstances may have changed and who may need immediate intervention.

3. Update the list of community resources available for students and families whose personal problems may be interfering with their development.

4. Conduct a systemwide inventory of materials counselors have successfully used in consultation with teachers and parents to help students resolve their problems.

Gysbers and Henderson (2000) describe the responsive services program element as that part of the organizational framework through which counselors address remedial needs. Due to the many circumstances that have the potential to interfere with students healthy development, the school has continuing needs for crisis counseling, individual and small-group counseling, diagnostic and remediation activities, and consultation and referral (Gysbers & Henderson, 2000). Responsive services prevent the escalation of problem areas and intervene to alleviate some of the immediate concerns of students.

Responsive services are often associated with crisis management in a school setting. Fairchild (1997) describes crises experienced by students as situational, transitional, or cultural/social. Situational crises may be environmental catastrophes such as a tornado, fire, or other natural disaster; personal/physical, such as an illness or accident resulting in disability; or interpersonal, such as family disruption through divorce or death. Transitional crises include such universal states as movement through developmental life phases or nonuniversal occurrences such as changes in social status. Finally, Fairchild describes cultural/social crises as those related to one's social or cultural milieu such as discrimination, and those resulting from a violation of social norms such as being the victim of abuse or some other type of crime.

Understanding the types of remedial needs students may have based on these categories, one can see that some issues have potential to negatively affect everyone in a school, some will be unique to particular groups of students and their families, and others affect individual students. School counselors are responsible for planning and implementing interventions that will help students resolve the dilemmas resulting from the crises so that students may take full advantage of their educational opportunities.

After reading and discussing this chapter, you should be able to

- Identify the interventions commonly used by school counselors to respond to the immediate and remedial concerns of students.
- Develop a weekly schedule that includes responsive services interventions at each of the three grade levels.
- Describe procedures for developing and implementing counseling plans for students who need remedial assistance.
- Distinguish between students who may benefit from direct interventions such as counseling and those who may be more appropriately assisted through indirect methods such as consultation and/or referral.

As in all program design, counselors need to consider both what is important to do and how much can be done. Gysbers and Henderson (2000) suggest that elementary and middle school counselors spend approximately 30 to 40 percent of their time working with this program element, whereas high school counselors spend slightly less, 25 to 35 percent. In the sections that follow, we will discuss the interventions most commonly associated with this program element: individual counseling, group counseling, crisis counseling, and consultation. Diagnosis and referral, as well as legal and ethical issues, will be discussed in the context of each intervention.

COUNSELING

The American School Counselor Association (ASCA) (2001) defines counseling as "a confidential relationship which the counselor conducts with students individually and in small groups to help them resolve or cope constructively with their problems and developmental concerns" (p. 17). Thompson and Rudolph (2000) offer a definition of counseling as "a process in which people learn how to help themselves and, in effect, become their own counselors" (p. 18). That statement could be interpreted to mean that school counselors would teach children to identify a problem, to recognize their associated feelings and thoughts, and to work toward a solution.

In their review of counseling outcome research, Sexton, Whiston, Bleuer, and Walz (1997) report that counseling with children and adolescents is as effective as it is with adults. They also note that we have too little information to identify which students benefit most from responsive services. The challenges for school counselors include how to identify students, how to incorporate responsive services into the counselor's day, how to conduct counseling, and how to determine the effectiveness of counseling interventions.

First, the counselor needs to distinguish between those students whose concerns may be appropriately addressed through school counseling and those requiring therapy from other professionals. The situational, environmental, and social/cultural crises described by Fairchild (1997) may all lead to student concerns that are appropriately addressed by either individual or group counseling in schools. Among other things, students may see a school counselor for academic and other school-related concerns, for coping with stress, and for relationship difficulties. Most problems students bring to school counselors can be understood in one or more of the following categories:

1. **Conflict with others.** The child has difficult relationships with parents, siblings, teachers, or peers. Counseling is focused on building better ways of relating. An example of the importance of this type of counseling intervention is the helpfulness of social skills training for all school levels noted by Sexton and colleagues (1997).
2. **Conflict with self.** A young person needs help with making a decision by clarifying alternatives and consequences. Counselors may find choice theory (Glasser, 1998) helpful with these children.
3. **Lack of information about self.** The child needs to understand personal abilities, strengths, interests, or values. Children may benefit from working with counselors using an Adlerian approach (Dinkmeyer, Pew, & Dinkmeyer, 1979) or rational-emotive-behavioral counseling (Ellis, 1996).
4. **Lack of information about the environment.** The young person needs information about skills for school success or career education. Many of the activities school counselors arrange for individual planning will address those concerns. However some students may require the one-on-one attention of individual counseling to help them make life choices. Solution-focused brief counseling (Walter & Pellar, 1992) may be helpful to these students.
5. **Lack of skill.** The child needs to learn a specific skill such as listening, studying, or asking for help. Many components of the guidance curriculum will focus on those skills. Once again some students may need additional practice or more-focused discussions, which could be accomplished in individual counseling or in small-group settings.

Ms. Pickens states, "The priorities of the program in my elementary school make it virtually impossible for me to provide long-term counseling for students. Because I have a limited amount of time available, 14 half hour slots each week for individual and 14 for group counseling, how might I decide who will be seen for counseling?" School counselors face the decision of when to refer a student to counseling outside the school. Serious disorders, personality problems, and other pervasive difficulties require more intensive therapy than most school counselors can provide. Some of the symptoms that may indicate a child needs longer term therapy from someone outside the school include eating disorders, intense sibling rivalry, intense preoccupation with sexual matters, extreme aggression with no apparent guilt, habitual lying or stealing, and sudden and unexplained changes in eating, sleeping, or behavior patterns. School counselors assess the frequency (how often the problem occurs), duration (how long it lasts), and intensity (how strong it is) to help them determine whether to work with the young person in school or to refer to another professional. Additionally counselors look at three other things when deciding whether to refer:

- Am I competent to deal with this concern?
- Do I have enough time and energy to work with this need?
- When in a counseling relationship, are we making enough progress? (Ehly & Dustin, 1989)

Lockhart and Keys (1998) urge school counselors to develop mental health counseling skills to address the range of student problems. According to these authors counselors need skills and knowledge about diagnostic criteria, managed care, child and family welfare systems, court system and juvenile services, residential programs, and the changing structure of accessing services. School counselors need to be familiar with the resources in their communities and make referrals based on the competence of the service providers (Remley & Herlihy, 2001). Counselors should compile a list of referral sources to provide students and parents. However, school systems have policy statements about how referrals are made and who coordinates or makes referrals in a given school. With few exceptions, referrals for counseling services are made with the understanding that any expense involved is the responsibility of the parents (Gysbers & Henderson, 2000). Consequently, it may be beneficial to parents if counselors include competent counselors who offer a wide range of payment options.

Mr. Wang, a middle school counselor, states that many referrals for counseling in his school come from persons other than the prospective counselee. Parents, teachers, administrators, and others in the community may believe, based on their interactions and or observations, that a student might benefit from counseling. Currently, Mr. Wang receives referrals from teachers written on the back of student homework, on sticky notes attached to other materials being returned to his mailbox, and frequently by incidental contact in hallways or restrooms. Parents frequently call or e-mail their requests that he meet with their children, sometimes leaving brief messages at the front office with student aides. He wishes to establish a system that allows him to receive referrals that are more informative and more confidential.

Finally, Ms. Lerner states, "I am concerned about confidentiality for my students. The school is different from agencies or private practice settings where the clients report to an office where they might expect some degree of privacy. My office opens onto a busy hallway and many students, teachers, and other staff may see who enters during group or individual counseling time. Additionally, students may not go wandering about the school independently. They must ask permission to leave a class to see me, or I must ask to see them. And, as I understand the laws, the students do not have the right to enter into a counseling relationship on their own and must have parental permission. Parents also have the right to know what is happening in our sessions. These circumstances make it very difficult for me to maintain my ethical responsibility to students."

Assume you have been seeing an adolescent whom you suspect has an eating disorder. Develop a list of referral sources in your community to provide to this student's parents.

Divide into small groups and develop a system for receiving and responding to requests for counseling services from students, teachers, parents, and others. Develop a referral form that would have the information needed to respond to the referral request, could be delivered to Mr. Wang in a confidential manner, and allows for a follow-up contact with the referring person. Be sure to include in your system how appointments will be scheduled, how students and teachers will be notified of the appointment, how students will get from classroom to counseling office and back to the classroom, and how missed assignments and instruction will be handled.

Mr. Terman clarifies, "Ms. Lerner, you are absolutely correct that it is a challenge to keep confidential that a particular student is being seen by a school counselor. However, it is possible to keep in confidence what occurs in those sessions with some exceptions as outlined in the ASCA Ethical Standards, section A.2. (see Appendix C). You are also correct that minors may not enter into contractual agreements with counselors. However, unless established by statute or school policy, the school counselor typically does not have to seek parental permission to provide counseling services to a student (Remley & Herlihy, 2001). The school counseling program and all of its elements, including responsive services, should be introduced to parents when their children enroll in school. They are advised at that time that their children will be participating in the program throughout their enrollment at varying levels. According to Remley and Herlihy parents who do not wish their children to receive counseling probably do have the right to request that counseling be discontinued."

Ms. Pickens adds, "Parents may also request information obtained from the child by the school counselor. I found something that helps me with that situation. Remley and Herlihy (2001) outline a five-step strategy for responding to such requests from parents or other responsible adults. The counselor tries the strategies in order, progressing to strategy two only if strategy one is not effective. The process begins with securing the minor's permission to disclose the information. Next, the counselor tries to convince the adult that maintaining the child's confidence will be more beneficial than revealing information obtained during counseling. Third, the counselor may act as a mediator of the information in a joint session with the child and adult. If the adult still wants the information and the child still does not wish to disclose, inform the child that disclosure will take place and when and where that will occur. The remaining option is to refuse to disclose the information, with the full support of the administration and with full knowledge that the parent may have a legal right to the information."

INDIVIDUAL COUNSELING

As counselors receive referrals for responsive services, they consider whether individual counseling or another intervention would be appropriate for the student. The following criteria (Blum, 1998) help guide the counselor:

- The student's concern is unique.
- Other students (in groups or classroom guidance) would not benefit from interventions aimed at resolving the problem.
- Confidentiality is essential.
- Individual assessment or interpretation is needed.
- The behavior under consideration would be considered deviant by others in the same age group.
- The student may experience distress talking about the concern in groups.

Schmidt (1999) also identifies some questions school counselors might ask to determine whether counseling is appropriate:

1. Does the student see the problem in a way that is similar to the one making the referral?
2. Is the student motivated toward change?
3. How much control does the student have over the situation leading to the problem?
4. What is the student's level of commitment to change?

As a summary of these considerations, the following factors influence whether to focus on individual counseling:

- Type of problem (school related, home related, other)
- Nature of problem (lack of skill, lack of information, conflict)
- Urgency of need (crisis, remedial, preventive)
- Age of student
- Willingness of student (voluntary, request by parent, teacher, etc.)
- Inner-directed or outer-directed problem (depression, aggression)

After school counselors receive the referral for counseling, they may seek out additional information if needed, and then schedule an initial interview with the student to attempt to answer the four questions Schmidt provided. In this initial meeting counselors assess the nature and extent of the problem based on the list above and decide, with the student, whether individual counseling might be helpful.

In fact, counselors assist students with their problems and developmental concerns in many ways. Selecting the approaches that may be most productive for which student is influenced by a number of factors. Specifically, the cognitive, social, and physical development of students largely determines the approach taken by the counselor. Table 8.1 summarizes ways some of these factors affect a counseling application. Additionally, the student's cultural identity (e.g., worldview, language, individual vs. group orientation) is important for the counselor to know and appreciate. Locke (1993) admonishes school counselors to learn about working with culturally different groups and to add specific techniques to their repertoire of skills. Table 8.2 contains criteria for counselors to use in assessing whether they are providing equitable counseling services. Finally, the counselor must have a good grasp of the major counseling theories and their applications with school-aged youth in order to develop effective counseling plans.

Person-centered counseling (Rogers, 1977, 1992) provides counselors with relationship skills for building rapport. Choice theory (Glasser, 1998), solution-focused brief counseling (Walter & Pellar, 1992), Adlerian counseling (Dinkmeyer et al., 1979), and rational-emotive-behavioral (Ellis, 1996) counseling are other theories used by many school counselors. Additionally Myrick (1997) has identified a problem-solving model for school counselors to use for individual counseling. His process includes deciding on the problem, identifying what the child has tried to do to solve the problem, generating some other possible solutions, and determining the child's next step. Keys, Bemak, and Lockhart (1998) recommend short-term models such as Myrick's problem-solving outline and Walter and Pellar's solution-focused counseling. That process leads to establishing goals for counseling that help counselors and students plan how to work together. The ASCA Ethical Standards (ASCA, 2000) (see Appendix C, Standard A3) state that a professional school counselor

TABLE 8.1 Development and Counseling Applications

Age	Typical Concerns	Situational Problems	Transitions	Counseling Considerations
Middle childhood (6–10)	Teacher and/or peer approval; being chosen last for a team; fear of being ridiculed; fear of losing a friend; school performance	Growing up in abusive or alcoholic home; living in poverty; adjustments to parental divorce and/or remarriage	Adjusting to school; missing parents; changes in friendships; too little or too much dependency	Help with problem-solving abilities; design interventions that are concrete, such as bibliotherapy, art, puppets, role-play, and games; talking less effective
Early adolescence (11–14)	Mood swings; relationships with friends and parents; worry about appearance; sexuality	Growing up in abusive or alcoholic home; living in poverty; adjustments to parental divorce and/or remarriage; pregnancy; substance abuse	Overwhelming feelings; moving to middle school; planning for their future	Confusion predominates; concrete strategies for cause and effect, alternative behaviors, and long-range implications
Middle adolescence (15–18)	Complex relationships; sexual intimacy; family stress	Growing up in abusive or alcoholic home; living in poverty; adjustments to parental divorce and/or remarriage; pregnancy; substance abuse	Changes in role, relationships, routine, and assessment of self; future	Be aware of ambivalence; use activities to illustrate points; bibliotherapy, journaling, and homework helpful

Source: Adapted from Vernon, A. (1999). Counseling children and adolescents: Developmental considerations. In A. Vernon (Ed.), *Counseling children and adolescents* (2nd ed.). Denver, CO: Love Publishing. Reprinted with permission.

works jointly with the counselee in developing integrated and effective counseling plans, consistent with both the abilities and circumstances of the counselee and counselor. Such plans will be regularly reviewed to ensure continued viability and effectiveness, respecting the counselee's freedom of choice. (p. 26)

Counseling plans consist of a statement of the concern or problem to be addressed in counseling; specific goals to be achieved that will resolve the problem; short-term objectives that, when accomplished, are likely to result in the achievement of the goal; activities or interventions to help the student achieve the short-term objectives; and a method for evaluating whether the objectives and goal(s) have been achieved. The heart of the counseling plan is the goal or the goals toward which you and the student are striving. The goals and the means of achieving them will be guided by the concern of the student and the theoretical approach of the

Using the three broad headings of crises articulated by Fairchild (1997), develop a list for each of the types of problems or concerns for which students might receive counseling referrals. Combine your list with those of your classmates to create a comprehensive list. Identify those issues that you believe would be most appropriate for individual counseling.

TABLE 8.2   Counseling Diverse Students—Criteria for Equity

Questions	Yes	No	Needs Improving
1. Am I, as the counselor, familiar with strategies that promote equity in a multicultural society (e.g., utilizing culturally/gender relevant counseling practices, empathizing with and understanding the students' world view)?	☐	☐	☐
2. Am I, as the counselor, familiar with and understanding of both verbal and nonverbal language patterns of different ethnic/racial groups?	☐	☐	☐
3. Do I, as the counselor, have high expectations for all students and assist students to acquire resources and opportunities necessary for success?	☐	☐	☐
4. In working with a diverse student population in counseling situations, do I, as the counselor, consider the interaction of gender differences, class differences, language differences, and cultural differences?	☐	☐	☐
5. Do I, as the counselor, provide career counseling on the basis of the students' abilities, interests, and skills rather than according to traditional roles based on gender, race, disability, or ethnicity?	☐	☐	☐
6. Do I, as the counselor, encourage students to take courses nontraditional to their gender, race, disability, or ethnicity if the student shows an interest in one of those areas (e.g., mathematics, science, computer technology for females, early childhood education for males)?	☐	☐	☐
7. Do I, as the counselor, assess my own values, attitudes, and beliefs and have the ability to refrain from imposing them upon the student?	☐	☐	☐
8. Do I, as the counselor, participate in in-service programs or special skill sessions for counselors dealing with culturally diverse students?	☐	☐	☐
9. Do I, as the counselor, meet with students outside of the office to show an interest in their needs beyond the classroom?	☐	☐	☐
10. Do I, as the counselor, use a multidimensional approach to identify the level and scope of a student's ability before recommending course selection, placement, and future schooling/career opportunities?	☐	☐	☐

Source: Greenberg, J. M., and Shaffer, S. (1991). *Elements of Equity: Criteria for Equitable Schools.* Mid-Atlantic Equity Consortium. Available on the World Wide Web: http://www.maec.org/. Reprinted with permission.

counselor. Person-centered counselors use empathy to create an environment that encourages children to become more self-aware. Counselors who use choice theory concentrate on children making better choices and teach young people a process for examining their behavior, considering alternatives, and planning for change. Solution-focused counselors help students identify and use their strengths to create differences in their lives. Adlerian counselors work on helping children take responsibility for their choices as they discover ways to contribute positively. Often Adlerian counselors involve other adults in counseling plans. Pryor and Tollerud (1999) explain some specific ways Adlerian principles can be used in schools with children and adults. Rational-emotive-behavioral counselors encourage children to identify and change their self-defeating thoughts and actions.

Young (2001) identifies several positive outcomes of goal setting, including the fact that goals help us stay focused on the concerns of the student. Clearly stated and understood goals help counselors evaluate whether they have the skills needed to assist the student or whether a referral would be more appropriate. Positively stated goals help students focus on success, specific goals provide a sound basis for making decisions about interventions, and measurable goals make it possible to determine whether counseling has been helpful to the student.

> Divide into groups of five. From each theoretical approach, write a goal statement appropriate for a student who is not completing homework. Compare and revise these goals after a group discussion.

Counseling Plan

Student: Tamikka Jones

Grade: 4th

Source of Referral: Parents

Reason for Referral: Grandmother died as a result of a violent crime. Since the funeral one month ago, Tamikka sleeps almost all of the time that she is not in school, eats less than usual, stays inside her room, and has withdrawn from activities previously enjoyed, including playing with friends and studying for school.

Goal: Tamikka will increase her waking time, the number of balanced meals she eats each week, and resume her previous level of social and school activity.

Short-term objectives:

1. Tamikka will stay awake between the time she gets home from school and her 9 P.M. bedtime.
2. Tamikka will play outside with her friends at least three afternoons each week until dinnertime.
3. Tamikka will eat a well-balanced meal at 6 P.M. each evening.
4. Tamikka will complete homework assignments between the end of dinnertime and 8 P.M. each evening.

Counseling Interventions:

1. Cognitive distraction will be used to have Tamikka think about a happy time she spent with her grandmother, replacing the thoughts about her grandmother's death. Tamikka will create a scrapbook to illustrate some of the happy memories.
2. Exercise and playing with friends will be used to help Tamikka leave the house and engage in physical activities instead of taking a nap before dinner.
3. Worksheets for rating her week with regard to meals, social activity, sleep, and completion of homework will be used to increase self-awareness of her behavior and track progress toward goals.

Evaluation: Counseling will be discontinued when Tamikka is sleeping no more than 10 hours per day, completing 90 percent of all homework assignments, spending at least 4 hours per week playing with friends after school, and eating at least two well-balanced meals per day.

Counselors have several options to build a caseload for individual counseling. They may wait for students to refer themselves. They may respond to parent and teacher referrals. They may seek recommendations from school administrators. And they may combine all these options. After their team's discussion of counseling, Ms. Pickens has decided to try a suggestion made by Myrick (1997). She is going to ask all the teachers at one grade level, the principal, and the assistant principals for the names of children who might need some individual attention. For this school year she will counsel with two of those named most frequently for a 6-week period. She will also work with 12 other students identified by several adults. For the rest of her individual counseling she will assist those who have self-referred and those referred by others. Many of those situations may be short term requiring one or two sessions only. However, she will schedule time for longer counseling relationships with four students during each grading period. She is now ready to consider the small groups offered in school.

COUNSELING IN SMALL GROUPS

In their summary of research, Roth and Fonagy (1996) state that with children "group psychotherapy . . . for a single term appeared to have the greatest effect over-all, and it was the most economical form of therapy offered" (p. 317). All of the counselors report that they enjoy working with students in small groups and view this strategy as efficient and effective. Even though they have only 14 half-hour slots available each week, they see six to eight students at the same time and the group process allows students to learn from each other. Thompson and Rudolph (2000) suggest several reasons for working with children in small groups. They recognize that children and adults exist as members of groups in many of their daily activities. The importance of other people's perceptions on our personal beliefs and perceptions constitutes another reason to use small-group work with children. Those authors state that group counseling creates a more reality-oriented situation than individual counseling. In groups children can replace their inappropriate behaviors with new ways of relating through the group interaction. Counselors may choose small-group counseling when they want to help students learn to work together. In a small-group setting the members can deal with their ideas, feelings, and behaviors. The members also have chances to build strong relationships among themselves.

Small-group counseling may be appropriate in a variety of circumstances such as when counselors want to address urgent needs, focus on a problem, or encourage student development. School counselors use the small-group format for both guidance (psychoeducational) goals and counseling (interpersonal) goals. These two types of groups differ in several ways. Guidance/psychoeducational groups have a learning orientation and may often be focused on the prevention of potential prob-

Remember a time when you worked with a group of your peers to explore and solve a problem. Describe the aspects that were and were not beneficial. Share experiences in small groups and develop a list of commonalities in "helpful" and "not help-ful" columns.

lems. Members are provided with information and practice skills that they can use in their lives. These groups may have an open format in which members can enter and leave or a closed format in which the same members stay through the entire schedule of group sessions. The leader facilitates the group process and teaches the content and skills. Activities are chosen that support the goals of the group. One example might be a guidance group that meets after school to improve academic skills. Some students may need all the lessons (study skills, time management, test-taking strategies, relaxation skills, organizational skills). Others may need only one or two of the lessons and attend only the sessions that are pertinent.

Counseling/interpersonal groups may also have the prevention orientation. These groups may focus on some identified stressors, a conflict, or a problem that distracts young people from learning. The problem may be individual or a common problem. These groups typically have a closed format. The leader uses counseling skills to help the members who are experiencing some disturbance because of the identified problem (e.g., divorce of parents, move to a new school, trouble making friends or managing anger). In groups members identify the particular problem(s) they are each having within the context of the central issue, explore solutions, and make decisions about how they will attempt to solve the problem(s). This parallels the problem-solving approach Myrick (1997) suggests.

The concerns around which groups are established are often identified through a needs assessment, or perhaps the counselor receives referrals around a similar issue for multiple students. Still other groups are offered routinely based on the counselor's knowledge of the developmental transitions with which students are most likely to need assistance. Group counseling plans are developed and goals are decided around the central organizing theme of the group. Table 8.3 lists some possible group themes.

> Develop a one-page survey with group topics typical of middle school students' transitional crises. Include topics associated with students' potential difficulties in academic and career development. Using the same plan format provided for Tamikka's individual counseling, work in small groups to develop a group plan for Tamikka and five other students who have experienced the death of a family member in the previous 6 months.

Stages in Groups

Groups usually evolve through four stages: beginning, transition, working, and leaving. In the beginning stage the counselor and group establish the ground rules and other guidelines for the group. The counselor helps set norms, models actions that lead to trust, and helps the members get acquainted. Certain rules and procedures are appropriate for all groups. For instance in the early sessions the leader should clarify the group purpose, members' responsibility, ground rules, and the importance of confidentiality. Guidelines such as only one person speaking at a time, listening to the person speaking, taking turns, and not making fun of each other are fundamental ground rules for groups in schools. Confidentiality in groups with minors can be problematic. The importance of members maintaining each others' confidentiality should be stressed, as well as any limits to the counselor's ability to maintain confidentiality. Remley and Herlihy (2001) advocate that counselors reiterate the limits when sensitive material surfaces in the group.

The goal during this first stage is for members to begin to build rapport. Students learn to care for each other, give each other attention, and begin to know and understand each other—conditions that lead to an atmosphere of trust. Additionally, students who have not previously participated in groups may need to acquire

TABLE 8.3   Possible Group Topics

Group Topics	Elementary	Middle	High School
Family Issues			
Alcoholic families	Yes	Yes	Yes
Divorce	Yes	Yes	Yes
Family transitions	Yes	Yes	Yes
Stepfamily	Yes	Yes	—
Interpersonal Issues			
Anger management	Yes	Yes	Yes
Communication skills	Yes	Yes	Yes
Conflict management	Yes	Yes	Yes
Peer pressure	—	Yes	Yes
Social skills	Yes	Yes	Yes
Valuing diversity	Yes	Yes	Yes
Personal Issues			
Death, grief, and loss	Yes	Yes	Yes
Health problems	Yes	Yes	Yes
Pregnancy education	—	Yes	Yes
Prevention for at-risk	Yes	Yes	Yes
Self-concept	Yes	Yes	Yes
Stress management	Yes	Yes	Yes
Time management	Yes	Yes	Yes
School Concerns			
Academic competition	—	Yes	Yes
Academic failures	Yes	Yes	Yes
Attitudes about school	—	Yes	Yes
Learning styles	Yes	Yes	Yes
New student	Yes	Yes	Yes
Responsible school behavior	Yes	Yes	Yes
Study skills	Yes	Yes	Yes

some group participation skills. Classroom rules for interaction among class members (e.g., talking to teacher, but not to each other) may not be conducive to group development.

What other classroom behaviors or rules may not be compatible with the aims of group counseling?

The transition stage involves group members testing each other. Some may be willing to participate and others may be more resistant to the group process. The counselor structures the group, clarifies the purpose of the group, and continues to model trust-building actions. As the members accept each other and learn to deepen their trust, the group moves to the working stage. During this stage, the members continue to focus of the concern, explore and clarify the issues on which they are working, set appropriate goals and identify new behaviors to practice in the group, move to practice the new behavior outside the group, and report back. During the working stage, the group leader monitors the group work for benefits, participation, cohesiveness, and trust. Finally, students evaluate their experience and progress, and leave the group. The group leader helps by summarizing what has been learned, checks for unfinished business, deals with feelings of separation, and evaluates the group experience.

Leading Groups

Group counseling leadership requires planning. An important early step for counselors is introducing group counseling to administrators and teachers (Blum, 1998). Such an orientation includes an explanation of how group counseling supports student achievement in school. Sharing the research of effectiveness provides support for including small-group work within responsive services. For example, Reeder, Douzenis, and Bergin (1997) used a small-group counseling intervention to improve racial relationships between second graders. Garrett and Crutchfield (1997) modified an idea from the Native American culture for a series of small-group sessions to help children develop positive self-images. Others have demonstrated the effectiveness of small-group work with low-performing students (Campbell & Myrick, 1990), with bereaved children (Zambelli & DeRosa, 1992), and with students who have been retained (Campbell & Bowman, 1993).

Counselors collaborate with teachers and administrators on the scheduling of groups to minimize disruption to instructional time. Logistical issues such as the number of times the group will meet and the length, setting, and frequency of the meetings are planned and communicated to teachers and prospective group members. In schools the groups' duration may be tied to a grading period of 6 to 9 weeks. Groups in early elementary grades usually meet for 20 minutes, in fourth or fifth grades, for 30 minutes, and in middle and secondary schools, for a class period (45 to 55 minutes). Groups may meet before or after school, during lunch, or during other times of the day as alternatives to class time. Group size depends on the age of the students and the purpose of the group. Myrick (1997) suggests groups of five to six with no more than seven to eight students.

Before finalizing the group, counselors screen potential group members. Screening is an important ethical issue (ASCA, 2000) intended to reduce the potential of psychological harm to a student who may not be ready for group participation. The selection of participants should involve a process during which the potential member receives information about the particular group and about a group member's role. The counselor and the student determine the suitability of that person for this group experience. Some students may be too hostile, too suspicious, or too fragile to be included. Students who are screened but not included in the group should be given the option of an alternative experience. Counselors may refer to the criteria noted for individual counseling to decide whether students who are not selected may see the counselor one-on-one.

Additionally, group leaders work to balance group sessions by working on both maintenance and task functions. How members are working together and helping each other are the maintenance functions. Movement toward the group goal is the task function (Blum, 1998). Group leaders serve as models to demonstrate group membership and communication skills. The group leader uses counseling skills and

Review your list of "helpful" group experiences. Identify the leadership skills or functions that were evident in each instance. Now, review the "not helpful" group experiences. Identify which of the leadership tasks or functions might have been used to make this experience or incident a more productive one.

techniques as well as the following tasks: directing communication traffic, guiding the group process, blocking harmful behavior, connecting ideas, reaching a consensus, moderating discussion, summarizing, and supporting (Thompson & Rudolph, 2000).

A straightforward model, SIPA (structure, involvement, process, and awareness), suggested by Gladding (1999) helps school counselors focus on their leadership responsibilities. Structure occurs when counselors ask students to listen and/or to do activities according to the guidelines related to the group's goal. Involvement takes place as the counselor draws in members of the group and they become active participants. The process consists of group members sharing ideas, and awareness relates to the group leader and members consolidating what has been learned.

CRISIS COUNSELING

One school district's safety plan can be found at http://www.wa.gov/ago/ourschool/5_plan/pearl.htm. Visit the website and compare this plan to the one for your local school district.

A crisis may occur through either natural disasters (e.g., harm to students, teachers, or parents by flood, wind, or fire) or personal disasters (e.g., harm to members of the school community by a violence, suicide, or accidents). Whatever the cause, crises in schools and their surrounding communities require intervention. Crisis implies that the impact of the event is experienced immediately and needs an immediate response. An appropriate response to a schoolwide crisis is based on a previously developed plan. Unlike individual or group counseling for the concerns we have already discussed, one cannot develop an effective plan and strategy for responding to a crisis in the midst of the crisis.

The counselors at Washington County Schools have a crisis plan in place. The plan is updated annually, outlines specific responsibilities and who is responsible for carrying them out, is distributed to every staff member, and is evaluated periodically through mock drills (Blum, 1998). Their plan was implemented most recently when a car that did not yield to the stop sign displayed by a school bus struck and killed a 6-year-old first grader. The accident was witnessed by all the elementary school children riding the bus. Because there was a crisis plan in place, the employees of the school and system knew exactly to whom they should refer all inquiries from the press. One person was responsible for calling in counselors from the other schools and community agencies to assist with small-group and individual counseling sessions for the children riding the bus and those in the deceased student's classroom. The teachers throughout the school system were responsible for telling the students in each of their classrooms what had happened, and they knew to provide factual information in developmentally appropriate language. Parents were invited to the school to participate in sessions with other adults. The children who witnessed or were affected by this traumatic event needed assistance with their concerns and perceptions about self. The parents needed assistance in addressing their concerns and fears for their children and their children's safety (Junhke, 1997).

Even though crisis counseling may occur in large groups, in small groups, and with individuals, it is a decidedly different intervention than individual or small-group counseling. Working in small groups, discuss the differences between individual and small-group counseling and crisis counseling.

Classroom announcements and activities were used to keep students informed; provide them an opportunity to express their feelings of sadness, fear, helplessness, and so forth; and attend to their needs for reassurance regarding their own physical safety. Outside consultants were brought in on the third day following the accident to debrief the adults who provided support and services for the children. Follow-up activities were scheduled at predetermined intervals, and the counselors provided staff development training for teachers about the behaviors students might display that would indicate a need for additional intervention.

CONSULTATION

Mr. Terman and his team of counselors recognize that one of the advantages of working in schools is the opportunity to work with other adults who work with students. School counselors work as consultants providing an indirect service when they help teachers, administrators, parents, and others who have responsibilities for a third party (students) find ways to solve problems. Consultation includes three people: the consultant (school counselor), the consultee (the person with whom they have direct contact), and the recipient (the person who benefits from the indirect assistance). Dougherty (2000) explains that the goal of consultation is to solve problems related to a situation that needs attention. School counselors who share their expertise and skills help both the consultees and the people with whom the consultees interact.

Mr. Terman's team reviewed their many opportunities to work as consultants. They listed some of their previous year's experiences that could be classified as consulting activities. They worked with teachers who wanted counselors to give them ideas for working with students who were having academic difficulties. Teachers also asked for help in understanding children's behaviors and in creating positive classroom environments. The counselors helped teachers develop skills in working with parents and in including materials related to children's personal/social, academic, and career development into their curriculum. Administrators consulted with counselors about students with special needs as well as about relationships with parents and the community. Counselors also consulted with administrators on some schoolwide programs and with other counselors when they needed assistance resolving ethical dilemmas or assistance from a more experienced colleague. Parents requested help in understanding developmental and academic concerns experienced by their children. The counselors conducted one parent education group and wanted to extend this way of consulting with parents. The group realized all those examples illustrated some of the many ways consultation fits into the responsive services component of a school counseling program.

Consultation can be approached in different ways. Kurpius and Fuqua (1993) listed the following as four descriptions of modes of consulting:

1. **Provision.** Within this mode the consultee has a specific need and works with the counselor/consultant who provides services to meet the need. One of the counselors in Mr. Terman's school had worked with a teacher who wanted to integrate some information and skills about emotional intelligence in her class. The counselor helped the teacher find some materials and then co-taught three classes with the teacher.
2. **Prescription.** Consultation in this way involves the counselor/consultant working as an expert who analyzes the situation by collecting information, making an expert diagnosis, and then giving directions for remedying the difficulty. An

example of this occurred last year, after three meetings of a small group for first-year teachers. The counselor who was facilitating the group wondered whether the classroom environments the teachers described could be improved and offered to observe the classes. Based on what she saw, she suggested that the teachers could improve their classrooms by responding to students more consistently. The counselor recommended that these first-year teachers practice this skill and helped them find some resources to show them examples.

3. **Collaboration.** This is a partnership mode of consultation in which the consultee and the counselor/consultant work together in defining, designing, and implementing the solution. A distraught parent had come to the counseling office one day after receiving the news that her partner was terminally ill. She did not know how to prepare her child for what the family was going to be facing. The counselor helped the parent think through the different things that needed to be done such as telling the child, determining how much information is needed, planning for emergencies, and explaining changes that would be happening at home. They next generated a list of possibilities for each of those and the advantages and disadvantages of each alternative. After that process they made a tentative plan with provisions for following up.

4. **Mediation.** This mode of consultation involves the consultant establishing a way for individuals or groups who are disagreeing to listen to each other's viewpoints and helping them come to a mutually agreeable resolution. An example of this type of consulting occurred when three teachers on a team were at odds about some of the arrangements in a classroom they shared. The counselor/consultant brought all three together and moderated their discussion until they reached an acceptable agreement.

Counselors have choices about ways to implement the consulting process. They may use an education/training consultation model to provide information (Gallessich, 1982; Lippitt & Lippitt, 1986). They may use behavioral consultation when the goal is a change in behavior (Lutzker & Martin, 1981). They may implement mental health consultation when the goal is to help solve a current problem as well as similar future problems (Meyers, Brent, Fahery, & Modafferi, 1993; Brown, Pryzwansky, & Schulte, 1998). They may also work as Adlerian consultants to help adults understand a child's behavior and to improve those patterns of behavior (Doughtery, 2000). Finally Kahn (2000) suggests a model of solution-focused consultation. According to Rosenfield and Gravois (1993), the skills necessary when using any of these approaches include

- Understanding and using information about context or culture.
- Using effective interpersonal and communication skills.
- Understanding and implementing effective problem-solving steps.
- Developing and evaluating interventions.
- Applying the skills and relationship factors in practice situations.
- Reflecting on the situation and evaluating one's own skills.
- Understanding the ways ethical codes apply to consultation practice.
- Applying ethical principles appropriately.

In a group identify another example of situations in schools that could be addressed by each of the consultation modes.

Assume that your superintendent has asked you to provide training for new teachers at the end of their first semester on classroom management. Prepare a plan for the consultation activity, including a description of the training event, the goals or objectives of the training, the interventions used to achieve the goals, the resources you would use in the training, and a method of evaluating the event.

Caplan (1970) suggests that consultants consider four areas when determining how to approach consultation. The consultee difficulty may be a result of lack of knowledge. In this case the consultee may not have sufficient understanding of the problem or of some other factor that is relative to the case. The consultant may deal with this by supplying the information. Another problem that consultees may present is a lack of skill. In these situations the consultee understands the relevant factors in the case but does not have the skill to intervene effectively. The consultant works by helping the consultee explore the problem, what has been tried, and what other possibilities exist. They then determine the skills needed to work with the situation and explore ways to develop those skills. The difficulty of lack of confidence presents a third source of difficulty for consultees. These consultees need support and encouragement. The consultant would serve as one source as both worked to identify other support systems available. Lack of professional objectivity occurs when consultees lose professional distance in their work and therefore block the use of their skills with a person. The consultant helps the consultee identify and lessen the impact of the interference.

Systematic Facilitative Approach to Consultation

Myrick (1997) explains a how-to model that gives counselors a framework for practice. The steps of the model are as follows:

1. Identify the problem by listening carefully and helping the consultee explain the situation.
2. Clarify the situation by identifying
   a. The consultee's and the client's feelings.
   b. The specific behaviors of both.
   c. The expectations of the consultee.
   d. What has been done up to this point.
   e. Strengths of the consultee.
3. Determine the goal or outcomes by specifying them as behaviors.
4. Observe and record behaviors (when needed).
5. Develop an action plan that can be done in 2 weeks by the consultee by considering possible interventions, identifying the most appealing, and discussing how it might work and when it will start.
6. Implement the plan.
7. Follow up for evaluating and revision as well as discussion of the next steps.

> With one of your classmates talk about a work problem using the steps of Myrick's model. Then practice by developing a consultation plan that might be used with the parents of Tamikka.

Consultation with Teachers

Counselors may work with teachers in large groups, small groups, and individually. Possibilities for large-group meetings in which information is presented are topics such as classroom management, standardized tests, conflict-resolution skills, parent conference skills, and strategies for different types of learners. Blum (1998) recommends that successful staff development depends on responding to specific needs, having voluntary attendance, and scheduling the session according to the teachers' preferences. The topic should be relevant and the session short and well planned.

Counselor/consultants may work on child study teams or screening committees. They may do case studies with teachers, identify teacher's expectations, and share learning strategies for students. As suggested earlier, counselors may also form support groups for teachers. School counselors also need strategies for consulting with parents (Conroy & Meyer, 1994; Norwood & Atkinson, 1997). Counselors may work with parents in large groups to provide information about subjects such as transitions, orientation, college, financial aid, and the counseling program. Concerns about child rearing, developmental descriptions, and school expectations may also be addressed. In a review of outcome research related to consultation, Sheridan and Welch (1996) found evidence to support this as an effective approach in schools.

SUMMARY

In this chapter, you have read about responsive services and the interventions typically associated with such services. Specifically, individual and group counseling, crisis counseling, and consultation in the school setting were described. Some of the more pertinent legal and ethical issues regarding working with minors were presented.

PORTFOLIO COMPONENTS

1. Develop a counseling plan for a middle school student with the same problems as Tamikka and one for a student in high school. Discuss the differences in objectives and activities based on developmental life stage.
2. Create a sample crisis plan that is flexible enough to be implemented in a school, regardless of the disaster leading to the crisis.
3. Prepare a reflection statement describing how you might feel and respond to a crisis such as the one described in this chapter. How do you view death? How would you address the questions of first graders about death from a culturally sensitive perspective, acknowledging the importance of family beliefs and values?
4. Identify a student concern that would be considered a situational crisis. Develop a list of resources to be used by counselor, student, parent/guardian, and teacher to assist the student in remediating the difficulties associated with the crisis.

C H A P T E R   9

System Support

CASE STUDY

SYSTEM SUPPORT: THE FRAMEWORK

Mr. Terman and the TK–12 team are once again meeting to have their year-end review/planning session. They report surprising findings with regard to responsive services. Because they more fully implemented the program elements of individual planning and the guidance curriculum, the counselors across grade levels report having more time to provide responsive services than in previous years. Mr. Terman reports that he spent much more time providing individual and group counseling to students with remedial needs, as well as serving as a consultant to teachers and parents, in addition to meeting program objectives related to students' life and career goals. All counselors report similar experiences, and Ms. Lerner observes that she spent less of her responsive services time slots each week in crisis counseling than she had in the past as well. They are eager to pursue planning and implementation activities related to the fourth program element, system support.

The counselors know that to continue to increase their efficiency and productivity, they must have a strong support system for their program. Their goals for the coming year are

1. To set specific goals for the management of their programs.

2. To collaborate with each other and distribute the effort for the program element so that all counselors are providing some aspect of the support, but no one is responsible for all of the support.

3. To be deliberate in the collection, analysis, and distribution of research and information that supports the comprehensive program.

4. To identify areas where their skills need to be updated and pursue professional development opportunities as needed.

To accomplish these goals, the counselors decide to meet several times during the summer in grade-level teams to complete assessment and prioritizing activities for this program component. They hope to begin implementation in the new school year.

System support includes the management activities necessary for effective program implementation. Although system support is the smallest of the four program components articulated by Gysbers and Henderson (2000) in terms of allocation of time, 10 to 15 percent, it is one of the most important. An analogy might be the function served a building by interior walls (load bearing walls) that support the roof by connecting it to the building's foundation. Although only a few of the walls in a building are load bearing, as long as these walls remain in place other walls may be moved or removed, and new ones added, without decreasing the building's structural integrity. Without these walls, a building may stand temporarily but the roof will eventually sag and may even cave in from its own weight. The detrimental effects of weather and other environmental degradations will have a negative impact on the building. In other words, the building will not withstand the test of time. Similarly, with strong system support the school counseling program may be "remodeled" (or revised) as needed to accommodate the changing needs of the school community without losing its basic integrity. Without strategic system support, the counseling program will not be strong enough or flexible enough to withstand the pressures of the environment. System support activities allow school counselors ways to sustain their programs as well as enlist support from others for the school counseling program.

After reading and discussing this chapter, you should be able to

- Explain the importance of research and evaluation in program maintenance.
- Design an activity to educate school and community members about comprehensive developmental school counseling.
- Design an activity to forge alliances with community businesses, industries, and social service agencies.
- Identify appropriate opportunities to participate in educational planning teams/committees.

ASSESSMENT AND PRIORITIZATION

The counselors decided to meet in grade-level teams (K–5, 6–8, and 9–12) to create a list of the work activities currently performed by counselors that might be classified as system support. Once their inventory is complete, they will rank each of the items in order of importance and congruence with the overall goals of the school counseling program. Then, they will discuss ways that the tasks might be accomplished more efficiently. The overall goal of this first phase of planning is to reduce the time each counselor spends in system support activities to no more than 10 percent of total time (4 hours/week) in elementary and middle schools and 15 percent (6 hours/week) in high schools.

The counselors review the system support categories identified by Gysbers and Henderson (2000), so that they may more accurately assess how what they are (and are not) currently doing fits with a well-recognized standard in the field.

1. Research and development activities include program evaluation, follow-up studies, and outcome studies associated with program interventions.
2. Professional development activities involve assessing the skills and competencies one needs to acquire or update to practice school counseling effectively.
3. Staff and community public relations involves communicating with others about the goals, activities, and outcomes of the school counseling program.
4. Committee and advisory boards refers to the counselor's involvement in school and community planning and development activities to benefit students and their families.
5. Community outreach activities are those by which counselors establish and maintain relationships with agencies and employers that offer opportunities and services for students and families.
6. Program management activities are those tasks that support the planning, implementation, and evaluation of the school counseling program.

7. Fair-share responsibilities refer to the contributions school counselors make, along with other professional staff, to ensure that the school runs smoothly and that the students are safe.

Planning Inventory of System Support Tasks by Grade Level

Elementary	Middle	High
New student registration	Preregistration advisement	Preregistration advisement
Test coordination	Test coordination	Schedule adjustments
Student assistance	Test interpretation (teachers/parents)	Graduation credit checks
Team coordinator	Student assistance	Reference letters
Student referrals	Team coordinator	Test coordination
Member grade-level team	Student referrals	Test interpretation (teachers/parents)
Special testing	Member grade-level team	Student assistance
Disciplinary hearings	Schedule parent/teacher conferences	Team coordinator
Gifted education	Disciplinary hearings	Student referrals
Oversee student records	Vocational education	Member grade-level team
After-school tutoring	Progress reports	Liaison with outside agencies
Coordinator guidance program	Record keeping	Guidance clerk
Management	Attendance follow-ups	Supervision
• Assessing needs	Liaison with outside agencies	Advanced placement/joint enrollment
• Planning	Guidance clerk	Business-industry-education committee
• Scheduling	Supervision guidance program	Progress reports
• Evaluating	Management	Record keeping
	• Assessing needs	Disciplinary hearings
	• Planning	Vocational education guidance
	• Scheduling	Program management
	• Evaluating	• Assessing needs
		• Planning
		• Scheduling
		• Evaluating

In small groups, discuss these tasks and group them into the categories identified by Gysbers and Henderson. Which categories seem to be overloaded and which seem to be underdeveloped? How might some of the tasks in the overloaded categories be accomplished through differential staffing or assignment to other professionals, paraprofessionals, or volunteers? What activities would you add at each of the grade levels? Remember, the activities retained by the counselors should account for approximately 10 to 15 percent of their time and be of the highest priority.

SETTING GOALS

Their experiences planning other components of school counseling programs lead the counselors into beginning with outcome statements. They want to know what their expectations are so they can plan more carefully. Therefore, the counselors decided to set goals, by grade level, in each of the seven categories associated with this program element. After they refined their definitions of the different areas, the entire counseling staff established and approved the following goals.

Research and Development

The counselors determined that this area includes the collection and analysis of data that could provide information for program and school decisions. They would accomplish this by working on the following goals.

Goal 1: Counselors at each grade level will design an instrument to evaluate the four program elements: guidance curriculum, individual planning, responsive services, and system support (see Figure 9.1 for an example).

Goal 2.a: Counselors will complete an evaluation of the program annually by using a random sample of parents, teachers, and students who respond to a comprehensive program evaluation instrument. The high school counselors will also survey graduates and school dropouts.

Goal 2.b: The program will be evaluated annually by all of the counselors and principals. Program components with less than a satisfactory rating by 75 percent or more of the respondents will be revised. Focus groups will be conducted to help the counselors and their advisory committees identify potential ways of revising and of improving.

Goal 3: Comprehensive needs assessments will be conducted every 3 years to survey all parents, students, teachers, and administrators regarding program priorities. Annual needs assessments will be conducted with students and teachers to identify program priorities for small-group counseling interventions. Activities in each program area selected as important by fewer than 50 percent of the respondents will be reviewed for relevance and revised accordingly. Activities identified by 75 percent or more of the respondents as important will be implemented or continued (see Figure 9.1).

Goal 4: Each counselor will participate annually in a formal evaluation based on the performance appraisal instrument designed for school counselors by the state department of education. Areas designated as less than satisfactory will serve as the basis for counselor developed professional improvement plans to increase knowledge, skill, and or competence in the designated area(s) (see Table 9.1 for an example).

FIGURE 9.1 Delivery of School Counseling Program Evaluation

School Counselor Competencies	Met	Unmet	Performance Indicator
Provides a comprehensive guidance curriculum			
• Orients constituents to program and curriculum			
• Provides large- and small-group activities fostering personal/social development			
• Provides large- and small-group activities enhancing career development			
• Provides large- and small-group activities to develop educational plan that supports career choices			
• Collaborates with teachers to deliver curriculum			
• Provides information to teachers, parents, students, and others			
Conducts individual planning			
• Helps students assess skills, abilities, interests, and achievements			
• Provides activities to enhance student awareness of educational opportunities			
• Advises students and parents in self-appraisal, educational and career planning, and acquisition of labor market information			
• Assists students in making transitions			
• Assists students with course selections and class placement			
• Helps students find resources and support services needed in new educational, community, and employment settings			
Provides responsive services			
• Orients constituents to school counseling program and services			
• Consults with students, parents, teachers, and other educators to identify strategies to help students			
• Conducts personal counseling on a small-group or individual basis			
• Provides crisis counseling and support to students and families facing emergency situations			
• Assists with school crisis management planning and activities			
• Serves as a resource to professional staff and parents/guardians in areas of intervention and provision of activities for the development of students			
• Refers students and families to appropriate community agencies when assistance is needed			
• Serves as a resource to professional staff, parents/guardians, and others in areas of assessment and analysis of standardized test data			

FIGURE 9.1 *continued*

School Counselor Competencies	Met	Unmet	Performance Indicator
• Trains teachers to administer tests and interpret test data when appropriate			
• Assists teachers and administrators in communicating and interpreting assessment and test results to parents and others			
Develops system support			
• Establishes appropriate goals and objectives for program			
• Plans for delivery of program			
• Selects resources for program implementation			
• Orients constituents to the program			
• Consults regularly with teachers, administrators, and other staff to provide information and support			
• Serves on committees and advisory boards that support other programs in the school and community to gain support for the school counseling program			
• Visits businesses, industries, and community agencies to become knowledgeable of opportunities and resources available			
• Manages resources effectively			
• Provides for maintenance of program			
• Evaluates program			
• Monitors program and activities			
• Conducts research useful to the guidance and counseling program			

Source: Adapted from Alabama State Department of Education (1996). *The revised comprehensive counseling and guidance model for Alabama's public schools.* Bulletin 1966, No. 27. Montgomery, AL: Author. Reprinted with permission.

Goal 5: Outcome measures to determine the extent to which intervention goals are met will be included in each program component and the associated counseling or guidance activities. For all goals not met by at least 75 percent of the students participating, the activities and strategies currently being used will be reviewed and revised.

Professional Development

The counselors defined professional development as their attendance and involvement in activities that increase their knowledge and skills. Their abilities to refine their practices because of their involvement would serve as evidence of their professional development.

Goal 1: All counselors will attend a minimum of one school counseling conference annually to address those individual professional development needs identified

TABLE 9.1 Counselor Evaluation Matrix

	Ineffective	Marginal	Skillful	Exemplary
Has Knowledge of the Content of Counseling and Instructional Program	Applies information contradictory to current knowledge in field	At times applies information that is not current	Keeps current in the field and in the school program and applies knowledge in counseling	Keeps current in the field, applies knowledge, and shares information with colleagues
	Misuses Counseling Program Handbook in providing counseling program	Does not use Counseling Program Handbook and guidelines in providing counseling program	Demonstrates a working knowledge of Counseling Program Handbook	Integrates principles in Counseling Program Handbook to help students realize the interrelationship of the curriculum
	Frequently presents inaccurate, inadequate information	Occasionally presents inaccurate information without considering multiple points of view	Presents accurate information recognizing multiple points of view	Presents accurate information recognizing multiple points of view and uses strategies and techniques that encourage students to consider the full range of academic and career possibilities
	Frequently misconstrues the relationship between concepts/strategies offered and the students' current knowledge	Misses opportunities to demonstrate the relationship between concepts offered and students' current knowledge	Highlights the relationship between concepts offered and students' current knowledge/needs	Interrelates counseling program and career planning concepts/strategies and involves students in discovering and exploring the relationships between goals and current knowledge/skills
Provides Appropriate Learning and Counseling Experiences	Inappropriately applies principles of learning to the counseling process	Inconsistently applies principles of learning to the counseling process	Applies appropriate principles of learning to support the educational, career, and personal development of students	Applies appropriate and varied principles of learning to support the educational, career, and personal development of all students, and uses a variety of principles of learning to enhance the level of students' involvement and interaction

TABLE 9.1   *continued*

	Ineffective	Marginal	Skillful	Exemplary
	Uses techniques and strategies that do not facilitate students' ability to meet the program objectives	Employs techniques and strategies that are inconsistent with program objectives	Uses a variety of techniques and strategies that encourage students to meet program objectives	Uses a variety of techniques and strategies to individualize instructions and maximize students' involvement and interaction in meeting program objectives
	Makes no attempt to accommodate for difference in learning styles and levels	Frequently misses opportunities to meet and accommodate differences in learning styles and levels	Accommodates differences in learning styles and levels	Accommodates differences in learning styles and levels and encourages students to develop their individual learning styles
	Selects objectives that are inappropriate for students' needs and abilities	Frequently selects objectives that do not recognize students' needs and abilities	Recognizes students' needs and abilities in selecting objectives at the appropriate level of maturity	Recognizes students' needs and abilities in selecting goals; encourages students to recognize and match objectives to the level of their maturity
Demonstrates Counseling and Guidance Skills	Does not implement individual and group counseling/guidance services	Does not consistently implement individual and group counseling services	Implements productive individual and group counseling services	Implements productive and creative counseling services for students with a variety of learning styles
	Does not establish and/or communicate consistent and fair expectations to students and/or parents	Does not routinely establish and/or communicate consistent and fair expectations to students and/or parents	Establishes and communicates fair and consistent expectations to students and parents	Encourages students' and parents' involvement in the development and communication of consistent and fair expectations
	Does not keep students on task during group guidance activities	Does not consistently keep students on task during group guidance activities	Keeps students on task during group guidance activities	Uses a variety of strategies that keep students on task by matching strategies to individual and group needs

TABLE 9.1 *continued*

	Ineffective	Marginal	Skillful	Exemplary
	Makes no attempt to provide for smooth flow of events in counseling sessions	Does not consistently provide for the smooth flow of events in counseling sessions	Provides for the smooth flow of events in counseling sessions	Seeks students' ideas on providing for smooth flow of events in counseling sessions
	Does not establish productive group and individual guidance routines	Does not consistently establish productive group and individual guidance routines	Establishes productive group and individual guidance routines	Encourages students' involvement in establishing productive group and individual routines in counseling
	Does not organize daily schedule to allow for adequate counseling services	Does not consistently organize daily schedule to allow for adequate direct counseling services	Organizes daily schedule to allow time for adequate direct counseling services	Organizes daily schedule to allow for maximum direct counseling services
Demonstrates Appropriate Planning	Frequently misuses and/or misinterprets individual and group data in prescribing strategies	Misses opportunities to prescribe appropriate strategies based on individual and group diagnostic data	Diagnoses individual and group needs and prescribes appropriate strategies to meet those needs	Diagnoses individual and group needs, prescribes appropriate strategies, and capitalizes on the strengths of individual students to implement varied goals
	Rarely establishes short-term and long-range goals	Inconsistently establishes short-term and long-range goals	Establishes short-term and long-range goals that take into account sequencing of instructional objectives and/or individual students' development	Encourages students' participation in establishing short-term and long-range goals that take into account sequencing of instructional objectives and/or individual students' development
	Rarely has material and/or records organized and available	Inconsistently has material and/or records organized and available	Maintains appropriate and accurate records and creates, selects, and adapts materials to accommodate students' differences	Maintains appropriate and accurate records; creates, selects, and adapts materials to accommodate students' differences; encourages students to organize their own materials

TABLE 9.1 *continued*

	Ineffective	Marginal	Skillful	Exemplary
Demonstrates Human Relations and Communication Skills	Rarely communicates or communicates inappropriately with students, parents, and school staff	Inconsistently communicates or communicates inappropriately with students, parents, and school staff	Maintains consistent and appropriate communication with students, parents, and school staff	Uses a variety of methods to communicate and interact with students, parents, and school staff
	Rarely or inconsistently provides for needs of diverse students	Frequently misses opportunities to provide for needs of diverse students	Provides for needs of diverse students	Provides for needs of diverse students and encourages understanding of diversity
	Takes little or no responsibility for the total school program or goals	Frequently misses opportunities to contribute to the total school program or goals	Shares responsibility for the total school program and goals by incorporating the school goals in the counseling program	Shares responsibility for the total school program and goals by incorporating the school goals in the counseling program and involves others in understanding and participating in achieving schoolwide goals
	Is disrespectful of and insensitive to the diversity among individuals	Is frequently disrespectful of and insensitive to the diversity among individuals	Demonstrates respect for and sensitivity to the diversity among individuals	Through modeling and counseling strategies, encourages respect for and sensitivity to the diversity among individuals; promotes schoolwide efforts to increase mutual respect for and sensitivity to diversity
	Rarely builds positive relationships with students, parents, and school staff	Misses opportunities to build positive relationships with students, parents, and school staff	Builds positive relationships with students, parents, and school staff	Builds positive relationships with students, parents, and school staff and promotes a positive atmosphere
	Rarely promotes team efforts among school staff, parents, and community agencies	Misses opportunities to promote team efforts among school staff, parents, and community agencies	Promotes team efforts among school staff, parents, and community agencies	Promotes and encourages colleagues to promote team efforts by being a resource to school staff, parents, and community agencies

TABLE 9.1 *continued*

	Ineffective	Marginal	Skillful	Exemplary
	Rarely provides information and orientation for students, parents, and school staff	Misses opportunities to provide information and orientation for students, parents, and school staff	Provides information and orientation for students, parents, and school staff	Provides information and orientation for students, parents, and school staff and develops programs for students, parents, and school staff
Monitors and Evaluates Student and Program Outcomes	Does not use a variety of information sources to monitor students' outcomes	Inconsistently uses a variety of information sources to monitor students' outcomes	Uses a variety of sources, such as student interviews, students' records, and parents' conferences, to monitor and evaluate students' outcomes	Uses a variety of information to monitor and evaluate students' outcomes; designs activities to meet students' needs
	Uses student evaluation procedures in violation of county public schools policy	Frequently does not follow appropriate student evaluation procedures	Selects and follows appropriate student evaluation procedures	Selects appropriate student evaluation procedures, assesses the information, and uses the information for planning
Uses Available Resources	Does not consult with teachers	Seldom consults with teachers	Regularly consults with teachers	Regularly consults with teachers and uses data to provide counseling services and involves students, parents, and teachers in implementing individualized activities for students
	Does not use or misuses the services of school-based and/or community resources	Seldom uses the services of school-based and/or community resources	Regularly uses the services of school-based and/or community resources	Uses the services of school-based and/or community resources and capitalizes on resources to increase learning and/or involvement in counseling services
	Does not provide a variety of counseling materials to students, teachers, and parents	Seldom provides a variety of counseling materials to students, teachers, and parents	Provides a variety of appropriate counseling materials to students, teachers, and parents	Researches new counseling materials, assesses materials for timeliness and appropriateness, and develops

TABLE 9.1 *continued*

	Ineffective	Marginal	Skillful	Exemplary
				innovative activities for students, teachers, and parents
	Does not take advantage of staff development opportunities	Seldom takes advantage of staff development opportunities	Uses available staff development opportunities	Capitalizes on staff development opportunities to provide more effective practices
Fulfills Professional Responsibilities	Does not demonstrate a professional attitude toward the accomplishment of building, area, and division level goals	Seldom demonstrates a professional attitude toward the accomplishment of building, area, and division level goals	Consistently demonstrates a professional attitude toward the accomplishment of building, area and division level goals	Participates actively in program development, changes, and implementation of building, area, and division level goals; serves as a role model for peers in promoting the accomplishment of these goals
	Does not work cooperatively with staff in the school program	Misses opportunities to work cooperatively with staff in the school program	Works cooperatively with staff in the school program	Works cooperatively with staff in the school program and shares expertise and ideas with colleagues
	Consistently demonstrates behaviors that show a lack of commitment to the educational profession	Frequently demonstrates behaviors that show a lack of commitment to the education profession	Participates in activities that demonstrate a commitment to the educational progression	Initiates activities that demonstrate a commitment to the educational profession; provides leadership in such activities
	Demonstrates behaviors that are detrimental to students and/or the school image	Does not serve as a role model for students	Serves as a role model for students	Serves as a role model; provides opportunities for students to act as role models for their peers
	Does not participate in self-assessment activities and/or does not use resources available for professional growth	Does not appropriately use staff development activities and/or other resources available for professional growth	Participates in self-assessment activities and uses resources available for professional growth	Participates in self-assessment activities, uses resources available for professional growth, and demonstrates leadership in staff development activities

Source: Fairfax County Public Schools (1992). *Counselor Evaluation Matrix.* Fairfax, VA: Author. Reprinted with permission.

in the annual performance appraisal. Satisfactory evaluation in the designated area at the time of the next annual review will be the criterion for determining success.

Goal 2: All school counselors will participate in systemwide professional development activities to meet common goals. For example, during the coming school year, all counselors will participate in four crisis response training sessions. Counselors will score 90 percent or higher on a posttest designed to assess their understanding of the content of the training sessions and will receive satisfactory ratings on the crisis management section of the responsive services program component annual evaluation.

Staff and Community Public Relations

The activities in this area relate to informing others about the school counseling program—what is done, how it is done, and by whom. These documents and presentations explain and illustrate the parameters of the school counseling program.

Goal 1: To orient interested stakeholders to the goals, activities, and outcomes of the school counseling program, school counselors will prepare a professional presentation appropriate for school and community groups and present to at least one group per grading period.

Goal 2: To inform interested stakeholders about the ongoing efforts of counselors and the benefits of the school counseling program, school counselors will publish two editions of a newsletter to be distributed to each household of a currently enrolled student; all teachers, administrators, and school board members; key community leaders; and associated agencies. Newsletters will be archived on the school counseling program home page of each school.

Goal 3: Counselors will develop a brochure. The design will include elements common across all school levels with sections to be standardized for elementary, middle, and high school programs. The brochures will be distributed during school orientation sessions.

Goal 4: On a rotation basis the school counselors will write a column to be submitted to the local newspaper and for the home page of each school. The column will include parenting tips, developmental milestones, and other information useful for parents.

Committee and Advisory Boards

Participation with others who work on children's concerns provides school counselors with opportunities to improve lives within and beyond the school setting.

Goal 1: Each school counseling program will hold at least one meeting each semester with the program's advisory board.

Goal 2: All school counselors will participate in grade-level planning teams for those students for whom they provide programs.

Goal 3: All school teams and committees that require school counselor participation will be identified, and one representative from the school's counseling staff will be recommended for membership.

Goal 4: All community teams and committees that require school counselor participation will be identified, and one representative from the system's school counseling staff will be recommended for membership.

Community Outreach

The counselors determine ways to establish more connections with community agencies and business.

Goal 1: Agencies that offer supportive services for students and families will be identified, and one counselor at each grade level will be designated to develop a list of contacts and procedures for referral for each.

Goal 2: Employers in the community will be identified, and one counselor at each grade level will be designated to develop a list of contacts at each to identify possible areas of collaboration to improve supportive services provided students and families.

Program Management

The complexities of operating a school counseling program require skills in organization and implementation. The counselors choose these goals for their focus.

Goal 1: Tasks that support the planning, implementation, and evaluation of the school counseling program will be identified and responsibility for each at elementary, middle, and high school will be assigned. Differential staffing will be used to decrease the amount of time any one counselor spends on the tasks.

Goal 2: Annual calendars will be developed to identify on a month-by-month basis the systemwide activities to be implemented as part of each of the four program elements at elementary, middle, and high school.

Fair-Share Responsibilities

Good citizenship within the school community includes participation in some activities that are not identified with school counseling. Counselors want to decrease the likelihood of those fair-share responsibilities interfering with their work with the school counseling program.

Goal: Each counselor, in collaboration with the principal of his or her school, will identify and participate in two nonguidance school assignments that contribute to the effective and efficient operation of the school.

IMPLEMENTATION

Before full implementation of the system support goals can occur, the counselors may need some additional knowledge or training. Mr. Terman suggests that they conduct an informal needs assessment to identify the counselors' specific questions or concerns. Some concerns may be addressed immediately through sharing information and resources, whereas others may require knowledge or skill development more appropriately acquired through more formal professional development opportunities. Through discussion, the counselors expressed the following concerns about their day-to-day functioning. Mamie Young has agreed to summarize their conversation. She has listed their concerns within the goal categories as one way of organizing the many issues they discussed and studied. She also includes information about the differences for the elementary, middle, and high school levels. Her notes will provide them with a record they can use as they begin the next school year.

RESEARCH AND DEVELOPMENT/STAFF AND COMMUNITY PUBLIC RELATIONS

Promoting the Program

The school counselors in Washington County know they have a unique role in the education of students and that their contributions are central to the academic mission of schools. They want to help everyone in the school community understand the importance of the school counseling program. They also want to determine what components of their program are working best. Accountability strategies will serve the multiple purposes of evaluating what works well and communicating the results of their evaluations to the interested public. The presentation of the material they gather and disseminate may vary by school level, but the substance will be consistent across levels.

Johnson (2000) suggests a contemporary schematic for a strategic, three-phase initiative designed to use enhanced accountability practices to promote the professional identity of the school counseling program. Those phases move from agreeing about program goals and priorities, to evaluating their program, and finally to promoting the program. The counselors will use this framework as their guide.

AGREEING

The counselors have begun to accomplish the first step by affirming their commitment to the mission of the school counseling program. They have defined the mission through well-articulated goals and objectives. Additionally, they have identified through what program elements the goals may be addressed and have allocated time and resources needed to implement the program.

They also have a procedure and schedule for conducting needs assessments. The information they gather from students, parents, and teachers will be used to determine annual priorities. They decide some modifications may enhance the helpfulness of the survey they currently use. First they want to revise the instrument to allow the participants to respond both to how important they consider the service and how well the service was provided. Lusky and Hayes (2001) provide a useful sample of such a survey that includes the counseling program's services of providing information, individual planning, counseling interventions, and consultation. The counselors will modify the language and length of the survey for the elementary and middle school levels but will focus on the same areas K–12 for consistency. The counselors may now use their revised survey as a needs assessment and as an evaluation instrument. Second, they want to expand the groups that are completing the survey and will include some of their business partners and some of the agency personnel with whom they will be working more closely.

Finally, the counselors want to understand the perceptions held by others of the school counseling program. Specifically, they wish to gauge the extent to which the students, parents, teachers, and others' perceptions agree with the articulated program. For this more open-ended process they are going to contact a professor at a local university and ask if some counselors-in-training would conduct focus groups and interviews with constituent groups to compile a summary description. Where the descriptions differ from the stated program, efforts will be made to understand the reasons and to formulate a response to them.

EVALUATING

Systematic evaluations provide evidence of the work and outcomes of the school counseling program (Gysbers & Henderson, 2000). Information about what the program does to aid student success as well as how students have benefited from the activities is crucial. The counselors maintain daily time and task analysis logs so that they may regularly check to be sure that they are implementing all phases of the program and in the agreed upon balance of program elements. These daily logs are summarized weekly and monthly. Based on the monthly summaries, counselors identify program elements in which they may be over- or undercommitted and make adjustments as necessary. An additional benefit of the daily time and task analysis logs is that counselors can easily see (and share) the numbers of students they have seen individually, in small groups, and through classroom guidance. They can also keep track of those who have been assisted indirectly through teacher, parent, and administrator consultations and by referral to other resources in the school or community. And they are able to identify whether their interventions were aimed toward academic, career, or personal/social development. Therefore, these data help the counselors determine and describe what they are doing and if they are delivering the program they planned and articulated.

In a small working group, develop a one-page time and task analysis log that would enable counselors to keep track of their daily activities and the time spend in each, categorized by program element and developmental concern.

A second purpose of evaluation is to determine the extent to which goals are met. The counselors have identified specific competencies for students in grades K–12 in the three domains on which the program is based: academic, career, and personal/social development. Further, the counselors have identified through which program element—guidance curriculum, individual planning, responsive services, or system support—each competency is to be addressed (VanZandt & Hayslip, 2001). Results-oriented evaluation will determine whether students who participate in the program demonstrate these competencies (e.g., goals, outcomes) at a predetermined criterion level. Or stated another way, evaluation tells us how many students (criterion level) will be able to demonstrate a specific ability (competency, outcome, or goal) at either the conclusion of an intervention or some other specified time. To evaluate outcomes, one devises a method (or methods) for checking students' performance to determine if the specified number of students has achieved the desired outcome or demonstrated the specified competency. Outcome measures help counselors determine the impact of their program. Parents will be interested in information related to student assistance. Administrators will want to have comparative measures for across-the-school impact, and the school board members will be concerned with the cost effectiveness of the program. Three outcome measures that are meaningful and understandable to anyone are student grades, student attendance, and discipline referrals. Counselors can monitor these three areas for the students with whom they work for outcome results.

Ms. Pickens states, "I understand the importance of evaluation and that guidance for the evaluation is found in the stated objective. However, I am still uncertain about how to analyze the data for evidence of meaningful change once it has been collected."

Some examples of accountability measures and their connection to impact that have been provided by Johnson (2000) may help Ms. Pickens answer her concerns.

- A pre/post assessment of the effects on students' study skills habits as they participate in a classroom guidance unit on that topic.
- Evaluative feedback from parents collected from a questionnaire regarding their child's explanation and use of the study skills learned.
- Tabulation of the number of at-risk students persisting in K–12 school and beyond.
- A pre/post assessment of the effects of participating in the peer mediation program.
- Case study documentation of "multiple failure" students who have reversed that trend in academic performance after collaborative interdisciplinary team efforts initiated by school counselors.
- An experimental group design (treatment group vs. no-treatment group) on the effects of small-group counseling of children who are experiencing divorce.
- Feedback from classroom teachers about the change in behaviors of children who receive individual and/or small-group counseling.

Select one intervention typically used to deliver the school counseling curriculum. Identify two ways to evaluate whether the intervention you selected has been successful. How would the evidence you need to convince parents, teachers, principals, students, and school board members be different?

The data from these measures are generally analyzed to produce descriptions. Descriptive statistics are simple and straightforward and yield useful information such as means or averages, percentages, most frequent responses, range of scores for each response, and so forth. Other tests such as t-tests are used to compare differences between pre- and postintervention scores. The counselors agree that their master's level research course prepared them to conduct these types of data analysis. They will consult with others, such as counselor educators at the local university, if they wish to perform analyses for which they are unprepared.

PROMOTING

The counselors realize that they will be able to gradually incorporate this accountability system into their daily work. They will build a realistic time line as they expand the data they gather, interpret, and use. They do not want to delay all their strategies to build awareness of their program, however. They are studying the suggestions offered by Johnson (2000) to create a plan of action to be implemented this year. She provides samples of strategies that can be used to inform different constituent groups (students, parents, teachers, administrators, community) about the role and utility of the counseling program as it relates to student success. She offers the following suggestions for school counselors to consider as they advocate for their programs:

- Conduct presentations that outline the role, services, and outcomes of the program as they relate to the school mission.
- Develop a booklet that highlights the best practices of the school counseling program.
- Develop a brochure and/or flyer that promotes the program.
- Introduce the program and services in all grade classrooms.
- Hold "accountability conferences" with the principal to discuss the program and to provide data that documents user statistics, comparative measures of success and deficiency, needs assessments, and recommendations.

- Write a "Dear Counselor" column for the school newsletter to respond to student academic concerns.
- Sponsor informational workshops for parents on topics such as learning styles and developmental milestones.
- Offer in-service workshops to teachers in areas such as motivation and test anxiety.
- Develop a professional portfolio for school counselors.
- Create a department Web site with informational links for students and community.
- Develop and distribute a quarterly calendar of services and functions.

These strategies help people understand a school counseling program and the effects that effort has on student success. School counselors who identify the program goals and determine if and how well those goals are being met will have convincing evidence to support and sustain a school counseling program. Mr. Terman's team acknowledges that any of these strategies can be used across any school level with slight modifications in language.

> Using the suggestions above and others your group creates, develop a 5-year time line of program advocacy activities aimed toward at least four different audiences (students, parents, teachers, administrators, school board, community). Identify modifications that would be needed for elementary, middle, and high school levels.

PROFESSIONAL DEVELOPMENT

School-Based Teams

Mr. McDougal moves the group to a discussion of management of the internal referral process. Students who experience academic or behavioral difficulties and who are not in special education classes may be referred to the building-based student advisory team (also known as student assistance team, student support team, child study team, intervention assistance program, multidisciplinary teams) to examine reasons the student is not succeeding in school (Blum, 1998) and to recommend interventions that may be implemented by the regular education teachers (Rathvon, 1999). Generally, membership includes a counselor, school psychologist, special education teacher, teachers from each grade level or subject area, and an administrator. Depending on the referral, outside agency representatives may also be asked to attend. Additionally, parents of referred students are invited to attend, as well as the referring teacher if he or she is not a permanent member of the team. When appropriate, the student being referred is also invited to participate.

Rathvon (1999) identifies four stages of the student assistance team process: problem definition, problem analysis, plan implementation, and plan evaluation. In stage one, the teacher's request for assistance is reviewed to ensure that all pertinent information is provided, student and parents are consulted, the problem is clarified, and baseline data is obtained. In stage two, factors contributing to the maintenance of the problem are identified, intervention strategies are evaluated and selected, and implementation procedures are planned. The intervention is implemented and progress monitored during the third stage. Finally, the effectiveness of the intervention is reviewed by comparing postintervention data with the baseline data. If the intervention is not successful, further intervention is planned and implemented. If committee members agree that efforts have been exhausted and change is unlikely, a request may be made to assess the student's eligibility for special education services. The information gathered by the team is included in the special education referral. Permission from parents is necessary to proceed with such a referral.

Two of the more positive outcomes associated with school-based teams are decreased number of referrals to special education and improved teacher attitudes toward diverse learners (Rathvon, 1999). However, Mr. McDougal states, "Many teachers are frustrated by the lack of innovative intervention strategies suggested by the team." This is consistent with research reported by Rathvon (1999) that teachers perceive the interventions offered them by teams as low in quality and lacking in variety. One reason for this is that many educators do not receive training in prereferral intervention strategies as part of their education, nor do team members typically receive training in effective school interventions. The counselors agree that there is a need for professional development focused on training team members to select interventions that teachers can use in the regular education classroom with difficult-to-teach students. The training will focus on identifying interventions that are proactive, can be used with an entire class to enhance the learning of all students as well as the targeted child, are easily taught, can be implemented with regular classroom resources, and can be easily evaluated (Rathvon, 1999). Mr. McDougal will identify an outside consultant with experience in intervention selection and skills in consultation and collaboration as assistance delivery methods.

Shepard-Tew and Creamer (1998) describe a case management process for the school-based, multidisciplinary team to follow. A referral is received and before a problem has been identified, a team member is randomly assigned as the case manager. A variety of forms are used to record any assessment, interventions, progress, and termination or referral status. The forms are designed to provide quick and accurate recording methods for accountability. The case manager begins an assessment by gathering information that may include discussions with teachers, parents, and significant others; a review of the school records and disciplinary records; an interview with the child; and formal testing. The case manager organizes the collected data using the prepared forms and then presents the case to the team. The team collaboratively develops an intervention plan for the child with the goal of diminishing the behaviors that were causing academic failure. The team works with home and school by initiating a plan for change in the behavior in both settings. The case manager coordinates and refers appropriate interventions to each team member for implementation. Each time the case is reviewed, a termination/referral summary form documents the interventions completed, the student's progress, and the recommendations for follow-up. The authors documented their successes in implementing this approach to integrated services to students by reporting that more than 70 percent of the parents, teachers, and children involved saw some improvement in behavior and academic success. The procedures are appropriate for all grade levels.

Mr. McDougal and the counselors agree that the format described by Shepard-Tew and Creamer (1998) would provide more structured and perhaps more productive meetings than they have led in the past. Additionally, assigning a manager from the team membership on a rotating base for each student case results in greater shar-

Develop a list of the three or four problems for which you believe students will be referred to school-based student assistance teams. As a class, reach consensus on the top three. Divide into three teams and provide training for each other in intervention strategies that have empirical support for each of the three problems identified. Be sure that your interventions meet these criteria: are proactive, can be used with an entire class to enhance the learning of all students as well as the targeted child, are easily taught, can be implemented with regular classroom resources, and can be easily evaluated.

ing of responsibility for the administrative tasks of the committee or team. Mr. McDougal agrees to present their ideas to the system-level student assistance teams coordinator. If she agrees, the counselors in each school will describe the approach during the first team meeting of the year for consideration by the other team members. Included in the proposed change will be a systematic method of collecting follow-up information about the students served by these teams, including those who are referred to outside agencies.

COMMITTEE AND ADVISORY BOARDS/ COMMUNITY OUTREACH

Student Referrals

Mr. Garrett McDougal, an elementary school counselor, will be responsible for coordinating student referrals and conducting follow-up activities for students who experience some circumstance that impedes academic progress but cannot be addressed by the school alone (Schmidt, 1999). He will collect the initial paperwork for referrals to programs in the school, and he will also make contact with outside agencies when an external referral is warranted.

Mr. McDougal and some of his colleagues are in the process of identifying key people at each outside agency with which they have routine contact regarding services for school-aged youth: law enforcement officials, juvenile and family courts, child protective services, mental health services, hospice, physicians, hospitals, health department, and in-patient psychiatric and drug and alcohol rehabilitation facilities for children and adolescents. Another group of counselors is compiling a list of organizations that do not provide counseling services but do offer resources and support to families such as local churches, food and clothing banks, recreational programs, and civic organizations. Additionally, community sources that provide academic support for students (e.g., volunteer tutors, learning centers, programs available through local colleges and universities) and those that provide challenging programs for advanced students are being identified. A Community Resource Directory with the contact information and the services and resources provided by each outside agency, as well as a description of their procedures and requirements for referrals, will be disseminated to all of the school counselors in the system prior to the beginning of the school year. The resource directory will be updated in May of each year by mailing each directory entry a copy of their current information and requesting that corrections be made and returned no later than June 15 of each year.

> In a small group, identify the sources you might use to identify the resources available in your community. What types of resources might be needed for elementary, middle, and high school levels? Develop a "script" that could be used for an initial contact with each individual or agency to introduce yourself, explain the reason for your call, and elicit the information you need to complete your resource directory.

Multiple Services

Ho (2001) reports that federal agencies that document existing services to children tend to segment children and families into rigid categories, are crisis oriented, are unable to develop comprehensive solutions, focus on weaknesses and problems, and lack systems for functional communication among agencies. She suggests that many professionals in the education, health, mental health, and social services fields recognize that current social problems need to be addressed with an integration of services that connect the school, family, and community. Therefore, the counselors in the Washington County system wish to increase their contact with the persons in associated agencies beyond the development of a comprehensive referral resource directory. They believe that students are best served if the various entities involved in promoting the development of youth collaborate, share information, and develop an intervention plan that is comprehensive but does not include overlapping or redundant services. They will begin by honing their collaboration skills.

Collaboration

Collaboration provides a way that the school counselors and others in the community can fully access the resources of schools, communities, and homes. Taylor and Adelman (2000) explain that a group designed to link school, the families of its students, and other entities of the community may be called a collaborative. Collaboratives may include representatives from the agencies included in the resource directory. Members may share facilities such as schools, parks, and libraries. One example of such valuable partnerships teams child welfare services, juvenile justice systems, and behavioral health care with schools (see also Bemak, 2000). Luongo (2000) explains how such a partnership adds value to the educational enterprise. He notes that achieving the integration requires reorienting policy, practice, and activities to outcomes and explains evidence such as the following to indicate the reorientation:

- Shared decision making
- Budgeting and priority setting that acknowledges the shared responsibilities
- Transdisciplinary teams composed of members from all institutions
- Focus on the child and family
- Mechanisms for cross-training
- Shared goals

School counselors begin by becoming familiar with the ways these institutions work and by helping the personnel in those agencies learn about schools. Visits to the sites and participation in combined professional development provide other methods for school counselors to advance these collaborative efforts. Additionally, the counselors wish to pursue staff development training in electronic collaboration methods, such as synchronous voice conferencing. Using this medium, persons would be able to meet from a location of their choosing, in real time, share documents and ideas, and move forward with plans when face-to-face meetings are not possible (Sabella, 2000).

To become more adept at building and maintaining these integrated services as a part of their system support component, the counselors review three sets of integrative-services training competencies identified by Ho (2001). The training areas are integrated infrastructures, interprofessional team building, and family-centered approaches. Ms. Nu has volunteered to gather more information about this training and to identify potential partners to build these integrated services teams. She and the other counselors believe the effort they expend on this initiative will multiply student successes, their ultimate goal.

PROGRAM MANAGEMENT

Student Records

Ms. Nu, a middle school counselor, states that her principal wants her to coordinate activities related to the maintenance of student records as part of her fair-share responsibilities. She has copies of the systemwide policy stating that the semester grades, standardized test scores, and attendance for all students will be printed on labels that records clerks will affix to the students' cumulative folders. Blum (1998) points out that such policies should also provide guidance regarding the procedures for amending or correcting a record, the content of the records, proper guidelines for maintenance and storage of records, procedures for reviewing records, and the identification of persons who have the right to access and review student records.

Aspects of records management about which Ms. Nu is unclear include who can actually handle and work with records containing confidential student information and under what circumstances records can be reviewed by or released to others. Generally, clerical personnel who work with counselors may have access to records as needed to accomplish the requirements of their employment (Remley & Herlihy, 2001). In fact, Schmidt (1999) points out that it is imperative to have clerical staff assigned tasks associated with records maintenance and management, with the school counselor making certain that the local, state, and national regulations are followed. If counselors are responsible for supervising these employees, they have a responsibility to make them aware of the importance of maintaining confidentiality of records. Ms. Lerner offers clarification on another issue related to viewing student records. Any parent, custodial or noncustodial, has the right to inspect the records of his or her child unless there is a court order to the contrary (Schmidt, 1999).

Additionally, the Family Educational Rights and Privacy Act (FERPA), or the Buckley Amendment, provides that the parents of minor children have the right to inspect students' records and that their written authorization is required before the records can be transferred to a third party (Remley & Herlihy, 2001). Some notable exceptions are the exclusion of the written authorization from parents to release records to another school in which the student is enrolling, to a court that issues a valid subpoena for records, and to other agencies such as medical or law enforcement personnel in an emergency situation that requires the release of information to ensure the safety of the student or others.

The counselors also keep personal records of their counseling sessions. They may keep administrative records that enumerate appointments and services received. Other types of administrative records include copies of correspondence, intake forms, or other routine papers. Counselors use case notes to help them remember particulars about the students and the content of their sessions. Remley and Herlihy (2001) recommend that counselors assume the notes they take will be read. The assumption that the notes will become public will help counselors be cautious about deciding what should be included. They advise keeping the purposes of providing quality services and of documenting decisions and actions that have been made. Counselors can use the acronym SOAP to guide them in what to include in case notes (Baird, 2002):

- Subjective information is what the client reports.

- Objective data refers to the results of any assessments that have been given.
- Assessment includes the counselor's perceptions.
- Plans are the identification of the problem and intervention plan.

These personal notes are kept in a secure place and should not be left unattended unless locked in a drawer or cabinet. The notes should be destroyed after an agreed-upon amount of time. The notes are not included in school records. The counselors decide that they want to begin writing a procedures manual for the counseling office and will include these guidelines for case notes and for student records in that manual. A subcommittee chaired by Ms. Lerner will provide leadership to this effort.

Program Coordination

ASCA (2000) defines coordination as a leadership process for organizing, managing, and evaluating the school counseling program. There are many other areas for which counselors may be asked to serve as coordinators. Counselors are logical persons in the school to identify for these tasks because they have a comprehensive overview of the school program. Additionally, they have specialized training in facilitating group development, typically are well organized, and possess leadership skills that lead to success in their coordination efforts. All the responsibilities associated with coordination are one part of the system support program element. Therefore, counselors must be selective about the number of programs other than school counseling for which they take responsibility. Borders and Drury (1992) suggest that the coordination activities of school counselors be limited to those specific to planning, implementing, and evaluating the school counseling program. In many systems, school counselors will be asked to take on other tasks as their "fair share" of tasks involved in smooth, efficient running of the school (Gysbers & Henderson, 2000).

The school counselors realize the importance of balancing their responsibilities. They recognize that their coordination skills are crucial in the system support component of their school counseling program. They must plan well in order to have time to perform the activities to sustain the counseling program as well as their functions in enlisting and assisting others in the educational enterprise. Consequently, they have decided to generate a 5-year plan that focuses on some interwoven aspects of system support. First they want to generate a description of the counseling program that incorporates needs assessments, program implementation, and outcome data. They will use that information to prepare a public awareness strategy to help others better understand the scope and effects of their program. Next, they will institute a process for building integrated service teams to overcome the fragmentation that occurs when students are receiving, or need to receive, services from multiple sources. The counselors know that concentrating on these efforts will consume most of the time they have allocated to system support and hope that this focus will streamline some other responsibilities they have. To work more efficiently, they request some training sessions from the instructional resource personnel in their system in the use of electronic databases and spreadsheets, coordinated scheduling software, and some word-processing applications such as merge files and mail merge functions.

Assume that you have agreed to coordinate one major committee such as the student assistance team or testing program at your school, and your principal has just asked you to coordinate the special education referral process. With another member of your class, describe how you might decline this request in an assertive and professional manner. Now in groups of three, role-play your response and provide feedback to each other on the effectiveness of your response. Role-play a second time incorporating the feedback from your peers. What types of activities or interventions might you incorporate into your program to prevent being asked to exceed the 10 to 15 percent of allotted time to this program element?

FAIR-SHARE RESPONSIBILITIES

Student Testing

Mr. Terman asks whether counselors are overwhelmed with responsibilities associated with the schoolwide testing program. Ms. Lerner responds "I am the coordinator at my school as my fair-share role. In that capacity, I assist with maintaining security of the tests while they are in my building, and I communicate with the system test coordinator to identify the numbers of tests we need in each grade. I schedule the classroom guidance lessons associated with test-taking strategies for the 9-week grading period preceding the spring administration of our standardized achievement tests. Additionally, when test results are returned, I conduct a session for teachers on interpreting and using test results to help plan instruction. I also offer group interpretation sessions for parents at various times of the day and evening over a 2-week period. I enjoy the opportunities to work with the parents, teachers, and students and remember to begin with thinking about the counseling program student competencies as I plan for those sessions. Often I can create lessons with objectives aimed at two or more of those outcomes."

Another counselor commented that she too had student testing as her fair-share role and that she was overwhelmed with the duties. Her school did not have a coordinator so she was responsible for the entire testing process. She also regretted that what often failed to happen were interpretive sessions. After the counselors discussed her frustration, she decided to keep careful logs of the amount of time she was spending with the testing process and with that information, approach her principal for a more equitable distribution of the work.

> Teachers often feel a great deal of stress during the testing period because in the era of "high-stakes testing" they are held accountable for the scores of their students. What types of activities might you offer or coordinate that would help reduce teachers' stress levels?

SUMMARY

In this chapter, you have read about the activities common to the system support element of a comprehensive school counseling program. Sample goals for each activity have been presented. Some typical concerns of practicing school counselors have been presented and suggestions made for responding to the concerns. Procedures for designing a plan for promoting the school counseling program, evaluating the activities, and working within integrated teams to improve efficiency and effectiveness in service delivery to students and their families have been presented. Finally, you have been challenged to consider ways to fulfill the responsibilities of this program element within the recommended time allotment of 10 to 15 percent.

PORTFOLIO COMPONENTS

1. Build a master calendar for the school year identifying the responsibilities associated with coordinating the school counseling program to be completed each month.
2. Identify an area of professional competence in which you need more knowledge and skill. Develop a goal statement that includes exactly what you wish to

accomplish with regard to this area. Identify the steps you will take to meet your professional development goal. When you have completed the identified activities, write a reflection statement describing your progress toward the goal and how you feel about your accomplishment.

3. Outline a procedure for identifying community resources and possibilities for partnerships that would benefit students and their families.

Elementary School Counseling Program: Culmination of Intensive Planning

═══════════════ **CASE STUDY** ═══════════════

PUTTING IT ALL TOGETHER IN THE ELEMENTARY SCHOOL

The counselors at Northside Elementary School, Mr. Goldberg and Ms. Sara, are preparing a presentation and handout to describe the elementary school counseling program at their school. The presentation will be made during the first school board meeting of the academic year. The local cable television channel broadcasts school board meetings so, in addition to those officials and interested parents in attendance, many parents, students, and other community leaders will also view the presentation. In consultation with their leadership team, Mr. Goldberg and Ms. Sara have decided to describe the planning efforts undertaken by the team during the past 3 years to update and revise the program so that it more accurately meets existing standards and current student needs. As an organizational strategy, the counselors will describe the five-step plan used to revise the program: discussion, awareness, design, implementation, and evaluation.

The Northside leadership team views this invitation from the school board as an opportunity to further two of their program goals. First, they will inform school and community constituents of their role and that of the school counseling program in the total educational enterprise. Second, they will demonstrate the accountability strategies built into the program design. Their hope is that the school board will have a better understanding of their contributions to the academic success of students after viewing this presentation. Although elementary school counselors are mandated at the state level, no state funding is provided for schools to hire them. Consequently, each time financial resources are threatened in the system, reduction of the number of elementary school counselors on staff is considered as a budget reduction strategy. The Northside leadership team hopes that by demonstrating that they are a value-added resource, the school board will instead look at ways to keep them working in the system.

Elementary school counseling programs are integrally linked with the key developmental tasks of early and middle childhood. Specifically, children from 6 to 11 years old are learning the physical skills needed to play ordinary games; developing wholesome attitudes toward self and others; learning to get along with peers; learning social and gender roles; developing the skills needed to read, write, and calculate; developing concepts necessary for everyday living; developing an understanding of right and wrong; achieving independence; and developing attitudes toward social groups and institutions (Havighurst, 1953, cited in Muro & Kottman, 1995). A developmentally based elementary school counseling program helps students acquire the skills and attitudes that are necessary for success in school and in life.

Additionally, the need for early identification and intervention for at-risk youth has received considerable attention in the education literature. Researchers have identified specific behavioral, situational, and attitudinal precursors to such risk factors as substance abuse, school dropout, and aggressive and violent behavior toward self or others. These precursors are often manifested during the elementary years. For example, McWhirter and colleagues, (1998) state that students who fail to complete high school express a dislike for school and the perception that school is irrelevant to their needs; exhibit poor grades and low academic achievement; live in poverty; and feel that they do not belong in school, that is, that no one cares about them. All four of these factors are linked to self-esteem and self-concept, a major focus of elementary school counseling programs. Successfully implemented elementary school counseling programs will both facilitate optimal development for students and result in the identification of those students who experience barriers to their normal, healthy development.

After reading and discussing this chapter, you should be able to

- Identify a list of key members for an elementary school counseling leadership team.
- List the sources of information necessary for creating an awareness of the needs of elementary school students in a particular school district.
- Select and prioritize student competencies to be accomplished as a result of participating in the elementary school counseling program.
- Identify at least two interventions appropriate for elementary school aged youth to facilitate mastery of a specified student competency.
- Identify who in the school will be responsible for each of the competencies identified and how and when related activities will be implemented.
- Identify at least three methods used to determine whether program goals have been reached and student competencies have been mastered.

SCHOOL BOARD PRESENTATION: PUBLICITY AND ACCOUNTABILITY

Ms. Sara and Mr. Goldberg are introduced by the superintendent and describe their program using a Power Point slide presentation and an accompanying handout. They are well aware that they are fulfilling two of the program goals they established as part of their system support functions. One, they are informing their constituent groups about the goals, and methods used to achieve them, of the Northside Elementary counseling program. Two, by reporting program outcomes and providing accountability data, they are demonstrating the importance of the program relative to the school mission statement.

Slide 1

**Northside Elementary School
Counseling Program**

Ms. Sara & Mr. Goldberg,
Professional School Counselors

Ms. Sara: "I am Naomi Sara and this is my colleague Jason Goldberg. We have been working together at Northside for 3 years. We appreciate the opportunity to share with you the results of our 5-year school counseling program revision plan and the current status of our program. In the handout you have been provided, you will find copies of each of these slides and some additional supporting materials that we will refer to in this presentation. Should you have questions about any points please feel free to ask them. For the members of the home audience who are viewing this presentation on cable television, you may ask questions by contacting us at school via phone or email. We also have a Web page on which we describe our program, post our calendar of activities, answer frequently asked questions, and have links to e-mail addresses and homework hotlines, as well as online referral forms. At the end of each day, we respond to e-mail requests for information and referrals."

Assume that a member of the audience has asked why the decision was made to revise the program. Prepare a slide that provides the rationale for making the transition from a service-oriented to a program-oriented school counseling program. What three points are important to make to the audience?

Slide 2

Job Description

- The elementary school counselor provides a comprehensive counseling and guidance program for elementary school students; consults and collaborates with teachers, parents, and staff to enhance their effectiveness in helping students; and provides support to other elementary educational programs.

"We will start our presentation with a general job description for elementary school counselors. To facilitate our work in the elementary school, Mr. Goldberg and I are each assigned responsibility for exactly half the students at each grade level. Mr. Goldberg addresses the needs and responds to requests from or about students in the first half of the alphabet, and I respond to those in the other half. This organizational strategy was in place when we came to Northside, and we, with subsequent agreement from our planning team and school staff, determined that it was an efficient way to split the student assignments. Maintaining this aspect of the program was very helpful to us in making certain we continued to deliver comprehensive services in our school while undertaking the planning activities associated with program revision. There is a more complete job description in the handout that includes some of the key functions and tasks for which we are responsible" (see Figure 10.1).

Slide 3

Leadership Team
Community Members

- Phyllis O'Neill, Pediatrician
- Harriet Goldman, Social Worker
- Arthur Adams, Attorney
- Hailey Central, Marketing Vice-President
- Jason Frank, Parent
- Melanie Jones, Parent

"The first phase of planning—discussion—led us to constitute a leadership team intended to represent those persons in the school and community with whom school counselors work to meet the needs of Northside students. Representatives of the health, legal, and social work professions; the business community; parents; and teachers have met monthly for the past 3 years to engage in a five-phase planning process that has resulted in the program you are going to hear about tonight. The process we agreed to use for planning is presented in the American School Counselor Association publication, *Vision into Action: Implementing the National Standards for School Counseling Programs* (1998). This planning effort has been extensive and collaborative. We would like to take this opportunity to thank all on the team as well as those who have made other contributions."

Prepare a list of potential members of an elementary school leadership team. Who are the key providers of services to elementary school children and their families in your community? Who or what professional and community groups do you have represented on your list that are not found among the Northside members? Discuss your rationale for including these persons.

FIGURE 10.1   Sample Handout No. 1

Northside Elementary School Counselor Job Description

Primary Function

The elementary school counselor provides a comprehensive counseling and guidance program for elementary school students; consults and collaborates with teachers, parents, and staff to enhance their effectiveness in helping students; and provides support to other elementary school educational programs.

Major Job Responsibilities and Illustrative Key Duties:

1. *Implement the elementary school counseling and guidance program curriculum:* Conduct counseling and guidance learning activities in each teacher's classroom and/or systematically conduct counseling and guidance activities for each grade level during the year in collaboration with the teaching staff; consult with and be a resource to teachers. Take a leadership role in seeing the infusion of counseling and guidance content into the regular education curriculum.

2. *Guide and counsel groups and individual students through the development of personal, social, educational, and career plans:* Collaborate with middle school personnel to assist students in making a smooth transition from elementary school to middle school; provide orientation activities for incoming students and their parents; inform students and parents of test results and their implications for educational planning; provide resources and coordinate the implementation of personal, social, educational, and career learning activities; provide individual assistance to students regarding personal, social, educational, and career issues.

3. *Counsel small groups and individual students:* Conduct structured, goal-oriented counseling sessions to meet the identified needs of individuals and groups of students.

4. *Consult and collaborate with teachers, staff, and parents in understanding and meeting the needs of students:* Participate in staff and team meetings; plan and conduct staff development programs and activities; facilitate conferences with teachers and/or parents and/or students; plan and conduct parent education programs; assist families with school-related problems and issues; write articles for newsletters and other publications.

5. *Refer students with problems and their parents to appropriate specialists, special programs, or outside agencies:* Consult and collaborate with in-district specialists such as school psychologists, social workers, and nurses; consult with and refer to community-based resources including psychologists, psychiatrists, physicians, service agencies, and others.

6. *Participate in activities that contribute to the effective operation of the school:* Cooperate and collaborate with other professionals in enhancing the education of students; establish and maintain effective relationships with grade levels and administrators; cooperate with other school personnel in placing students with special needs in appropriate programs; interpret group test results to faculty and administration for use in enhancing instruction; communicate with administrators, teachers, staff, students, parents, and the community regarding the counseling and guidance program and its role in the educational program; participate in the implementation of the school system assessment program.

7. *Plan, evaluate, and revise the counseling and guidance program:* Review the counseling and guidance program annually with the counseling and guidance department staff and counseling and guidance program advisory committee; communicate regularly with other counseling and guidance staff to establish and maintain a sequential comprehensive counseling and guidance program; identify student needs periodically and use the results for program planning; establish a planning calendar for counseling and guidance program activities; evaluate the counseling and guidance program.

8. *Pursue professional growth:* Attend local, state, and national staff development programs; join professional counseling and guidance associations; attend local, state, and national workshops and conferences sponsored by professional organizations; read professional journals; complete postgraduate courses.

Source: Alabama State Department of Education. (1996). *The revised comprehensive counseling and guidance model for Alabama's public schools.* Bulletin 1966, No. 27. Montgomery, AL: Author. Reprinted with permission.

Slide 4

Leadership Team
School Members

- Darla Winningham, Kindergarten
- Marie Foster, Third Grade
- Harrison Hemphill, Fifth Grade
- Martavius Daniels, Special Education
- Ora Lindsay, Administration

"As you can see, we have representatives from across school programs on the leadership team. Putting the team together was critical to a successful planning outcome. We wanted to have a diverse group of members, representing as many points of view as possible. We would like to emphasize that while the educators on this list have been instrumental in the planning process, the school counseling program is a result of collaboration with the entire school community. At regular intervals, parents, teachers, and administrators were asked for information and direction with regard to program priorities."

Slide 5

Vision Statement

The Northside Elementary School counseling program will support the development of skills, attitudes, and knowledge needed to become effective learners, productive citizens, and respectful, responsible members of a diverse community.

Mr. Goldberg: "Our first task as a group was to develop a vision statement that clearly stated what we wanted to happen for students as a result of participating in the school counseling program at Northside. Our statement is a reflection of the value our school places on learning, preparing for future careers, and getting along with others in a multicultural world. The vision statement was posted in our conference meeting room, and we returned to it frequently as we moved through subsequent planning phases. The statement is consistent with the mission of Northside Elementary School."

Slide 6

Increasing Awareness of Needs

- Review National Standards for School Counseling Programs (ASCA Standards)
- Review current school counseling program competencies (district and state)
- Review key data from school and community resources

"To find out what challenges exist that prevent all students from achieving the goals inherent in our vision statement, we went to multiple sources to gather as much information and data as we could. This stage took several months as we needed to access, compile, and analyze the information we believed would be helpful."

Slide 7

Results

- The ASCA standards included all of our previously articulated student competencies and added competencies we believed would help us achieve our vision.

- The data from our school and community helped us identify some particular groups of students who might need special assistance to meet these competencies.

Ms. Sara: "The ASCA national standards for school counseling programs address each of the following areas of student development: academic, career, and personal/social. School counselors have long emphasized these areas or domains of development as integral to students' school success. The national standards-based approach to school counseling has been embraced by counselors across the nation and endorsed by nearly all professional groups concerned with student achievement (e.g., the National PTA and the National Associations for both Secondary and Elementary School Principals) (Campbell & Dahir, 1997). The standards-based approach for school counseling programs mirrors the approach for other curricular areas. These standards served as the organizing tool for developing/revising our program.

"There are nine standards in all, three in each developmental area. You see here those related to academic development. For each of the nine standards, ASCA has identified a number of student competencies or outcomes. For example, one of the outcomes for all students listed in the Career Development Standard A is that students will develop career awareness. There are also specific performance indicators, skills or behaviors students will be able to demonstrate, for each competency that will help us evaluate whether our program has been successful. For example, a student outcome for the competency we just mentioned might be that 90 percent of students in second grade will be able to name at least five careers and describe them in general terms. The counselors and second-grade teachers teach students about careers in classroom guidance units. These units are delivered to second graders during September of each academic year, immediately following Labor Day, a federal holiday intended to honor the contributions of those who participate in the U.S. workforce."

Slide 8

ASCA National Standards: Academic Development

- *Standard A:* Students will acquire the attitudes, knowledge, and skills that contribute to effective learning in school and across the life span.

- *Standard B:* Students will complete school with the academic preparation essential to choose from a wide range of substantial postsecondary options, including college.

Mr. Goldberg: "Under academic Standard A, the first competency is that students will improve academic self-concept. To determine whether students' academic self-concept has improved, we look to the expected outcomes of having developed a positive academic self-concept. For example, 90 percent of students will identify at least five attitudes and behaviors they exhibit that lead to successful learning (Dahir, et al, 1998).

"Standard B competencies include students demonstrating the ability to plan to achieve goals. One performance indicator is that 90 percent of students will establish at least three academic goals annually and develop a realistic plan to achieve those goals."

Slide 9

Academic Development
(continued)

- *Standard C:* Students will understand the relationship of academics to the world of work and to life at home and in the community

"Standard C, students will relate school to life experiences, will be judged met if 90 percent of the students who participate in a designated guidance unit develop an essay describing how current academic success related to future career and vocational opportunities."

Slide 10

Student Characteristics
(N = 754)

- 50% white; 50% students of color (35% African American; 15% Latino)
- 65% female; 35% male
- 2 languages spoken
- Latino population transient
- 45% of students receiving free or reduced lunch

Ms. Sara: "We reviewed local and school data to try to increase our understanding of student needs based on the characteristics of our students, our school, and our staff. We found these characteristics about our student population. We are particularly concerned about our Latino children, because we know that they are at higher risk for dropping out of school than either the white or African American students. We believe that risk might be compounded among our students, because they typically change schools at least two times during the academic year and exhibit a high rate of absenteeism. Therefore, we put these children on our list of those who may not meet some of the specified competencies without special intervention."

Ms. Sara recognized a member of the audience who posed a question, "I have three grandchildren who move with their parents who are migrant farm workers. I am worried about their education and their future. What can you do to help them so they won't always be behind when they enroll in a new school?"

Mr. Goldberg: "We have introduced one new program just for the children you describe. It is a peer-tutoring program in which students in upper elementary grades serve as tutors for those who are younger. We hope that by identifying academically successful Latino students to work with the younger students who are not experiencing as much success, they will learn the academic material and will benefit from having positive role models as well. Additionally, we are going to offer several small groups designed to increase students' study skills. We have a new homework hotline that students and parents can call to get missed assignments, and we are working on setting up some special parent programs at the site of their employment to teach them some self-advocacy skills that will help them access the programs and resources they need for their children as they move from one community to another."

> Identify at least two other strategies that you might use to work with the children described.

Slide 11

> # School Staff Characteristics
>
> - 80% white; 20% persons of color (15% African American; 5% Latino)
> - Two languages spoken (English and Spanish)
> - 50% have 10 or more years of teaching experience; 40% have fewer than 3 years of teaching experience.

"There are 30 regular education and 5 special education teachers in the school. Additionally, there are 2 counselors, a school nurse, and 15 support staff (clerical, transportation, sanitation). Although 50 percent of our student body is made up of

In the intervening time, what might you suggest to involve more persons of color in the school program?

students of color, only 20 percent of our staff is made up of persons of color. We have relayed this information to our school planning team, and they have developed a plan to recruit more diverse faculty and staff."

Slide 12

School Characteristics

- Class size 25:1
- Persons of color underrepresented in gifted program; overrepresented in students retained
- Latino students overrepresented in special education, truancy cases

"We also found that 33 percent of the students missed 15 percent or more of the school year. Of these, 69 percent were students of color. However, the patterns of absenteeism tend to develop in the second grade. Based on findings such as these, the leadership team and the Northside faculty decided to focus on academic skill development among kindergarten and first-grade students and their parents. We wish to increase the school attendance of all students, especially students of color, and have added this focus to our program.

"We concluded the awareness phase of planning with an agreement to organize the program to meet the ASCA standards. We compiled the lists of student competencies and outcomes and asked all teachers and parents to prioritize the competencies according to those they viewed as most important. At the conclusion of this needs assessment, we had nine standards grouped in three developmental domains. Each standard was accompanied by a list of student competencies and performance indicators, ordered from most important to least important. We asked for additional information on special topics of importance that would guide the development of our small counseling groups. These topics were based on those typically associated with difficulties experienced by elementary-aged students. The prioritizing form we used is in your handout" (see Figure 10.2).

FIGURE 10.2 Sample Handout No. 2

Northside Elementary School Counseling Program Priorities Planning Form

Parents and teachers of Northside students please help us prioritize the competencies we wish students to be able to demonstrate as a result of participating in the school counseling and guidance program. Simply rank the competencies with 1 being the highest, or the one you believe is most important in each section. Following the competencies, we have listed some special topics. Please circle all that you believe are important to include in the program for selected students.

Academic Development

_____ Improve student's academic self-concept

_____ Acquire skills for improving learning

_____ Achieve academic success

_____ Improve learning

_____ Plan to achieve goals

_____ Relate school to life experiences

Career Development

_____ Develop career awareness

_____ Develop employment readiness

_____ Acquire career information

_____ Identify career goals

_____ Acquire knowledge to achieve career goals

_____ Apply skills to achieve career goals

Personal/Social Development

_____ Acquire self-knowledge

_____ Acquire interpersonal skills

_____ Apply self-knowledge

_____ Acquire personal safety skills

Special Topics

- Grief/loss
- Divorce/remarriage
- Families
- Truancy
- Peer problems
- Discipline

- New to school
- Behavior
- Academics
- Moving
- Substance abuse
- Hygiene/self-care

Thank you!

Slide 13

> **Designing the Program**
>
> - Consolidation of competencies
> - Program structure
> - Strategies to reach all students
> - Support from stakeholders

"The data were gathered and analyzed to prioritize competencies and special group needs. Next, we needed to identify a program structure that would allow us to address these competencies and special requirements in a systematic, deliberate, and collaborative way. After reviewing several models of school counseling, we proposed the adoption one we believed would work for us. Once again, we presented our ideas to the school community for their input and approval."

Slide 14

> **Program Structure**
>
> - Guidance Curriculum (35–45%)
> - Individual Planning (5–10%)
> - Responsive Services (30–40%)
> - System Support (10–15%)

"The program design or structure we decided to follow is based on the model developed by Gysbers and Henderson (2000). This model is comprehensive, is flexible, and has established support in the school counseling literature. The overall program is composed of four program elements through which counseling and guidance services are systematically delivered at each grade level. The guidance curriculum is the vehicle for delivering guidance lessons and planned programs at each grade level. Most of the student competencies identified with the ASCA national standards will be addressed through this program delivery component. Individual planning refers to advisement, assessment, placement, and follow-up activities. Responsive services is the umbrella term for services that are not needed by every student but are available for targeted groups and individuals. Most of the special topics we asked teachers and parents to help us identify will constitute our program offerings in this area. System support is the program element through which administration of the program, outreach, public relations, and community consultations are achieved.

"The percentages you see here in parentheses are the recommended allocations of an elementary school counselor's time across the program elements. In your supplementary handout materials, you will find an overview of the program model and the types of programs and services that each covers (see Figure 10.3). The specifics change, as well as the time allocations, as students move into middle and high school programs."

Slide 15

Reaching All Students

- *Classroom guidance*
  Near 50% of our time is spent in the classroom directly supplementing regular instruction for all students.

- *Teacher/parent referral procedures*
  Referral and follow-up procedures are in place so parents and teachers can easily refer identified students for responsive services such as individual or group counseling or consultation. Each person making a referral is kept informed of progress.

"We developed an annual calendar that details the types of classroom guidance activities/lessons we will be presenting in each class during the year (Wittmer, 2000). The calendar is posted on our Web page and is in the school newsletter (see Figure 10.4). It is revised as planning continues and activities are added. Guidance lessons are intended to provide learning opportunities for students to acquire or demonstrate the specified competencies in all three developmental areas. Some of the competencies are covered in the regular curriculum and some of them are

FIGURE 10.3 Sample Handout No. 3

Northside Comprehensive School Counseling and Guidance Program

Guidance Curriculum	Individual Planning	Responsive Services	System Support
Provides guidance content in a systematic way to all students, K–12.	Assists students in planning, monitoring, and managing their personal and career planning.	Addresses the immediate concerns of students.	Includes program, staff, and school support activities and services.

Purpose

Student awareness, skill development, and application of skills needed in everyday life.	Student educational and occupational planning, decision making, and goal setting.	Prevention and intervention.	Program delivery and support.

Areas Addressed

Educational	*Educational*	*Educational*	*Educational*

Motivation to achieve
Decision making
Goal setting
Planning
Problem-solving skills
	Acquisition of study skills
	Awareness of educational opportunities
	Appropriate course selection
	Lifelong learning
	Utilization of test data
		Academic concerns
		Physical abuse
		Sexual abuse
		Emotional abuse
		Grief, loss, and death
		Substance abuse
		Family issues
		Sexuality issues
		Coping with stress
		Relationship concerns
		School-related concerns:
		  tardiness, absences
		  and truancy,
		  misbehavior, school
		  avoidance, dropout
		  prevention
			Guidance program development
			Parent education
			Teacher and administrator consultation
			Staff development for educators
			School improvement planning
			Counselor professional development
			Research and publishing
			Community outreach
			Public relations

Career	*Career*		
Awareness of educational opportunities Knowledge of career opportunities Knowledge of vocational and technical training	Knowledge of career opportunities Knowledge of vocational and technical training Need for positive work habits		
Knowledge of Self and Others	*Knowledge of Self and Others*		
Self-esteem development Interpersonal effectiveness Communication skills Cross-cultural effectiveness Responsible behavior	Development of healthy self-concepts Development of adaptive and adjustive social behavior		

Counselor Role

Structured groups Consultation Guidance curriculum implementation	Assessment Planning Placement	Individual counseling Small-group counseling Consultation Referral	Program development and management Consultation Coordination

Note: These lists are exemplary and not exhaustive.

Source: Alabama State Department of Education. (1996). *The revised comprehensive counseling and guidance model for Alabama's public schools.* Bulletin 1966, No. 27. Montgomery, AL: Author. Reprinted with permission.

FIGURE 10.4 Sample Handout No. 4

Annual and Monthly Calendar for Northside Elementary School

	Guidance Curriculum	Individual Planning	Responsive Services	System Support
August	Orientation to program (K–5); respect for individual differences (K–5)	Referrals for peer tutoring program; advisement; placement and follow-up (student support team)	Small groups: making friends; academic concerns	School board presentation; calendar distribution; tutoring program training
September	Career awareness (K–5)	Referrals for peer tutoring program; advisement; placement and follow-up (student support team)	Small groups: family concerns; academic concerns; school-related concerns Peer tutors: study skills in subject area	Leadership team meeting; program management; lesson planning; peer tutor coordination; grade-level team meetings
October	Work habits and study skills (K–5)	Referrals for peer tutoring program; advisement; placement and follow-up (student support team)	Small groups: academic concerns; school-related concerns; relationship concerns Peer tutors: time management strategies in subject area	Leadership team meeting; program management; lesson planning; peer tutor coordination; grade-level team meetings
November	Goal setting (K–5)	Referrals for peer tutoring program; advisement; placement and follow-up (student support team)	Groups: Stress reduction; grief/loss; academic and school concerns Peer tutors: subject area skill development	State counselor conference; leadership team meeting; program management; lesson planning; peer tutor coordination; grade-level team meetings
December	Skills for academic success (K–5);	Referrals for peer tutoring program; advisement; placement and follow-up (student support team)	Groups: substance abuse; bullying; academic and school concerns Peer tutors: planning for the holidays	Leadership team meeting; program management; lesson planning; peer tutor coordination; grade-level team meetings
January	Understanding self and others (K–5)	Referrals for peer tutoring program; advisement; placement and follow-up (student support team)	Small groups: making friends; academic concerns	Leadership team meeting; program management; lesson planning; peer tutor coordination; grade-level team meetings
February	Career information (K–5); schoolwide career fair	Referrals for peer tutoring program; advisement; placement and follow-up (student support team)	Small groups: family concerns; academic concerns; school-related concerns; Peer tutors: study skills in subject area	Local staff development training; Leadership team meeting; program management; lesson planning; peer tutor coordination; grade-level team meetings

(continued)

FIGURE 10.4   *continued*

Annual and Monthly Calendar for Northside Elementary School

	Guidance Curriculum	Individual Planning	Responsive Services	System Support
March	Test-taking skills (K–5)	Referrals for peer tutoring program; advisement; placement and follow-up (student support team); Test preparation	Small groups: academic concerns; school-related concerns; relationship concerns; Peer tutors: time management strategies in subject area	Leadership team meeting; program management; lesson planning; peer tutor coordination; grade-level team meetings; counseling conference
April	Stress busters (K–5)	Referrals for peer tutoring program; advisement; placement and follow-up (student support team)	Groups: stress reduction; grief/loss; academic and school concerns Peer tutors: subject area skill development	Leadership team meeting; program management; lesson planning; peer tutor coordination; grade-level team meetings
May	Safety survival skills (K–5)	Test interpretations; advisement; placement and follow-up (student support team); middle school registration (5)	Groups: substance abuse; bullying; academic and school concerns Peer tutors: planning for the summer holiday	Leadership team meeting; program management; lesson planning; peer tutor coordination; IEP meetings
June	Transitions (K–5)	Referrals for peer tutoring program; advisement; placement and follow-up (student support team)	Follow-up and evaluation activities for group and tutoring program participants	Leadership team meeting; program management; lesson planning; peer tutor coordination; grade-level team meetings

covered in the guidance curriculum. We also post a weekly schedule (see Figure 10.5) to keep all constituencies informed about our activities.

"We depend heavily on teachers and parents who see these children daily to notice changes in behaviors, performance, or attitudes that might signal the need for more individualized intervention than can occur in the context of classroom guidance. Each referral is pursued by the assigned counselor."

FIGURE 10.5 Sample Handout No. 5

Northside Weekly Calendar

	Monday	Tuesday	Wednesday	Thursday	Friday
7:30	Consultation	Consultation	Consultation	Consultation	Consultation
8:00	Individual counseling	Individual counseling	Individual counseling	Individual counseling	Individual counseling
8:30	Classroom guidance (K)	Small groups	Classroom guidance (K)	Small groups	Classroom guidance (K)
9:00	Classroom guidance (K)	Small groups	Classroom guidance (K)	Small groups	Classroom guidance (1)
9:30	Classroom guidance (1)	System support	Classroom guidance (1)	System support	Classroom guidance (1)
10:00	System support	Classroom guidance (5)	System support	Classroom guidance (5)	System support
10:30	Classroom guidance (2)	System support	Classroom guidance (2)	System support	Classroom guidance (5)
11:00	Classroom guidance (2)	System support	Classroom guidance (2)	System support	Classroom guidance (5)
11:30	Lunch w/selected students	Lunch w/selected students	Lunch w/selected students	Lunch w/selected students	Lunch w/selected students
12:00	Consultation with teachers/ parents	Consultation with teachers/ parents	Consultation with teachers/ parents	Consultation with teachers/ parents	Consultation with teachers/ parents
12:30	Small groups	Classroom guidance (3)	Small groups	Classroom guidance (4)	Small groups
1:00	Individual planning	Classroom guidance (3)	Individual planning	Classroom guidance (4)	Individual planning
1:30	Small groups	Classroom guidance (3)	Small groups	Classroom guidance (4)	Small groups
2:00	System support	Classroom guidance (3)	System support	Classroom guidance (4)	System support
2:30	Individual counseling	Individual counseling	Individual counseling	Individual counseling	Individual counseling
3:00	Counseling/ consultation	Counseling/ consultation	Counseling/ consultation	Counseling/ consultation	Counseling/ consultation
3:30	Return calls/ e-mails	Return calls/ e-mails	Return calls/ e-mails	Return calls/ e-mails	Return calls/ e-mails

Slide 16

Support

- Teachers, parents, administrators, and students are more likely to support the implementation of a program that is based on identified priorities, supports the mission of the school, clearly reflects input of all consumers, is integrated across the curriculum, and includes measurable indicators of performance.

Ms. Sara: "We have made extraordinary efforts to understand the needs and values of the persons who will benefit from the school counseling program. As you will see in just a few moments, we have an annual review process in place that will ensure continued input from all constituent groups as our program grows or changes to accommodate the changing needs of our school community."

Slide 17

Five-Year Plan for Implementation

- *Year one:* Planning activities, leadership team, vision, increasing awareness

- *Year two:* Design activities, identify and prioritize competencies, distribute and gain support for ideal program model, identify changes needed (allocation of time, etc.)

"These are examples of some of the activities that have already taken place (we are in year three) and an idea of what will be added in the next 2 years."

Slide 18

Time line, *continued*

- *Year three:* Implement special programs (peer tutoring, conflict resolution training), fully implement revised guidance curriculum, publicize program, identify staff development needs
- *Years four & five:* Evaluate counselor performance, evaluate program, initiate revision activities as needed.

Slide 19

Evaluation: Accountability & Improvement

- Program design evaluation (every 3rd year)
- Program effectiveness evaluation (every year)
- Individual activity evaluation (each activity)
- Time and task analysis (daily)
- Counselor's performance evaluation (each year)

"Evaluation activities are necessary in order to determine whether the program is effective and program goals are met, as well as whether individual activities used to meet identified competencies are effective. These data are gathered systematically and used to plan for needed changes in the program design. Additionally, time and task analysis data maintained by each counselor allows us to see how consistently we are adhering to our time allotments. Finally, counselor performance evaluations are necessary to identify strengths as well as areas where additional professional development is needed. All of these evaluation activities can also be helpful in deeming what additional resources might be necessary for full program implementation. Mr. Goldberg is now going to answer questions that you have."

A school board member wishes to know, "What have been your findings with regard to effectiveness?"

Mr. Goldberg: "We have established through the daily time and task analysis logs that Ms. Sara and I are operating within the recommended time allotments established for program delivery. This is an improvement over our first 2 years when we consistently had difficulty fully implementing our guidance curriculum due to the inordinate amount of time we spent in crisis management. It has taken a real effort on the part of teachers, administrators, and students to learn conflict resolution and mediation skills so that many of the crises could be handled without counselor intervention. Additionally, we learned that teachers believe the program is effective and that we are effective program managers. They rated the program 4.2 on a 5-point scale on overall achievement of goals. They rated counselors 4.5 on a 5-point scale on overall effectiveness. Areas of strength were the guidance curriculum and individual planning activities. An area where we need improvement is responsive services, specifically individual counseling interventions. The small groups based on special topics are working well as perceived by teachers and student evaluations, too. However, teachers and parents who refer students with problems for individual counseling do not see the kind of improvement they would like in a timely manner. This finding has led Ms. Sara and myself to conduct a self-audit of our counseling skills. As a result of teacher opinion and this self-examination, we will be attending a 3-day seminar on solution-focused counseling. We have also purchased a book that describes a solution-focused approach for working with students, teachers, and parents and are meeting weekly to discuss our readings and plan ways to incorporate these strategies into our day-to-day operations (Metcalf, 1995).

"Regarding student outcomes, we have an identified performance indicator for every student competency addressed in our program. As a result of the increased attention to academic skill development in K–1, we have seen a 10 percent decrease in the number of retentions in both those grades, a 17 percent rise in achievement test scores, and improved grades for 15 percent of the students. The school attendance of Latino youth, many of whom are children of migrant farm workers, has improved and their parents are participating in their education at a higher rate than before we began visiting them in their workplace. Last school year, for example, we had 25 parents who had never been to the school before attend parent information night. While these numbers are modest, they are real improvements that we expect to continue, and compound, throughout a student's educational career. Are there other questions? Yes, our contact information is in the handout packet. Thank you for this opportunity and for your attention. We will be available after the meeting for additional questions or comments."

SUMMARY

This chapter has presented a snapshot of a comprehensive developmental school counseling program in an elementary school. The emphasis has been on the results of each part of the five-phase program planning process presented earlier in this text. A sample presentation was used to illustrate how to publicize one's program, and sample forms and informational documents typical of elementary school counseling program planning activities were provided.

PORTFOLIO COMPONENTS

1. Based on the program described in this chapter, develop a program evaluation instrument that can be used annually by teachers, parents, and administrators to provide feedback on whether the program vision is being realized, the extent to which the national standards are being implemented, and the perceived effectiveness of the four elements for program delivery.
2. Develop a lesson planning form that includes the competency being addressed, the activities used to address the competency, when the lesson is delivered and by whom, resources, and the measurable indicator(s) of student success.
3. Prepare a reflection statement that describes your strengths and weaknesses, both personal and professional, as a prospective elementary school counselor.

Middle School Counseling Program: Parent Orientation

===== **CASE STUDY** =====

MIDDLE SCHOOL MATTERS

The faculty and staff at Monroe Middle School decided to expand their orientation program from a one-night open house to a series of sessions that spotlighted different segments of the middle school learning experience. The extended orientation gave the school staff more time to explain their activities and to interact with the parents.

Ms. Hernandez, Ms. Clark, and Mr. Al-Mabuk, the counselors at Monroe Middle, have developed a slide presentation to outline the people and processes that lead to a schoolwide project they coordinated as well as other elements of the school counseling program. They also had a packet containing more detailed information for any parents or students who wanted the printed material. The presentation and the supporting materials were posted on the school's Web page.

Ms. Hernandez, Ms. Clark, and Mr. Al-Mabuk have discovered that their participation in this orientation every year helps them and the new sixth-grade students and parents. Everyone has a clearer idea of the goals of the counseling program and the ways those goals are achieved. People who attend this presentation can identify the leadership team, the calendar of activities, and the ways they can be involved in the counseling program.

Middle school counseling programs focus on the key developmental tasks of sixth-, seventh-, and eighth-grade students. Vernon (1999) provides an overview of the development of the middle school adolescent. Children in early adolescence (ages 11 to 14) experience rapid physical changes. Changes in the body associated with puberty begin. Those changes are followed by the appearance of secondary sex characteristics and generally a growth spurt. The variations in the rate of this physical maturation among children in this age group may result in self-consciousness and anxiety. Both genders may become clumsy and uncoordinated because of the disproportion of their hands and feet to their body. The common desire of early adolescents to be like everyone creates another source of anxiety. Likewise the physical and hormonal changes in their bodies may cause the adolescent confusion.

The cognitive shift from concrete thinking to formal operational thought starts during early adolescence. This gradual change allows adolescents to think more abstractly, reason more logically, and predict consequences. They will be more able to identify inconsistencies, think about the future and various possibilities, and imagine a logical sequence of events. As with physical changes, there are great variations in cognitive development in adolescents. Adults should take care not to overestimate the maturity of adolescents' thought processes.

The search for self-definition begins in early adolescence, often leading them to push for autonomy in spite of their immaturity and lack of experience. These contrasts may cause an increased vulnerability and dependence. Adults may be faced with a young person who does and does not want their adult companionship. Those and other contradictions may accompany early adolescence. They want to be distinctive and they want to blend in to the crowd. They may be self-conscious about feeling awkward and about feeling they are the center of attention. They may also be egocentric, seeing themselves as more important than others and assuming no one else shares similar experiences. An emotional roller coaster of moodiness, emotional outbursts, and troublesome emotions may accompany this age. Peer relationships may be pleasurable sources of support. Those relationships may also be negative, a source of humiliation and a major stressor of this age.

That overview of development hardly captures the energy with which most middle school students embrace life. Monroe Middle School, like so many other middle schools, contains students who are curious about themselves, excited about the future, and eager to investigate the world. Adults in the school found a way to capitalize on those attributes.

After reading and discussing this chapter, you should be able to

- Identify a list of key members for a middle school counseling leadership team.
- List the sources of information necessary for creating an awareness of the needs of middle school students in a particular school district.
- Select and prioritize student competencies to be accomplished as a result of participating in the middle school counseling program.
- Identify at least two interventions appropriate for middle-school-aged children to facilitate their mastery of a specified student competency.
- Identify who in the school will be responsible for each of the competencies identified and how and when related activities will be implemented.
- Identify at least five methods used to determine whether program goals have been reached and student competencies have been mastered.

PRESENTATION TO PARENTS

The teaching teams at Monroe integrated communication, math, social science, and science in their instruction. The school counseling program was also incorporated into this curriculum in a comprehensive project that the school counselors explained to parents of entering sixth graders by using the following presentation.

Slide 1

Monroe Middle School

Counseling Program

Ms. Tonia Hernandez

Mr. Ra Al-Mabuk

Ms. Janet Clark

Ms. Hernandez: Welcome to Monroe Middle School. As you may have learned by now, we have a student body of around 900. Our school consists of three teams at each grade level. Your sixth grader will spend his or her days with a group of teachers who plan and work together to help your child learn and grow throughout the school year. The teams within and across grade levels also plan, design, and put into practice educational programs and activities for our students.

This year our extended student/parent orientation allows us to have more time to highlight some of these fine activities taking place at Monroe Middle. We have the privilege of outlining one project that involves the students, faculty, and counseling program at Monroe Middle School. This project combines all subject areas. It not only reaches each student but also includes community activities and family involvement. Our urban location has many easy-to-reach resources that we use in this project, which is a yearlong learning opportunity.

During our time together in this orientation we want (1) to introduce ourselves—the counselors at Monroe and the school itself; (2) to explain the steps we used to plan this project; and (3) to describe the project itself.

We started our work with steps suggested by Dahir, Sheldon, and Valiga (1998) in *Vision into Action: Implementing the National Standards for School Counseling Programs*. Those steps include discussing, becoming aware, designing, implementing, and evaluating. We formed a committed team of leaders.

Slide 2

Leadership Team

- R. Al-Mabuk, school counselor
- T. Hernandez, school counselor
- J. Clark, school counselor
- A. Sherrill, 6th grade teacher
- T. Wu, 7th grade teacher
- J. Palmero, 8th grade teacher
- M. Wilkens, parent
- N. Morgan, assistant principal
- L. Johnston, business partner

Mr. Al-Mabuk: "The team began by having long talks. As you can see from this list the team includes school counselors, a teacher from each level, a parent, an administrator, and an executive of the school's business partner. Some members of the team volunteered and others were asked to help us. We wanted to make sure we had several views on all our decisions. Each person on this team has a group of three advisors who listen, respond, and guide, too. These advisors give us even more valuable insights and suggestions to our efforts. The advisors' names can be found in your handouts. The team worked for 2 years to develop the project. We'll be explaining the process and the outcomes for you.

Slide 3

Mission

Our school counseling program weaves activities of our total community to provide opportunities for every student to develop and use the attitudes, knowledge, and skills they need to live, work, and learn successfully.

"Our leadership team spent several meetings thinking about what was necessary. This mission statement captures what we decided was most important. As you can see, we share a commitment to every student being prepared for a successful life, our ideal outcome. As we work with the students at Monroe Middle, we use different learning activities to help them develop the skills, use information, and work with a problem-solving attitude for today and all their tomorrows.

With some classmates, write two variations of the mission statement.

Slide 4

We care about

- Children
- Their world
- Their successes now
- And their promising future

"As we talked we continued returning to these core beliefs. We reminded ourselves that young adults enter our school full of possibilities. We must nurture that promise and help them on their journeys to discover the best of themselves. We recognize that the worlds of our students do not begin and end in our hallways. We want a healthy, productive community surrounding them, and we want them to participate with and contribute to that neighborhood. We know some things create barriers to learning and growing. We are dedicated to recognizing and limiting those stumbling blocks by being alert to warning signs and immediately taking preventive and remedial actions. Finally we realize that we need to help our young people focus on and be better informed about their future.

"With these ideals in mind, the leadership team next decided what information was needed to carry out our mission. We looked for ways to increase our awareness of our school, our community, and our student's needs."

Slide 5

We investigated

- Our community profile
- Our school
- *National Standards for School Counseling Programs*
- North Carolina *Standard Course of Study*
- Information gathered from needs assessment

Ms. Clark: "As we mentioned, we wanted to determine some ways of understanding our students. We needed to know in what kind of world they existed, what needs they have, and the best way of meeting these needs.

"We looked at our community. The Chamber of Commerce and city hall helped us gather statistics on the rising unemployment rate in our city, the increase in children living in poverty, demographic variables of the population, and the many employers in our surroundings. We worked with some agencies that work with children to determine the extent of some risk factors such as the juvenile crime rate, teenage pregnancy rates, and the number of foster home placements.

"We also looked closely at our school. We reviewed the characteristics of our students and faculty. We looked at the numbers of discipline referrals, absences, and placement in any special services. We also looked at the patterns of students' high school courses, staying in school, and academic successes and failures.

"Next we reviewed our professional standards. We built a summary of those guidelines in a grid that became a working document for the next step of our planning.

"Our next project was asking students, parents, and teachers what they needed. We modified some needs assessment and integrated those results to build our project plan.

Find a state curriculum Web page and identify the counseling program competencies from that state. Compare and contrast the state competencies to the National Standards.

Slide 6

School Counseling Program Guiding Principle

- Students will use their academic skills and experiences, their personal qualities, and information about the world of work to make informed decisions, to set goals, and to accomplish those goals.

"After we had all this information, we looked at all areas we had investigated. The leadership team discussed our findings with other parents, teachers, students, and administrators. We now knew that students had trouble connecting the things they learned in school with things people did at work. We wanted to make that connection very obvious. We also realized that students did not understand that they could identify their personal learning style, their preferred working environment, and other preferences that relate to a career choice. We wanted to help them begin understanding themselves in those ways. We also needed to find ways for them to see that how they worked at school was important to their plans for the future.

"We created a project that allowed students to work individually, with other students, with community members, and with a great deal of information. The project would help in our middle school by giving students chances to work with students in different grades, by having students work together to complete projects, and by using the community as part of the learning environment. We wanted students who were leaving middle school to make careful decisions about their high school course work and their goals for education beyond high school. We were convinced that the information they gathered about careers and future possibilities would help. We also hoped the project would encourage students to be more connected to their community. Finally we believed that working with their fellow students and with people in the community would help students polish their interpersonal skills.

Slide 7

"Our guiding vision became constructing promising days for our children. We used a column to symbolize our focus on support as well as the many different kinds of that support. So far each year the eighth graders have designed an emblem as part of the celebration of their accomplishments in the project."

Slide 8

Priority Student Competencies

- *Academic*
  Students will incorporate curricular, cocurricular, and community experiences into their academic learning.
- *Career*
  Students will explain the relationship of personal skills and attitudes to different careers.
- *Personal/social*
  Students will demonstrate their abilities to gather information, detail priorities, and set goals related to their future.

Ms. Hernandez: "In more specific terms, we designed the project to help students focus on their academic advancement, their career potential, and their person/social skills. We know how quickly children who move through adolescence change physically as well as how they think and how they interact. Children in this age range have a great chance to see how things they are learning fit into the larger world. We want our students to be thoughtful about the many decisions they will be making, using skills and information they need to make careful choices.

What competencies from the National Standards have been collapsed into the three listed?

"We reviewed what we knew about career counseling in schools (Zunker, 2002) and used that information to build a program with strategies that could help middle school students explore, gain insights, and apply planning skills.

Slide 9

> # Discovering Possibilities for a Promising Future
>
> - Schoolwide effort
> - Combining knowing about me and knowing about world of work
> - Two career clusters/year
> - Three-year cycle
> - Clusters include transportation, education, medical, etc.

"The project centers on self-knowledge, exploring careers, investigating how to prepare for a career, and then combining the information. Over the 3 years the students attend Monroe Middle, they will be exposed to six broad categories of careers.

"In this project every person in the school is involved. Every student has responsibilities for self and for others. Many adults guide this learning. And to our delight more and more members of the community and more and more parents are contributing by talking in classes, having students visit their work, and being interviewed.

Find different classification systems of occupational information that could be used for this study. What criteria would you use in recommending one or the other?

Slide 10

> # Key Components to Project
>
> - Skills to locate, understand, and use information
> - Skills to interact with others
> - Knowledge about interrelationships of work and self
> - Skills to make decisions
> - Team approach across grade levels
>   - Eighth graders lead
>   - Seventh graders gather
>   - Sixth graders prepare

"Student teams plan, gather data, and present several displays of career information. We want to build these investigative skills, improve their interpersonal work styles, increase their understanding of the connections between work and self, and expand their abilities in decision making. This project has many opportunities to train, practice, master, and refine those components.

"The investigation involves many activities. The students have different roles based on their grade levels. Eighth graders direct the year-end presentations. They decide what information and other things they need. Eighth graders give the responsibility of gathering what is needed to the seventh graders. Working with teachers, eighth graders teach sixth graders how to gather information from several places. The eighth graders design and complete some kind of display to highlight the information that has been gathered about the two career clusters. We invited the community, parents, and entire school to the presentation.

"Seventh graders do the research on the career cluster by gathering the information the eighth graders have requested. Often the seventh graders decide to expand what they are studying as they do the research. They work at this in many ways: they interview, shadow people on jobs, collect census data, talk with professional organizations, use print and computer databases, and so forth. After they have finished gathering, they put the information together and give their findings to the eighth graders.

"The sixth graders learn about ways to gather information and practice those methods. They learn about teams, interviewing, developing questions, and classifying data. They have opportunities to practice with students, their family members, and school staff."

> With your classmates list as many tasks related to this type of project that could be realistically assigned to sixth, seventh, and eighth graders. After you have compiled the list, cluster the responsibilities and decide what kind of support and training they would need from counselors and teachers.

Slide 11

Discovering Possibilities for a Promising Future

- Interviews with community members, data from government and other sources, job shadowing, and service learning projects are some student activities involved.

- Career fairs, career modules, career portfolios, and video and computer presentations are some of the displays that have been created.

Mr. Al-Mabuk: "Here are some other examples of what the students have accomplished.

Slide 12

> # School Counselors' Participation
>
> - Coordinating efforts
> - Supporting training
> - Identifying resources

"As you can see the leadership team has designed a comprehensive project. We counselors coordinate the master calendar of events with all the responsibilities clearly designated. We teach teachers about career clusters, the career development process, and other specialized information they need. We work with the media specialist and our community liaison to locate resources for this program.

Slide 13

> # School Counselors Activities/Strategies
>
> - Teaching – 30% (12 hours/week)
> - Planning – 20% (8 hours/week)
> - Responding – 40% (16 hours/week)
> - Supporting – 10% (4 hours/week)

"This previous slide showed some ways we contribute to this project in our coordination role. The counseling program involves four strategies. We dedicate 50 percent of our time to the possibilities project. The other 50 percent falls into the same activities but may not have as clear a tie to the project. We want you to understand the types of activities we may be leading and the ways we will be working with you and your child. The next slides have more details about our parts in this particular project. Hopefully those details will help you picture what we do in the school counseling program.

Slide 14

> # Teaching
>
> - Focused Groups
>   - Interview teams
>   - Task group leaders
>   - Components of careers
>
> - Classroom Presentations
>   - What's a future?
>   - How do I listen so people will speak?
>   - Team building 101

"These are some classroom instructions we conducted related to the Discovering Possibilities project.

Slide 15

> # Planning
>
> - Advising
>   - Large-group course selection activities
>   - Small-group guidance activities
>   - Individual advisement for special assistance
>
> - Assessment
>   - Tests of working/learning styles
>
> - Placement and Follow-up
>   - Service learning screening
>   - Follow-up on placements in sites

"Besides delivering the curriculum with teachers and by ourselves, we help students with individual planning. These will give you some ideas of the activities we do to work with students when they need that kind of assistance."

Design a brochure for the school counseling program. What would you include? Compare your list to the lists of your classmates. Make yourself a checklist for your school program.

What kinds of assessment would you recommend for a middle school student who could not identify any interests related to careers?

Slide 16

> # Responding
>
> - Individual Counseling
>   - Skill building
>   - Choices
>   - Friendships
> - Small-Group Counseling
>   - Newcomers, skills
> - Consultation
>   - Parent involvement training
>   - Teacher education
> - Referral

Ms. Clark: "One component of the project we have not discussed is the self-assessment activities. Students gather materials about themselves over their 3 years here. They find evidence of their strengths, interests, and skills. They keep a diary of their working styles for a week each year, write a want-ad tailored to their abilities, find their "model" worker and compare that person to themselves, and discover their "styles" when working with ideas, people, and things. They combine these into a portfolio that consists of their summaries of what they have learned related to the careers they have investigated.

"Some students may need some individual attention to identify their strengths. Others may have trouble working on teams and may need to learn those skills. Others may be dealing with some problems that are so overwhelming they cannot accomplish anything. These are a few of the cases in which we might establish a counseling relationship with a child with goals related to their concerns.

Write out two or three sentences that you could use to explain your approach to counseling to a group of parents.

Slide 17

> # Supporting
>
> - Consultation
>   - Resource identification
>   - Process observer
>   - Problem solving
> - Outreach
>   - Community resources
>   - Updates
> - Information
>   - Career
>   - Teaming
>   - Child development

"Another part of the counseling program involves supporting the many systems in the school, and this slide gives you some examples of ways we do that. One joy of this project is our close alliance with businesses who have done most of the scheduling for students to visit and who have compiled several lists of resources.

Slide 18

How do we know it works?

- Students can explain the characteristics of an identified career, the preparation for that career, and the reasons their skills and abilities match or do not match that career.

"We began by telling you about what we thought was important—the students and promises for their future. As we worked on this project, we constantly asked, 'How will we know if this works?' Our answers were on two levels. The first level is about what students can do. They can tell us about a career by explaining the work done, the skills needed, and the training required. They can complete a realistic review of their own skills and abilities with evidence to support their evaluation. They can explain their dreams for their future and the pathways to making those hopes come true. Finally they can identify the matches and mismatches between themselves and different careers.

"Students show us another level of success when they plan for their high school courses and beyond. We look at how many stay in high school and the courses they take there as markers of their success in making decisions.

Slide 19

Indicators of Success

- Increase in daily average attendance
- Decrease in discipline referrals
- Stable and improving end-of-grade test scores
- Increase in community involvement in school
- Increase in parent participation at Monroe Middle School

With your classmates write a list of questions and answers that could be titled Questions Parents Frequently Ask School Counselors.

"We have also found that since the project began we have had some differences in the school. We have looked at the areas listed on the slide and see some positive trends since we began 2 years ago. We are convinced that this chance to work together closely has made Monroe Middle School even stronger than it already was.

Slide 20

Summary

- How we started
- What we designed
- How it proceeds
- What students do
- What counselors do
- How we know it works

"In conclusion, we have tried to show you the ways we planned a project and how it works in our school. We wanted you to see the things you can expect your child to be doing related to this project and how we check to see whether this is working.

"We also want to welcome you to Monroe Middle School and to encourage you to call us if you have any questions or concerns. We have provided a copy of our job description (see Figure 11.1) so that you can have a better idea of how the coun-

FIGURE 11.1 Counselor Job Description

Job Description for a Middle School Counselor

Reports to: Principal and/or Counseling Supervisor

Purpose: To help all students develop skills in personal/social growth, educational planning, and career development.

As a member of a school educational team, the school counselor performs specific duties and responsibilities in deliver a comprehensive, developmental school counseling program.

DUTIES AND RESPONSIBILITIES:

Major Function: Program Planning

The school counselor establishes the school counseling program and develops activities and resources to implement and evaluate the program. The school counselor involves other school staff in making decisions about the school counseling program.

Major Function: Counseling

The school counselor provides the responsive services of individual and group counseling to meet the developmental, preventive, and remedial needs of students.

Major Function: Consulting

The school counselor consults with students, parents, teachers, and other school and community personnel to assist in meeting the needs of students.

Major Function: Coordinating

The school counselor coordinates all counseling services for students. The school counselor assists with the coordination and implementation of student services in the school. The counselor also assists teachers with the guidance curriculum.

Major Function: Student Appraisal

The school counselor accurately interprets test results and other student data. The counselor also assists teachers with the educational placement of students by using appropriate educational assessment strategies.

Major Function: Professional Practices and Development

The school counselor adheres to ethical standards of the counseling profession and abides by the laws, policies, and procedures that govern the schools. The counselor also participates in professional associations and upgrades professional knowledge and skills when needed.

Source: Adapted from Winston-Salem/Forsyth County Schools. (2002) *School counselor job descriptions.* Winston-Salem, NC: Author. Reprinted with permission.

selors at Monroe are involved in your child's education. A sample calendar has also been included in your materials (see Figure 11.2). When teachers, parents, counselors, and the community work for our children, great things happen."

FIGURE 11.2   Sample Counseling Calendar

CALENDAR	Teaching	Planning	Responding	Supporting
August	Introductions (6–8); Decision-making model (8)	Referrals for grade-level peer helpers; advising, follow-up	Small groups: problem solving (7); transitions (6); academics (8)	Parent orientation; calendar finalized; new teacher training
September	Knowing Me (6–8)	Referrals for tutoring program; advising; student services team	Individual counseling; small groups as above	Community resources updates; coordination and program mgmt.
October	Working Together (6–8); Making Choices (6–8)	Referrals for service learning; advising; student services team	Individual counseling; small groups on relationships (6–8)	Community resources updates; leadership team; coordination and program mgmt.
November	Working Together (6–8); Making Choices (6–8)	Referrals for service learning; advising; student services team	Individual counseling; small groups on school-related concerns (6–8)	Community resources updates; leadership team; coordination and program mgmt.
December	What's a Career? (6); Career Awareness (7–8)	Referrals for service learning; advising; student services team	Individual counseling; small groups on school-related concerns (6–8)	Community resources updates; leadership team; project coordination and program mgmt.
January	What's a Career? (6); Career Awareness (7–8)	Placements for service learning; advising; student services team	Individual counseling; small groups on academic concerns (6–8); study skills (6–7)	Community resources updates; leadership team; project coordination and program mgmt.
February	My Possibilities (6); My Working Self (7–8)	Placements for service learning, advising; student services team	Individual counseling; small groups on academic concerns (6–8); study skills	Community resources updates; leadership team; coordination and program mgmt.
March	My Possibilities (6); My Working Self (7–8)	Placements for service learning; advising; student services team	Individual counseling; small groups on academic concerns (6–8); stress mgmt.	Community resources updates; leadership team; coordination and program mgmt.
April	Entering High School (8); Careers and Me (6–7)	Service learning site wrap-ups; registration activities; advising; student services team	Individual counseling; small groups on stress mgmt. (6–8)	Community resources updates; leadership team; project coordination and program mgmt.
May	Putting it Together—Middle School Matters (6–8) Schoolwide Project Presentation	Registration activities; advising; student services team	Individual counseling; small groups—transitions (8)	Community resources updates; leadership team; coordination and program mgmt.

SUMMARY

This chapter has outlined a middle school counseling program. The focus has been on a project that evolved from a planning process that included discussing, gaining awareness, designing, implementing, and evaluating the program. A sample orientation program for parents illustrates one way to increase understanding of a middle school counseling program.

PORTFOLIO COMPONENTS

1. Create a needs assessment instrument you could use to identify the training needs of teachers related to career information.
2. Develop a lesson plan for eighth-grade students on decision making. Include the specific competency, expected student outcome, activities, timing, instructor, and necessary resources.
3. Provide a self-assessment of your potential as a middle school counselor.

Comprehensive Developmental School Counseling in the Secondary School

CASE STUDY

COMPREHENSIVE DEVELOPMENT SCHOOL GUIDANCE AND COUNSELING FOR SECONDARY STUDENTS: A MODEL PROGRAM

The counselors at G.W. Carver High School are preparing a 3-hour skill-building program they will deliver at a national conference for school counselors. The presentation is based on the transformation of their school program from a services-oriented approach to a comprehensive developmental program. Their challenge is to condense the information they gathered, synthesized, and produced over a 3-year period into a 3-hour program. They want the information they present to be relevant and explanatory enough to be helpful to others who are interested in transforming their secondary school programs.

They also want to realistically present the challenges they have experienced as well as the successes. Goals for the program are for participants to be able to:

1. Describe a planning process used to transform a secondary school counseling program.

2. Identify the constituent groups that need to be represented on a secondary school leadership team.

3. List sources for information that would help them determine what needs to change about their current program and what needs to be retained.

4. Describe the importance of the ASCA National Standards for School Counseling Programs to their constituents.

5. Identify/develop important student competencies to be included in their program.

6. Specify performance indicators or measurable student outcomes for all competencies included in the program.

Secondary school programs typically serve students in grades 9 through 12. This grade placement coincides with the developmental period of adolescence, identified by Erikson (1980) as a time of transition from childhood to adulthood. Steinberg (1996) describes the key markers of adolescence. Physically, adolescents experience the rapid changes associated with puberty during which time they become capable of sexual reproduction. Their cognitive abilities develop, resulting in more advanced, complex, and abstract reasoning abilities. Emotionally, they move toward greater autonomy from parents and establish separate and unique identities. Their interpersonal interests shift from relationships with their parents to peers. They develop the skills and capacities for achieving intimacy. Socially, they prepare for adult roles in society with regard to work, family, and citizenship. Steinberg also points out that these developmental markers do not emerge for each adolescent at the same chronological time, nor do individual adolescents demonstrate them simultaneously. Some students mature earlier than others and some achieve maturity in one or more area of development before they do in others. The tasks of adolescence are challenging for the adolescent and for the adults in their lives. School counseling programs need to be particularly responsive to the developmental demands faced by secondary school students.

After reading and discussing this chapter, you should be able to

- Identify a list of key members for a high school counseling leadership team.
- List sources of information necessary for creating an awareness of the needs of high school students in a particular school district.
- Select and prioritize student competencies to be accomplished as a result of participating in the high school counseling program.
- Identify at least two interventions appropriate for high-school-aged youth to facilitate mastery of a specified student competency.
- Identify at least two interventions grounded in theories about developmental tasks of adolescents.
- Identify who in the school will be responsible for each of the competencies identified and how and when related activities will be implemented.
- Identify at least three methods used to determine whether program goals have been reached and student competencies have been mastered.

PRESENTATION BY CARVER HIGH SCHOOL COUNSELORS

Slide 1

**Carver High School
Counseling Program:**

*Comprehensive, Developmental,
Standards-based*

JoAnne Moriarty, Kevin Coopersmith,
Jackson Brown, Anhurada Beim,
Kalais Moore, and Angela Lindsey

Ms. Moriarty: "Welcome to our presentation today. I am JoAnne Moriarty and these are my colleagues, Kevin Coopersmith, Jackson Brown, Anhurada Beim, Kalais Moore, and Angela Lindsey. We are professional school counseling staff of Carver High School (see Figure 12.1). Our purpose today is to describe a project that we began 3 years ago at our school."

Slide 2

Project Goal

- To respond to a state department of education mandate to create a balanced, comprehensive developmental school counseling program for high school students.

"In 1998, the state department of education, in response to advocacy efforts of the state school counseling organization, reviewed all policies and procedures related to school counseling and determined that while our elementary and middle school counseling programs were comprehensive and developmental, the secondary programs were not. The SDE mandated that high school counseling programs be revised to reflect this focus. This presentation is a summary of the transition efforts at Carver High School."

Slide 3

Purposes

- To implement a standards-based school counseling program designed to facilitate the academic, career, and personal/social development of all students.

- To identify and respond to the developmental and remedial needs of students who were not achieving their highest academic potential under the existing program structure.

FIGURE 12.1 Sample Handout No. 1

Job Description: Carver High School Counselor

Position: High School Counselor

Primary Function: As a member of the system's counseling and guidance staff, the high school counselor provides a comprehensive counseling and guidance program for high school students; consults and collaborates with teachers, parents, and staff to enhance their effectiveness in helping students; and provides support to other high school educational programs.

Illustrative Key Duties:

1. Implement the high school counseling and guidance program curriculum:

Conduct counseling learning activities in the classroom for each grade level during the year in collaboration with the teaching staff; consult with and be a resource to teachers to facilitate the infusion of counseling content into the regular education curriculum.

2. Guide and counsel groups and individual students through the development of educational and career plans:

Collaborate with middle school personnel to assist students in making a smooth transition to high school; provide orientation activities for incoming students and their parents; inform students and parents of test results and their implications for educational and career planning; guide students in updating their High School Four-Year Plans; plan and coordinate the registration of students; guide seniors to help them develop and implement appropriate steps regarding their post-high school educational and/or career plans; coordinate career assessments and interpret results to students to assist in their career and educational planning; guide all students to develop career/educational plans through the teaching and/or supervision of career development activities; provide for the systematic and efficient dissemination of current, accurate information needed by students and/or parents as they develop their educational or career plans; provide individual assistance to students regarding personal, social, educational, and career issues and plans.

3. Consult with small groups and individual students:

Conduct structured, goal-oriented counseling sessions to meet the identified needs of individuals and groups of students.

Slide 4

Initial Analysis

- **Strengths**
  - Support from local school personnel, central office personnel, and community
  - Clear vision of future program
    - Program goals
    - Student outcomes
    - Program model
  - Committed leadership team
  - State mandate for change

FIGURE 12.1   continued

4. Consult and collaborate with teachers, staff, and parents in understanding and meeting the needs of students:

Participate in staffing and team meetings; plan and conduct staff development programs and activities; facilitate conferences with teachers and/or parents and/or students; plan and conduct parent education programs; assist families with school-related problems and issues; write articles for newsletters and other publications.

5. Refer students with problems and their parents to appropriate specialists, special programs, or outside agencies:

Consult and collaborate with school system specialists such as school psychologists, social workers, and nurses; consult with and refer to community-based resources including psychologists, psychiatrists, physicians, service agencies, and others.

6. Participate in activities which contribute to the effective operation of the school:

Cooperate and collaborate with other professionals in enhancing the education of students; establish and maintain effective relationships with instructional departments and administrators; cooperate with other school personnel in placing students with special needs in appropriate pro-grams; interpret group test results to faculty and administration for use in enhancing instruction; communicate with administrators, teachers, staff, students, parents, and the community regarding the counseling and guidance program and its role in the educational program; participate in the implementation of the school system assessment program.

7. Plan, evaluate, and revise the counseling and guidance program:

Review the counseling and guidance program annually with the guidance department staff and guidance program advisory committee; communicate regularly with other counseling staff to establish and maintain a sequential comprehensive counseling and guidance program; identify student needs periodically and use the results for program planning; establish a planning calendar for counseling and guidance program activities; evaluate the counseling and guidance program.

8. Pursue professional growth:

Attend local, state, and national staff development programs; join professional counseling and guidance associations; attend local, state, and national workshops and conferences sponsored by professional organizations; read professional journals; complete postgraduate courses.

Source: Alabama State Department of Education. (1996). *The revised comprehensive counseling and guidance model for Alabama's public schools.* Bulletin 1966, No. 27. Montgomery, AL: Author. Reprinted with permission.

Mr. Coopersmith: "We identified several strengths in our initial discussions with the leadership team. Adequate support from interested publics was a key factor in our success. We made several presentations to school and community groups about the benefits of comprehensive developmental programs for students. Additionally, we knew that we wanted to implement the ASCA standards for school counseling programs and that we would adopt the model already used by the K–8 counselors in our system. Our leadership team membership was composed of school, business, related agencies, medical, legal, and religious community members. These individuals were committed to the change process and pledged to stay with the project throughout the 3 years we imagined the project would take to complete.

Slide 5

Initial Analysis, *continued*

- **Weaknesses**
  - Change is hard
  - Current program model adequately serves a very vocal group of consumers
  - Difficult to commit time to plan for change
  - Outdated job description

In small groups, plan an intervention/activity to use with parents who may be concerned that their children will receive less attention than they have in the past. Be sure to have a goal statement, the intervention, and person responsible for the intervention, when it will occur, and how it will be evaluated. Share your ideas in the large group.

"Even though we actively sought and built support for change, we knew that change would be hard for some people around some issues. We accepted this fact and made sure that we included a related agenda item in every team meeting. For example, Carver High School has historically had a large number of merit scholars and other academically talented youth who apply to very competitive colleges and universities. The counselors have spent a lot of time working with those students, and they and their parents have been pleased with the success rate for matriculation at highly selective schools. We anticipated that they might resist efforts to broaden the focus for college planning to include previously underserved students and to include more school-to-work interventions in our program. Consequently, we thought it would be wise to demonstrate that these students would not now be neglected or their needs subordinated, but that they might be met through interventions other than individual counseling sessions."

Slide 6

Team/Resources

- **We assumed that with a strong leadership team and adequate resources the weaknesses could be overcome.**
  - Team (school and community leaders, parents, and agency representatives)
  - Equipment (computers, presentation hardware and software)
  - Support and outside services (program development consultant; one full day of planning per month in addition to monthly team meetings)

Slide 7

> # Procedures
>
> - **Five-phase planning model:**
>   - Discussion
>   - Awareness
>   - Design
>   - Implementation
>   - Evaluation
>
> FOR MORE INFORMATION:
> Vision into Action: Implementing National
> Standards in School Counseling Programs (1998)

Ms. Biem: "The planning model we adopted was the one articulated in the publication you see here. For those of you unfamiliar with the planning strategy, we highly recommend that you review this one. We were very satisfied with our planning outcomes at each phase and felt that the model was explained well enough to make following it easy for all on the planning team. This was particularly important to us because not all of the members of our leadership team had taken part in such an extensive program revision before.

Slide 8

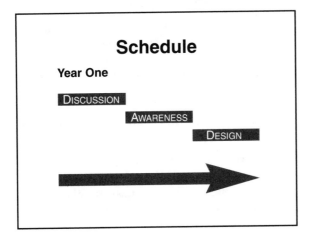

Slide 9

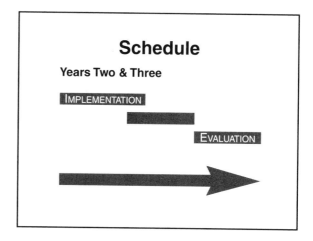

"Because evaluation leads to more planning, design, and implementation, the process we describe is a never-ending one. However, once you have identified what you want students to be able to do (student competencies) and your comprehensive program model, revisions will mostly focus on updating your competencies and replacing activities/interventions that are not successful."

Slide 10

> # Related Documents
>
> - ASCA National Standards
> - State-level student competencies for students in grades 9–12
> - Career development guidelines
> - Regional accreditation report and site visitor recommendations
> - Community and school profile

Ms. Moore: "These are the documents we used to help us in the second stage of planning, increasing our awareness of what needs to be changed. We reviewed available data and identified two areas of change on which we would focus: first, changes necessary for specific students or student groups to help them have a more successful high school career; and, two, changes that need to occur at the program level in order to implement a comprehensive developmental program."

What other organizing themes might be useful conceptualizations of necessary changes?

Slide 11

> ## What needs to change for students?
>
> Female students need to participate in math and science classes at higher rates.
>
> Students of color and students from low socioeconomic families need to participate in academically challenging curriculum at higher rates.
>
> All students need to have an accurate assessment of career interests and abilities as part of career development.

Slide 12

> ## Changes, *continued*
>
> Number of students persisting to graduation needs to increase.
>
> Number of teen pregnancies needs to decrease.
>
> Number of bias-motivated aggressive incidents among students on and off campus needs to decrease.
>
> Students in special needs classes need to participate in extracurricular activities at a higher rate.

Slide 13

What needs to change programmatically?

Program model needs to be more comprehensive and developmental than crisis oriented.

Some tasks historically completed by counseling department need to be redistributed to appropriate others.

Some procedures need to be streamlined, completed with increased efficiency, automated when possible.

Slide 14

Program changes, *continued*

To better serve all students, new programs need to be added, such as teacher-advisor, peer mediators.

School databases (absentee lists, discipline referrals and actions, enrollment patterns in particular courses, grades, achievement test scores) need to be viewed in a disaggregated fashion to get a clear picture of student needs.

Slide 15

Program changes, *continued*

Communication with students, parents, and teachers needs to be more systematic.

High school, career, and college planning resources need to be available in multiple formats (hardcopy, internet accessible)

More small groups need to be offered to address the developmental transitions inherent in middle adolescence.

Slide 16

Selected Student Competencies

Career	Educational	Personal/social
Form a career identity	Apply effective study skills	Gain self-awareness
Plan for the future	Set educational goals	Develop positive attitudes
Combat career stereotypes	Learn effectively	Make healthy choices
Analyze skills and interests	Gain test-taking skills	Gain responsibility
		Resolve conflicts

Ms. Lindsey: "The competencies our leadership team, teachers, students, and parents believed to be most important are listed here.

Slide 17

Program Model

Guidance Curriculum (25%)	Individual Planning (30%)	Responsive Services (30%)	System Support (15%)
Counselors teach and provide necessary information to parents and students	Counselors help students plan for their future	Counselors help students and parents address life issues	Counselors support the school and community and manage programs and their own growth

"This program model proposed by Gysbers and Henderson (2000) is comprehensive and flexible enough to provide us a structure for designing and implementing the program we envision. The design of this program helped us move away from our previous approach of simply identifying and providing services to a much more systematic approach for meeting the needs of all students. Responsibility for the program is shared by all of the professional staff in the school. In your handout, we have included a planning form (see Figure 12.2). This form was used for each student

FIGURE 12.2 Sample Handout No. 2

Program Planning Form
Carver High School Guidance and Counseling Department

National Standard: _____ Academic A B C _____ Career A B C _____ Personal/Social A B C
Competency: Student will apply effective study skills

	Strategies	Person Responsible	Resources	Evidence of Effectiveness
Freshmen	Classroom Guidance: Students will evaluate their study habits and develop a plan for change if needed.	Counselor	Computer lab with Internet access	90% of students will list five or more effective study strategies they plan to use during the current academic year.
Sophomores	Individual Planning: Students will evaluate how effective study skills can contribute to effective work habits in the future.	Teacher advisor	Lesson plan	90% of students will list at least five effective study habits and describe their relationship to effective work habits.
Juniors	Individual Planning: Students will review relationships between time spent on studying and academic success.	Teacher advisor	Lesson plan	90% of students will describe an academic experience in which effort and persistence positively affected learning.
Seniors	Classroom Guidance: Students will recognize that learning is a lifetime process.	Counselor	Lesson plan	90% of students will describe the application of study skills and habits to a nonacademic activity.

competency. The form helped us make sure we were addressing every competency and outcome for each grade level; that we articulated each intervention used to meet the competency; and that we knew who was involved, what resources were required, and when the activity was to be implemented. Each planning form also included the evidence of effectiveness, essential to our ability to demonstrate accountability and intervention/program efficacy."

Slide 18

Successes: Web Page

- **Departmental Information**
  - Counseling staff
  - Mission/vision statement
  - Definition and overview of program scope, sequence, and delivery methods
  - Methods for contacting counselors
  - Forms for requesting credit checks, transcripts, recommendations

---

Ms. Biem: "The Web page helped us with a number of the areas identified for change. We were able to streamline and disseminate information more effectively and update it more easily. The response from both parents and students has been positive."

Slide 19

Web Page

- **Educational Planning**
  - Graduation requirements
  - Annual planning calendars by grade
  - Four-year education plan forms
  - Guidance calendar including all test dates, deadlines, and schoolwide events related to educational planning
  - Links to sources of information on financial aid, college searches, and academic skills development.

Slide 20

Web Page

- **Career Planning**
    - Job shadowing
    - Career portfolio
    - Resumé writing
    - Interest inventories and career search programs
    - Military links
    - Links to career resources

Slide 21

Web Page

- **Focus on Parents**
    - **Tip Sheets**
        - Understanding your adolescent
        - Helping your adolescent be successful in school
        - Homework, study skills, and time management
    - **Links**
        - Educational planning
        - Career planning
        - Adolescent concerns

Mr. Brown: "We used several good resources to assist us in determining what would be on the Web page. First and foremost, we carefully examined parent, student, and teacher input about areas in which they felt underprepared. For example, parents expressed concern that they did not know how to help their children receive financial aid for postsecondary preparation. In response, we added numerous links to the top-rated financial aid Web sites. Students who were not college-bound indicated that they would like to have more help with planning their futures, so we have an expansive career planning section specifically for students who are planning to enter the workforce directly upon high school graduation (Harris-Bowlsbey, Dikel, & Sampson, 1998). In addition, we wanted to include all of the forms that are most frequently requested by students and parents. We found that this measure alone cut down dramatically on the flurry of activity in our office around specific activities such as requesting recommendations for employment or college."

Ms. Moriarty: "We also focused on the development of small groups designed to address some of the more important concerns identified by students, parents, and teachers. As you can see from our list, several are related to adolescent development (body image, planning for the future), whereas others are related to needs individuals may have at any phase of life (grief/loss). We survey students, parents, and teachers each spring to identify our small-group topics for the following academic year.

> Working in small groups, develop a brief needs assessment survey that could be used to identify and prioritize group topics. Share your lists and combine them to make a comprehensive needs assessment instrument.

Slide 22

> ## Small Groups
>
> - **Topics**
>   - Body image
>   - Dating relationships
>   - Family disruption
>   - Grief/loss
>   - College-bound athletes
>   - Academic success strategies
>   - Goal setting and decision making

"Groups are added to the annual calendar (see Figure 12.3) and scheduled in a staggered fashion so that students do not miss the same course more than twice during an academic term."

Slide 23

> ## Teacher Advisor Program
>
> - This program was perhaps the most challenging to develop but has yielded the greatest benefit for students, parents, and teachers in the educational and career planning area.

FIGURE 12.3 Sample Handout No. 3

Annual Calendar for Carver High School

	Guidance Curriculum	Individual Planning	Responsive Services	System Support	Special Events
August	Orientation (all); Future Perfect	Grade-specific teacher advisement; placement and follow-up	Individual counseling; small groups: academic success	Teacher advisor training; peer mediation training; leadership	
September	Careers and Me	Grade-specific teacher advisement; placement and follow-up	Individual counseling; small groups: academic success	Teacher advisor training; peer mediation training; leadership	Deadline for Oct. SAT; Senior Parents Meeting
October	Planning for the Future (goal setting)	College apps; placement and follow-up; teacher advisement	Individual counseling; small groups: goals and decisions	Leadership team; peer mediation coordination; program mgmt.	Register for PSAT; College Fair; ACT & SAT testing dates; Service academy applications due
November	Skills for School (study skills, test-taking skills)	College apps; placement and follow-up; teacher advisor; support teams	Individual counseling; small groups: goals and decisions; athletes	Leadership team; peer mediation coordination; program mgmt.	SAT; deadline for Dec. test dates; school/ community involvement days
December	Skills for School	Teacher advisor; placement and follow-up; support teams	Individual counseling; small groups: dating relationships; athletes	Leadership team; peer mediation coordination; program mgmt.	Financial aid forms available; ACT; deadline for Jan. tests
January	R-E-S-P-E-C-T	Teacher advisor; placement and follow-up; support teams	Individual counseling; small groups: families	Leadership team; peer mediation coordination; program mgmt	Financial Aid Night; Feb. ACT deadline
February	Deconstructing Stereotypes	Teacher advisor; placement and follow-up; support teams	Small groups: body image; individual counseling	Leadership team; peer mediation coordination; program mgmt	ACT; register for March SAT; Career Fair
March	Getting Along	Teacher advisor; placement and follow-up; support teams	Small groups: body image; individual counseling	Leadership team; peer mediation coordination; program mgmt	Register for April ACT and May SAT; SAT; Register for next year's courses
April	Healthy Choices	Teacher advisor; placement and follow-up; support teams	Small groups: grief-loss; individual counseling	Leadership team; peer mediation coordination; program mgmt	Register for June SAT; Junior Parent Night (college admissions panel)
May	Healthy Choices	Teacher advisor; placement and follow-up; support teams	Small groups: grief-loss; individual counseling	Leadership team; peer mediation coordination; program mgmt	Parents Breakfast; AP Testing
June	Transitions	Teacher advisor; placement and follow-up; support teams	Individual counseling	Leadership team; peer mediation coordination; program mgmt	ACT; Visit colleges of interest

Mr. Brown: "Teachers work with the same group of students throughout their high school careers to assist in the development and monitoring of the 4-year life-career plan. They provide information relevant to each grade level through weekly half-hour meetings with their advisees. A significant part of the guidance curriculum is delivered through this program."

Slide 24

Current Challenges

- Training peer mediators and implementing program
- Redistributing routine tasks
- Addressing issues related to sexuality and contraception
- Placing traditionally underserved students in academically challenging courses

---

Divide into four groups and assign one of the challenges to each group. Develop a plan to respond to each situation, and then discuss your plans in the large group. As a class, prioritize the four plans and develop a schedule for implementation.

Ms. Lindsey: "We have identified the four challenges most pressing for us at this time. Our leadership team is currently devising a plan to prioritize and address these four issues."

Slide 25

What's Next?

- Work with leadership team and school community to address current challenges
- Lobby school board for increase in budget and staff based on demonstrated effectiveness of program over last 3 years
- Increase number of volunteer staff to perform some of the system support tasks

---

Ms. Moriarty: "We would now be happy to answer any questions you might have about our project, program, and future plans."

One counselor in the audience states, "I am curious about the way that you evaluate the program. Please discuss your procedures." The purposes of evaluation are twofold in this program. First, to identify each competency and how it is addressed through the guidance program. Second, to assess whether students are meeting the competencies (Gysbers, 1995). The first part of the assessment procedure is easily accomplished by reviewing each planning form and having the person responsible indicate whether the planned activity took place (see Figure 12.2). Continuing to use the planning forms, the person responsible would indicate whether the stated criterion needed to determine success was met. In the most recent evaluation, all competencies were addressed through the program. However, not all competencies were mastered by 90 percent of the students. The counselors are now reviewing and revising the activities that were successful with fewer than 90 percent of the students.

> In small groups, identify additional questions that you would ask these counselors if you were present at the conference. Trade questions with another group in your class and brainstorm responses to all the items on their list. Based on your questions and answers, how would you alter the presentation?

SUMMARY

This chapter has presented an overview of the efforts of the counselors at one school to transform their program from a services-oriented program to a comprehensive developmental program. The emphasis has been on the use of a planning model to identify and implement changes necessary to accomplish the goals of change.

PORTFOLIO COMPONENTS

1. Based on the program described in this chapter, develop a program evaluation instrument that can be used annually by teachers, parents, students, and administrators to provide feedback about the extent to which the identified student competencies have been met and the perceived effectiveness of the four elements of the program for delivery of services.
2. Develop a lesson plan that would be easy for teachers to use to address any one of the student competencies identified by this program as important.
3. Prepare a reflection statement that describes your strengths and weaknesses, both personal and professional as a prospective secondary school counselor.

Appendix A
The Role of the Professional School Counselor

Approved June 1999

The professional school counselor is a certified/licensed educator who addresses the needs of students comprehensively through the implementation of a developmental school counseling program. School counselors are employed in elementary, middle/junior high, senior high, and post-secondary settings. Their work is differentiated by attention to age-specific developmental stages of student growth and the needs, tasks, and student interests related to those stages. School counselors work with all students, including those who are considered "at-risk" and those with special needs. They are specialists in human behavior and relationships who provide assistance to students through four primary interventions: counseling (individual and group); large group guidance; consultation, and coordination.

Counseling is a confidential relationship in which the counselor meets with students individually and in small groups to help them resolve or cope constructively with their problems and developmental concerns.

Large Group Guidance is a planned, developmental program of guidance activities designed to foster students' academic, career, and personal/social development. It is provided for all students through a collaborative effort by counselors and teachers.

Consultation is a collaborative partnership in which the counselor works with parents, teachers, administrators, school psychologists, social workers, visiting teachers, medical professionals, and community health personnel in order to plan and implement strategies to help students be successful in the education system.

Coordination is a leadership process in which the counselor helps organize, manage, and evaluate the school counseling program. The counselor assists parents in obtaining needed services for their children through a referral and follow-up process and serves as liaison between the school and community agencies so that they may collaborate in efforts to help students.

Professional school counselors are responsible for developing comprehensive school counseling programs that promote and enhance student learning. By providing interventions within a comprehensive program, school counselors focus their skills, time, and energies on direct services to students, staff, and families. In the delivery of direct services, the American School Counselor Association (ASCA) recommends that professional school counselors spend at least 70% of their time in direct services to students. ASCA considers a realistic counselor:student ratio for effective program delivery to be a maximum of 1:250.

Above all, school counselors are student advocates who work cooperatively with other individuals and organizations to promote the development of children, youth, and families in their communities. School counselors, as members of the educational team, consult and collaborate with teachers, administrators, and families to assist students to be successful academically, vocationally, and personally. They work on behalf of students and their families to insure that all school programs facilitate the educational process and offer the opportunity for school success for each student. School counselors are an integral part of all school efforts to insure a safe learning environment for all members of the school community.

Professional school counselors meet the state certification/licensure standards and abide by the laws of the states in which they are employed. To assure high quality practice, school counselors are committed to continued professional growth and personal development. They are proactively involved in professional organizations which foster and promote school counseling at the local, state, and national levels. They uphold the ethical and professional standards of these associations and promote the development of the school counseling profession.

Source: American School Counselors Association. (2000). *ASCA 2000–2001 membership directory and resource guide.* Gainesville, FL: Naylor. Reprinted by permission.

Appendix B
National Standards

ASCA's National Standards for School Counseling Programs help school systems identify what students will know and be able to do as a result of participating in a school counseling program; establish similar goals, expectations, support systems and experiences for all students; serve as an organizational tool to identify and prioritize the elements of an effective school counseling program; and provide an opportunity to discuss the role of counseling programs in school to enhance student learning.

The National Standards for School Counseling Programs facilitate student development in three broad areas: academic development, career development and personal/social development. Following are the nine national standards.

Academic Development

STANDARD A
Students will acquire the attitudes, knowledge and skills contributing to effective learning in school and across the life span.

STANDARD B
Students will complete school with the academic preparation essential to choose from a wide range of substantial post-secondary options, including college.

STANDARD C
Students will understand the relationship of academics to the world of work and to life at home and in the community.

Career Development

STANDARD A
Students will acquire the skills to investigate the world of work in relation to knowledge of self and to make informed career decision.

STANDARD B
Students will employ strategies to achieve future career success and satisfaction.

STANDARD C
Students will understand the relationship between personal qualities, education and training and the world of work.

Personal/Social Development

STANDARD A
Students will acquire the attitudes, knowledge and interpersonal skills to help them understand and respect self and others.

STANDARD B
Students will make desicions, set goals and take necessary action to achieve goals.

STANDARD C
Students will understand safety and survival skills.

Source: Retrieved 9/18/01, from the World Wide Web: http://www.schoolcounselor.org/content.cfm. Reprinted by permission of American School Counselor Association.

Appendix C
Ethical Standards for School Counselors

Revised June 25, 1998

Preamble

The American School Counselor Association (ASCA) is a professional organization whose members have a unique and distinctive preparation, grounded in the behavioral sciences, with training in clinical skills adapted to the school setting. The school counselor assists in the growth and development of each individual and uses his or her highly specialized skills to protect the interests of the counselee within the structure of the school system. School counselors subscribe to the following basic tenets of the counseling process from which professional responsibilities are derived:

- Each person has the right to respect and dignity as a human being and to counseling services without prejudice as to person, character, belief, or practice regardless of age, color, disability, ethnic group, gender, race, religion, sexual orientation, marital status, or socioeconomic status.
- Each person has the right to self-direction and self-development.
- Each person has the right of choice and the responsibility for goals reached.
- Each person has the right to privacy and thereby the right to expect the counselor-counselee relationship to comply with all laws, policies, and ethical standards pertaining to confidentiality.

In this document, ASCA specifies the principles of ethical behavior necessary to regulate and maintain the high standards of integrity, leadership, and professionalism among its members. The Ethical Standards for School Counselors were developed to clarify the nature of ethical responsibilities held in common by school counseling professionals. The purposes of this document are to:

- Serve as a guide for the ethical practices of all professional school counselors regardless of level, area, population served, or membership in this professional Association;
- Provide benchmarks for both self-appraisal and peer evaluations regarding counselor responsibilities to counselees, parents, colleagues and professional associates, schools, and communities, as well as to one's self and the counseling profession; and
- Inform those served by the school counselor of acceptable counselor practices and expected professional behavior.

A. Responsibilities to Students

A.1. Student Rights

The professional school counselor:

a. Has a primary obligation to the counselee who is to be treated with respect as a unique individual.
b. Is concerned with the educational, career, emotional, and behavioral needs and encourages the maximum development of each counselee.
c. Refrains from consciously encouraging the counselee's acceptance of values, lifestyles, plans, decisions, and beliefs that represent the counselor's personal orientation.
d. Is responsible for keeping informed of laws, regulations, and policies relating to counselees and strives to ensure that the rights of counselees are adequately provided for and protected.

A.2. Confidentiality

The professional school counselor:

a. Informs the counselee of the purposes, goals, techniques, and rules of procedure under which she/he may receive counseling at or before the time when the counseling relationship is entered. Disclosure notice includes confidentiality issues such as the possible necessity for consulting with other professionals, privileged communication, and legal or authoritative restraints. The meaning and limits of confidentiality are clearly defined to counselees through a written and shared disclosure statement.

b. Keeps information confidential unless disclosure is required to prevent clear and imminent danger to the counselee or others or when legal requirements demand that confidential information be revealed. Counselors will consult with other professionals when in doubt as to the validity of an exception.

c. Discloses information to an identified third party who, by her or his relationship with the counselee, is at a high risk of contracting a disease that is commonly known to be communicable and fatal. Prior to disclosure, the counselor will ascertain that the counselee has not already informed the third party about his or her disease and he/she is not intending to inform the third party in the immediate future.

d. Requests of the court that disclosure not be required when the release of confidential information without a counselee's permission may lead to potential harm to the counselee.

e. Protects the confidentiality of counselee's records and releases personal data only according to prescribed laws and school policies. Student information maintained in computers is treated with the same care as traditional student records.

f. Protects the confidentiality of information received in the counseling relationship as specified by federal and state laws, written policies, and applicable ethical standards. Such information is only to be revealed to others with the informed consent of the counselee, consistent with the counselor's ethical obligation. In a group setting, the counselor sets a high norm of confidentiality and stresses its importance, yet clearly states that confidentiality in group counseling cannot be guaranteed.

A.3. Counseling Plans

The professional school counselor works jointly with the counselee in developing integrated and effective counseling plans, consistent with both the abilities and circumstances of the counselee and counselor. Such plans will be regularly reviewed to ensure continued viability and effectiveness, respecting the counselee's freedom of choice.

A.4. Dual Relationships

The professional school counselor avoids dual relationships which might impair her or his objectivity and increase the risk of harm to the client (e.g., counseling one's family members, close friends, or associates). If a dual relationship is unavoidable, the counselor is responsible for taking action to eliminate or reduce the potential for harm. Such safeguards might include informed consent, consultation, supervision, and documentation.

A.5. Appropriate Referrals

The professional school counselor makes referrals when necessary or appropriate to outside resources. Appropriate referral necessitates knowledge of available resources and making proper plans for transitions with minimal interruption of services. Counselees retain the right to discontinue the counseling relationship at any time.

A.6. Group Work

The professional school counselor screens prospective group members and maintains an awareness of participants' needs and goals in relation to the goals of the group. The counselor takes reasonable precautions to protect members from physical and psychological harm resulting from interaction within the group.

A.7. Danger to Self or Others

The professional school counselor informs appropriate authorities when the counselee's condition indicates a clear and imminent danger to the counselee or others. This is to be done after careful deliberation and, where possible, after consultation with other counseling professionals. The counselor informs the counselee of actions to be taken so as to minimize his or her confusion and to clarify counselee and counselor expectations.

A.8. Student Records

The professional school counselor maintains and secures records necessary for rendering professional services to the counselee as required by laws, regulations, institutional procedures, and confidentiality guidelines.

A.9. Evaluation, Assessment, and Interpretation

The professional school counselor:

a. Adheres to all professional standards regarding selecting, administering, and interpreting assessment measures. The counselor recognizes that computer-based testing programs require specific training in administration, scoring, and interpretation which may differ from that required in more traditional assessments.

b. Provides explanations of the nature, purposes, and results of assessment/evaluation measures in language the counselee(s) can understand.

c. Does not misuse assessment results and interpretations and takes reasonable steps to prevent others from misusing the information.

d. Uses caution when utilizing assessment techniques, making evaluations, and interpreting the performance of populations not represented in the norm group on which an instrument is standardized.

A.10. *Computer Technology*

The professional school counselor:

a. Promotes the benefits of appropriate computer applications and clarifies the limitations of computer technology. The counselor ensures that: (1) computer applications are appropriate for the individual needs of the counselee; (2) the counselee understands how to use the application; and (3) follow-up counseling assistance is provided. Members of underrepresented groups are assured equal access to computer technologies and are assured the absence of discriminatory information and values in computer applications.

b. Counselors who communicate with counselees via internet should follow the NBCC Standards for Web-Counseling.

A.11. *Peer Helper Programs*

The professional school counselor has unique responsibilities when working with peer helper programs. The school counselor is responsible for the welfare of counselees participating in peer programs under her or his direction. School counselors who function in training and supervisory capacities are referred to the preparation and supervision standards of professional counselor associations.

B. Responsibilities to Parents

B.1. *Parent Rights and Responsibilities*

The professional school counselor:

a. Respects the inherent rights and responsibilities of parents for their children and endeavors to establish, as appropriate, a collaborative relationship with parents to facilitate the counselee's maximum development.

b. Adheres to laws and local guidelines when assisting parents experiencing family difficulties that interfere with the counselee's effectiveness and welfare.

c. Is sensitive to cultural and social diversity among families and recognizes that all parents, custodial and non-custodial, are vested with certain rights and responsibilities for the welfare of their children by virtue of their role and according to law.

B.2. *Parents and Confidentiality*

The professional school counselor:

a. Informs parents of the counselor's role with emphasis on the confidential nature of the counseling relationship between the counselor and counselee.

b. Provides parents with accurate, comprehensive, and relevant information in an objective and caring manner, as is appropriate and consistent with ethical responsibilities to the counselee.

c. Makes reasonable efforts to honor the wishes of parents and guardians concerning information that he/she may share regarding the counselee.

C. Responsibilities to Colleagues and Professional Associates

C.1. *Professional Relationships*

The professional school counselor:

a. Establishes and maintains professional relationships with faculty, staff, and administration to facilitate the provision of optimal counseling services. The relationship is based on the counselor's definition and description of the parameter and levels of his or her professional roles.

b. Treats colleagues with professional respect, courtesy, and fairness. The qualifications, views, and findings of colleagues are represented to accurately reflect the image of competent professionals.

c. Is aware of and optimally utilizes related professions and organizations to whom the counselee may be referred.

C.2. *Sharing Information with Other Professionals*

The professional school counselor:

a. Promotes awareness and adherence to appropriate guidelines regarding confidentiality; the distinction between public and private information; and staff consultation.

b. Provides professional personnel with accurate, objective, concise, and meaningful data necessary to adequately evaluate, counsel, and assist the counselee.

c. If a counselee is receiving services from another counselor or other mental health professional, the counselor, with client consent, will inform the other professional and develop clear agreements to avoid confusion and conflict for the counselee.

D. Responsibilities to the School and Community

D.1. Responsibilities to the School

The professional school counselor:

a. Supports and protects the educational program against any infringement not in the best interest of counselees.
b. Informs appropriate officials of conditions that may be potentially disruptive or damaging to the school's mission, personnel, and property while honoring the confidentiality between the counselee and counselor.
c. Delineates and promotes the counselor's role and function in meeting the needs of those served. The counselor will notify appropriate officials of conditions which may limit or curtail her or his effectiveness in providing programs and services.
d. Accepts employment only for positions for which he/she is qualified by education, training, supervised experience, state and national professional credentials, and appropriate professional experience. Counselors recommend that administrators hire only qualified and competent individuals for professional counseling positions.
e. Assists in developing: (1) curricular and environmental conditions appropriate for the school and community; (2) educational procedures and programs to meet the counselee's developmental needs; and (3) a systematic evaluation process for comprehensive school counseling programs, services, and personnel. The counselor is guided by the findings of the evaluation data in planning programs and services.

D.2. Responsibility to the Community

The professional school counselor collaborates with agencies, organizations, and individuals in the school and community in the best interest of counselees and without regard to personal reward or remuneration.

E. Responsibilities to Self

E.1. Professional Competence

The professional school counselor:

a. Functions within the boundaries of individual professional competence and accepts responsibility for the consequences of his or her actions.
b. Monitors personal functioning and effectiveness and does not participate in any activity which may lead to inadequate professional services or harm to a client.
c. Strives through personal initiative to maintain professional competence and to keep abreast of professional information. Professional and personal growth are ongoing throughout the counselor's career.

E.2. Multicultural Skills

The professional school counselor understands the diverse cultural backgrounds of the counselees with whom he/she works. This includes, but is not limited to, learning how the school counselor's own cultural/ethnic/racial identity impacts her or his values and beliefs about the counseling process.

F. Responsibilities to the Profession

F.1. Professionalism

The professional school counselor:

a. Accepts the policies and processes for handling ethical violations as a result of maintaining membership in the American School Counselor Association.
b. Conducts herself/himself in such a manner as to advance individual ethical practice and the profession.
c. Conducts appropriate research and reports findings in a manner consistent with acceptable educational and psychological research practices. When using client data for research or for statistical or program planning purposes, the counselor ensures protection of the individual counselee's identity.
d. Adheres to ethical standards of the profession, other official policy statements pertaining to counseling, and relevant statutes established by federal, state, and local governments.
e. Clearly distinguishes between statements and actions made as a private individual and those made as a representative of the school counseling profession.
f. Does not use his or her professional position to recruit or gain clients, consultees for her or his private practice, seek and receive unjustified personal gains, unfair advantage, sexual favors, or unearned goods or services.

F.2. Contribution to the Profession

The professional school counselor:

a. Actively participates in local, state, and national associations which foster the development and improvement of school counseling.
b. Contributes to the development of the profession through sharing skills, ideas, and expertise with colleagues.

G. Maintenance of Standards

Ethical behavior among professional school counselors, Association members and nonmembers, is expected at all times. When there exists serious doubt as to the ethical behavior of colleagues, or if counselors are forced to work in situations or abide by policies which do not reflect the standards as outlined in these Ethical Standards for School Counselors, the counselor is obligated to take appropriate action to rectify the condition. The following procedure may serve as a guide:

1. The counselor should consult confidentially with a professional colleague to discuss the nature of a complaint to see if she/he views the situation as an ethical violation.
2. When feasible, the counselor should directly approach the colleague whose behavior is in question to discuss the complaint and seek resolution.
3. If resolution is not forthcoming at the personal level, the counselor shall utilize the channels established within the school, school district, the state SCA, and ASCA Ethics Committee.
4. If the matter still remains unresolved, referral for review and appropriate action should be made to the Ethics Committees in the following sequence:
   • state school counselor association
   • American School Counselor Association
5. The ASCA Ethics Committee is responsible for educating—and consulting with—the membership regarding ethical standards. The Committee periodically reviews and recommends changes in code. The Committee will also receive and process questions to clarify the application of such standards. Questions must be submitted in writing to the ASCA Ethics Chair. Finally, the Committee will handle complaints of alleged violations of our ethical standards. Therefore, at the national level, complaints should be submitted in writing to the ASCA Ethics Committee, c/o the Executive Director, American School Counselor Association, 801 North Fairfax, Suite 310, Alexandria, VA 22314.

H. Resources

School counselors are responsible for being aware of, and acting in accord with, standards and positions of the counseling profession as represented in official documents such as those listed below:

American Counseling Association. (1995). *Code of ethics and standards of practice*. Alexandria, VA. (5999 Stevenson Ave., Alexandria, VA 22034) 1 800 347 6647 www.counseling.org.

American School Counselor Association. (1997). *The national standards for school counseling programs*. Alexandria, VA. (801 North Fairfax Street, Suite 310, Alexandria, VA 22314) 1 800 306 4722 www. schoolcounselor.org.

American School Counselor Association. (1998). *Position Statements*. Alexandria, VA.

American School Counselor Association. (1998). *Professional liability insurance program*. (Brochure). Alexandria, VA.

Arrendondo, Toperek, Brown, Jones, Locke, Sanchez, and Stadler. (1996). Multicultural counseling competencies and standards. *Journal of Multicultural Counseling and Development, Vol. 24*, No. 1. See American Counseling Association.

Arthur, G.L. and Swanson, C.D. (1993). *Confidentiality and privileged communication*. (1993). See American Counseling Association.

Association for Specialists in Group Work. (1989). *Ethical Guidelines for group counselors*. (1989). Alexandria, VA. See American Counseling Association.

Corey, G., Corey, M.S. and Callanan. (1998). *Issues and Ethics in the Helping Professions*. Pacific Grove, CA: Brooks/Cole. (Brooks/Cole, 511 Forest Lodge Rd., Pacific Grove, CA 93950) www.thomson.com.

Crawford, R. (1994). *Avoiding counselor malpractice*. Alexandria, VA. See American Counseling Association.

Forrester-Miller, H. and Davis, T.E. (1996). *A practitioner's guide to ethical decision making*. Alexandria, VA. See American Counseling Association.

Herlihy, B. and Corey, G. (1996). *ACA ethical standards casebook*. Fifth ed. Alexandria, VA. See American Counseling Association.

Herlihy, B. and Corey, G. (1992). *Dual relationships in counseling*. Alexandria, VA. See American Counseling Association.

Huey, W.C. and Remley, T.P. (1988). *Ethical and legal issues in school counseling*. Alexandria, VA. See American School Counselor Association.

Joint Committee on Testing Practices. (1988). *Code of fair testing practices in education*. Washington, DC: American Psychological Association. (1200 17th Street, NW, Washington, DC 20036) 202 336 5500

Mitchell, R.W. (1991). *Documentation in counseling records*. Alexandria, VA. See American Counseling Association.

National Board for Certified Counselors. (1998). *National board for certified counselors: code of ethics*. Greensboro, NC. (3 Terrace Way, Suite D, Greensboro, NC 27403-3660) 336 547 0607 www.nbcc.org.

National Board for Certified Counselors. (1997). *Standards for the ethical practice of webcounseling*. Greensboro, NC.

National Peer Helpers Association. (1989). *Code of ethics for peer helping professionals*. Greenville, NC. PO Box

2684, Greenville, NC 27836. 919 522 3959. nphaorg@aol.com.

Salo, M. and Schumate, S. (1993). *Counseling minor clients*. Alexandria, VA. See American School Counselor Association.

Stevens-Smith, P. and Hughes, M. (1993). *Legal issues in marriage and family counseling*. Alexandria, VA. See American School Counselor Association.

Wheeler, N. and Bertram, B. (1994). *Legal aspects of counseling: avoiding lawsuits and legal problems*. (Videotape). Alexandria, VA. See American School Counselor Association.

Note: Ethical Standards for School Counselors was adopted by the ASCA Delegate Assembly, March 19, 1984. The first revision was approved by the ASCA Delegate Assembly, March 27, 1992. The second revision was approved by the ASCA Governing Board on March 30, 1998 and adopted on June 25, 1998. Reprinted by permission of American School Counselor Association.

Appendix D
Competencies in Assessment and Evaluation for School Counselors

Approved by the American School Counselor Association on September 21, 1998, and by the Association for Assessment in Counseling on September 10, 1998.[1]

The purpose of these competencies is to provide a description of the knowledge and skills that school counselors need in the areas of assessment and evaluation. Because effectiveness in assessment and evaluation is critical to effective counseling, these competencies are important for school counselor education and practice. Although consistent with existing Council for Accreditation of Counseling and Related Educational Programs (CACREP) and National Association of State Directors of Teacher Education and Certification (NASDTEC) standards for preparing counselors, they focus on competencies of individual counselors rather than content of counselor education programs.

The competencies can be used by counselor and assessment educators as a guide in the development and evaluation of school counselor preparation programs, workshops, in service, and other continuing education opportunities. They may also be used by school counselors to evaluate their own professional development and continuing education needs.

School counselors should meet each of the nine numbered competencies and have the specific skills listed under each competency.

COMPETENCY 1. SCHOOL COUNSELORS ARE SKILLED IN CHOOSING ASSESSMENT STRATEGIES.

a. They can describe the nature and use of different types of formal and informal assessments, including questionnaires, checklists, interviews, inventories, tests, observations, surveys, and performance assessments, and work with individuals skilled in clinical assessment.
b. They can specify the types of information most readily obtained from different assessment approaches.
c. They are familiar with resources for critically evaluating each type of assessment and can use them in choosing appropriate assessment strategies.
d. They are able to advise and assist others (e.g., a school district) in choosing appropriate assessment strategies.

COMPETENCY 2. SCHOOL COUNSELORS CAN IDENTIFY, ACCESS, AND EVALUATE THE MOST COMMONLY USED ASSESSMENT INSTRUMENTS.

a. They know which assessment instruments are most commonly used in school settings to assess intelligence, aptitude, achievement, personality, work values, and interests, including computer-assisted versions and other alternate formats.
b. They know the dimensions along which assessment instruments should be evaluated, including purpose, validity, utility, norms, reliability and measurement error, score reporting method, and consequences of use.
c. They can obtain and evaluate information about the quality of those assessment instruments.

COMPETENCY 3. SCHOOL COUNSELORS ARE SKILLED IN THE TECHNIQUES OF ADMINISTRATION AND METHODS OF SCORING ASSESSMENT INSTRUMENTS.

a. They can implement appropriate administration procedures, including administration using computers.
b. They can standardize administration of assessments when interpretation is in relation to external norms.
c. They can modify administration of assessments to accommodate individual differences consistent with

publisher recommendations and current statements of professional practice.

d. They can provide consultation, information, and training to others who assist with administration and scoring.

e. They know when it is necessary to obtain informed consent from parents or guardians before administering an assessment.

COMPETENCY 4. SCHOOL COUNSELORS ARE SKILLED IN INTERPRETING AND REPORTING ASSESSMENT RESULTS.

a. They can explain scores that are commonly reported, such as percentile ranks, standard scores, and grade equivalents. They can interpret a confidence interval for an individual score based on a standard error of measurement.

b. They can evaluate the appropriateness of a norm group when interpreting the scores of an individual or a group.

c. They are skilled in communicating assessment information to others, including teachers, administrators, students, parents, and the community. They are aware of the rights students and parents have to know assessment results and decisions made as a consequence of any assessment.

d. They can evaluate their own strengths and limitations in the use of assessment instruments and in assessing students with disabilities or linguistic or cultural differences. They know how to identify professionals with appropriate training and experience for consultation.

e. They know the legal and ethical principles about confidentiality and disclosure of assessment information and recognize the need to abide by district policy on retention and use of assessment information.

COMPETENCY 5. SCHOOL COUNSELORS ARE SKILLED IN USING ASSESSMENT RESULTS IN DECISION-MAKING.

a. They recognize the limitations of using a single score in making an educational decision and know how to obtain multiple sources of information to improve such decisions.

b. They can evaluate their own expertise for making decisions based on assessment results. They also can evaluate the limitations of conclusions provided by others, including the reliability and validity of computer-assisted assessment interpretations.

c. They can evaluate whether the available evidence is adequate to support the intended use of an assessment result for decision-making, particularly when that use has not been recommended by the developer of the assessment instrument.

d. They can evaluate the rationale underlying the use of qualifying scores for placement in educational programs or courses of study.

e. They can evaluate the consequences of assessment-related decisions and avoid actions that would have unintended negative consequences.

COMPETENCY 6. SCHOOL COUNSELORS ARE SKILLED IN PRODUCING, INTERPRETING, AND PRESENTING STATISTICAL INFORMATION ABOUT ASSESSMENT RESULTS.

a. They can describe data (e.g., test scores, grades, demographic information) by forming frequency distributions, preparing tables, drawing graphs, and calculating descriptive indices of central tendency, variability, and relationship.

b. They can compare a score from an assessment instrument with an existing distribution, describe the placement of a score within a normal distribution, and draw appropriate inferences.

c. They can interpret statistics used to describe characteristics of assessment instruments, including difficulty and discrimination indices, reliability and validity coefficients, and standard errors of measurement.

d. They can identify and interpret inferential statistics when comparing groups, making predictions, and drawing conclusions needed for educational planning and decisions.

e. They can use computers for data management, statistical analysis, and production of tables and graphs for reporting and interpreting results.

COMPETENCY 7. SCHOOL COUNSELORS ARE SKILLED IN CONDUCTING AND INTERPRETING EVALUATIONS OF SCHOOL COUNSELING PROGRAMS AND COUNSELING-RELATED INTERVENTIONS.

a. They understand and appreciate the role that evaluation plays in the program development process throughout the life of a program.

b. They can describe the purposes of an evaluation and the types of decisions to be based on evaluation information.

c. They can evaluate the degree to which information can justify conclusions and decisions about a program.

d. They can evaluate the extent to which student outcome measures match program goals.

e. They can identify and evaluate possibilities for unintended outcomes and possible impacts of one program on other programs.

f. They can recognize potential conflicts of interest and other factors that may bias the results of evaluations.

COMPETENCY 8. SCHOOL COUNSELORS ARE SKILLED IN ADAPTING AND USING QUESTIONNAIRES, SURVEYS, AND OTHER ASSESSMENTS TO MEET LOCAL NEEDS.

a. They can write specifications and questions for local assessments.
b. They can assemble an assessment into a usable format and provide directions for its use.
c. They can design and implement scoring processes and procedures for information feedback.

COMPETENCY 9. SCHOOL COUNSELORS KNOW HOW TO ENGAGE IN PROFESSIONALLY RESPONSIBLE ASSESSMENT AND EVALUATION PRACTICES.

a. They understand how to act in accordance with ACA's *Code of Ethics and Standards of Practice* and ASCA's *Ethical Standards for School Counselors*.
b. They can use professional codes and standards, including the *Code of Fair Testing Practices in Education, Code of Professional Responsibilities in Educational Measurement, Responsibilities of Users of Standardized Tests*, and *Standards for Educational and Psychological Testing*, to evaluate counseling practices using assessments.
c. They understand test fairness and can avoid the selection of biased assessment instruments and biased uses of assessment instruments. They can evaluate the potential for unfairness when tests are used incorrectly and for possible bias in the interpretation of assessment results.
d. They understand the legal and ethical principles and practices regarding test security, copying copyrighted materials, and unsupervised use of assessment instruments that are not intended for self-administration.
e. They can obtain and maintain available credentialing that demonstrates their skills in assessment and evaluation.
f. They know how to identify and participate in educational and training opportunities to maintain competence and acquire new skills in assessment and evaluation.

Definitions of Terms

Competencies describe skills or understandings that a school counselor should possess to perform assessment and evaluation activities effectively.

Assessment is the gathering of information for decision making about individuals, groups, programs, or processes. Assessment targets include abilities, achievements, personality variables, aptitudes, attitudes, preferences, interests, values, demographics, and other characteristics. Assessment procedures include but are not limited to standardized and unstandardized tests, questionnaires, inventories, checklists, observations, portfolios, performance assessments, rating scales, surveys, interviews, and other clinical measures.

Evaluation is the collection and interpretation of information to make judgments about individuals, programs, or processes that lead to decisions and future actions.

Note: (1) A joint committee of the American School Counselor Association (ASCA) and the Association for Assessment in Counseling (AAC) was appointed by the respective presidents in 1993 with the charge to draft a statement about school counselor preparation in assessment and evaluation. Committee members were Ruth Ekstrom (AAC), Patricia Elmore (AAC, Chair, 1997–1998), Daren Hutchinson (ASCA), Marjorie Mastie (AAC), Kathy O'Rourke (ASCA), William Schafer (AAC, Chair, 1993–1997), Thomas Trotter (ASCA), and Barbara Webster (ASCA).

Source: Retrieved 5/3/01, from the World Wide Web: http://acc.ncat.edu/ Copyright 2001, Association for Assessment in Counseling. Reprinted by permission.

References

Abramson, J., & Rosenthal, B. (1995). Interdisciplinary and interorganizational collaboration. In R. Edwards (Ed.), *The encyclopedia of social work* (19th ed., pp. 1479–1480). Washington, DC: NASW Press.

Adelman, H., & Taylor, L. (1998). *Restructuring boards of education to enhance schools' effectiveness in addressing barriers to student learning.* Los Angeles, CA: Center for Mental Health in Schools, University of California at Los Angeles.

Alabama State Department of Education. (1996). *The revised comprehensive counseling and guidance model for Alabama's public schools.* Bulletin 1966, No. 27. Montgomery, AL: Author.

American Association of University Women (AAUW). (1992). *How schools shortchange girls: A study of major findings on girls and education.* Washington, DC: Author.

American Counseling Association. (1999). Ethical standards for Internet on-line counseling. Retrieved 9/18/01 from the World Wide Web: http://www.counseling.org

American Counseling Association. (1993). *Counseling minor clients.* Alexandria, VA: Author.

American Counseling Association. (2000). The truth about school counseling. *Advocacy Kit: School counseling legislation*, p. 5. Alexandria, VA: Author.

American School Counselor Association. (1999a). *1999–2000 Membership directory and resource guide.* Gainesville, FL: Naylor.

American School Counselor Association. (1999b). *Doing the right thing: Ethics and the professional school counselor.* Alexandria, VA: Author.

American School Counselor Association. (1999c). The role of the professional school counselor. Retrieved 5/23/02, from the World Wide Web: http://www.schoolcounselor.org

American School Counselor Association. (2000). *ASCA 2000–2001 membership directory and resource guide.* Gainesville, FL: Naylor.

Anderson, R. S., & Reiter, D. (1995). The indispensable counselor. *The School Counselor, 42*, 268–276.

Annie E. Casey Foundation. (2000). *Kids count data book: State profiles of child well-being.* Baltimore, MD: Author.

Apple, M. W. (1980). Analyzing determinations: Understanding and evaluating production of social outcomes in schools. *Curriculum Inquiry, 11*, 3–42.

Apple, M. W. (1988). *Teachers and texts.* New York: Routledge.

Artiles, A. J., & Trent, S. C. (1994). Overrepresentation of minority students in special education: A continuing debate. *Journal of Special Education, 27*, 410–437.

Association for Assessment in Counseling. (1998). Competencies in assessment and evaluation for school counselors. Retrieved 9/18/01, from the World Wide Web: http://aac.ncat.edu/documents/atsc_cmptncy.htm

Au, K. (1980). Participation structures in a reading lesson with Hawaiian children. *Anthropology and Education Quarterly, 11*, 91–115.

Aubrey, R. F. (1982). A house divided: Guidance and counseling in 20th century America. *Personnel and Guidance Journal, 61*, 198–204.

Baird, B. N. (2002). *The internship, practicum, and field placement handbook: A guide for the helping professions* (3rd ed.). Upper Saddle River, NJ: Prentice Hall.

Baker, S. B. (2000). *School counseling for the twenty-first century* (3rd ed.). Upper Saddle River, NJ: Merrill.

Ballantine, J. H. (1997). *The sociology of education: A systematic analysis* (4th ed.). Upper Saddle River, NJ: Prentice Hall.

Banks, J. A. (2000). The social construction of difference and the quest for educational equality. In R. S. Brandt (Ed.), *Education in a new era* (pp. 21–46). Alexandria, VA: Association for Supervision and Curriculum Development.

Basham, A., Appleton, V. E., & Dykeman, C. (2000). *Team building in education: A how-to guidebook.* Denver, CO: Love Publishing.

Basham, A., Appleton, V., & Lambarth, C. (1998). The school counselor's role in organizational team building. In C. Dykeman (Ed.), *Maximizing school guidance program effectiveness: A guide for school administrators and program directors* (pp. 51–58). Greensboro, NC: ERIC/CASS Publications.

Bemak, F. (2000). Transforming the role of the counselor to provide leadership in educational reform through collaboration. *Professional School Counseling, 3*(5), 323–331.

Bennis, W. (1995). The artform of leadership. In J. T. Wren (Ed.), *The leader's companion: Insights on leadership through the ages* (pp. 377–378). New York: Free Press.

Benson, P. L., Galbraith, J., & Espeland, P. (1998). *What kids need to succeed.* Minneapolis, MN: Free Spirit Press.

Bergmann, S. (1991). Guidance on the middle school level: The compassion component. In J. Capelluti & D. Stokes (Eds.), *Middle level education: Policies, practices and programs* (pp. 30–35). Reston, VA: NSSA.

Blanchard, K., & Johnson, S. (1983). *The one-minute manager.* New York: Berkley Books.

Bloom, B. S., Engelhart, M. D., Frost, E., Hill, W. H., & Krathwohl, D. R. (1956). *Taxonomy of educational objectives. Handbook 1: Cognitive domain.* New York: David McKay.

Blum, D. J. (1998). *The school counselors book of lists.* West Nyack, NY: Center for Applied Research in Education.

Borders, L. D., & Drury, S. M. (1992). Comprehensive school counseling programs: A review for policymakers and practitioners. *Journal of Counseling and Development, 70* (4), 487–498.

Bowers, C. A. (1984). *The promise of theory: Education and the politics of cultural change.* New York: Longman.

Bracey, G. W. (2000). The 10th Bracey report on the condition of public education. *Phi Delta Kappan, 82*(2), 133–144.

Brookfield, S.D. (1990). *The skillful teacher.* San Francisco: Jossey-Bass.

Brooks-Gunn, J., Klebanov, P., Liaw, R., & Duncan, G. (1995). Toward an understanding of the effects of poverty on children. In H. Fitzgerald, B. Lester, & B. Zuckerman, (Eds.), *Children of poverty: Research, health and policy issues* (pp. 3–36). New York: Garland.

Brown, D., Pryzwansky, W. B., & Schulte, A. C. (1998). *Psychological consultation: Introduction to theory and practice* (4th ed.). Boston: Allyn and Bacon.

Brown, D., & Srebalus, D. J. (1988). *An introduction to the counseling profession.* Upper Saddle River, NJ: Prentice Hall.

Brusselmans-Dehairs, C., Hencry, G. F., Beller, M., & Gafni, N. (1997). *Gender differences in learning achievement: Evidence from cross-national surveys.* Paris, France: UNESCO.

Bulach, C., & Lunenberg, F. C. (1995). The influence of the principal's leadership style on school climate and student achievement. *People & Education, 3,* 333–351.

Campbell, C. (2000). K-12 peer helper programs. In J. Wittmer (Ed.), *Managing your school counseling program: K-12 developmental strategies.* Minneapolis, MN: Educational Media.

Campbell, C., & Bowman, R. (1993). The "Fresh Start" support club: Small-group counseling for academically retained children. *Elementary School Guidance and Counseling, 27,* 172–185.

Campbell, C., & Myrick, R. (1990). Motivational group counseling for low-performing students. *Journal for Specialists in Group Work, 15,* 43–50.

Campbell, C. A., & Dahir, C. A. (1997). *Sharing the vision: National standards for school counseling programs.* Alexandria, VA: American School Counselor Association.

Caplan, G. C. (1970). *The theory and practice of mental health consultation.* New York: Basic Books.

Cecil, J. H., & Cobia, D. C. (1990). Educational challenge and change. In H. Hackney (Ed.), *Changing contexts for counselor preparation in the 1990s* (pp. 21–36). Alexandria: VA, Association for Counselor Education and Supervision.

Clark, M. A., & Stone, C. (2000). Evolving our image: School counselors as educational leaders. *Counseling Today, 21–46.*

Coleman, J. S., Campbell, E. Q., Hobson, C. J., McPartland, J., Mood, A. M., Weinfeld, F. D., & York, R. L. (1966). *Equality of educational opportunity.* Washington, DC: U.S. Government Printing Office.

Conger, R. D., Conger, K. J., & Elder, G. (1997). Family economic hardship and adolescent academic performance: Mediating and moderating processes. In G. Duncan & J. Brooks-Gunn (Eds.), *Consequences of growing up poor* (pp. 288–310). New York: Russell Sage Foundation.

Conroy, E., & Meyer, S. (1994). Strategies for consulting with parents. *Elementary School Guidance & Counseling, 29,* 60–67.

Corey, G., Corey, M. S., & Callanan, P. (1993). *Issues and ethics in the helping professions* (4th ed.). Pacific Grove: Brooks/Cole.

Cotton, K. (n.d.) *Research you can use to improve results.* Alexandria, VA: Association for Supervision and Curriculum Development.

D'Andrea, M., & Daniels, J. (1999). Youth advocacy. Retrieved 10/10/1999, from the World Wide Web: http://www.counseling.org/conference/advocacy5.htm

Dahir, C. A., Sheldon, C. B., & Valiga, M. J. (1998). *Vision into action: Implementing the national standards for school counseling programs*. Alexandria, VA: American School Counselor Association.

DeBlois, R. (2000). The everyday work of leadership. *Phi Delta Kappan, 82*, 25–27.

Dettmer, P. A., Dyck, N. T., & Thurston, L. P. (1996). *Consultation, collaboration, and teamwork for students with special needs* (2nd ed.). Boston: Allyn and Bacon.

Dinkmeyer, D., Pew, W., & Dinkmeyer, D., Jr. (1979). *Adlerian counseling and psychotherapy*. Monterey, CA: Brooks/Cole.

Dispelling the myth: High poverty schools exceeding expectations. (1999). Washington, DC: The Education Trust.

Dougherty, A. M. (2000). *Psychological consultation and collaboration in school and community settings* (3rd ed.). Pacific Grove, CA: Brooks/Cole.

Drug Abuse Office and Treatment Act. (1976). 42 U.S.C. 290§ 3 & 42 C.F.R. Part 2.

Drummond, R. J. & Ryan, C. W. (1995). *Career counseling: A developmental approach*. Englewood Cliffs, NJ: Merrill.

Education Trust (n.d.). *Education watch: Education Trust community data guide*. Washington, DC: Author.

Ehly, S., & Dustin, R. (1989). *Individual and group counseling in schools*. New York: Guilford Press.

Ellis, A. (1996). *Better, deeper, and more enduring brief therapy*. New York: Brunner/Mazel.

ERIC/CAPPS. (1990). *Building comprehensive school counseling programs*. Greensboro, NC: Author.

Erikson, E. (1980). *Identity and the life cycle* (2nd ed.). New York: Norton.

Esposito, C. (1999). Learning in urban blight: School climate and its effect on the school performance of urban, minority, low-income children. *School Psychology Review, 28*, 365–378.

Evans, H. H., & Burck, H. D. (1992). The effects of career education interventions on academic achievement. A meta-analysis. *Journal of Counseling and Development, 71*, 63–68.

Fairchild, T. N. (1997). School-based helpers' role in crisis intervention. In T. Fairchild (Ed.), *Crisis intervention strategies for school-based helpers* (2nd ed.). Springfield, IL: Charles C. Thomas.

Fall, M. (1994). Developing curriculum expertise: A helpful tool for school counselors. *The School Counselor, 42*, 92–99.

Family Educational Rights and Privacy Act. (1974). 20 U.S.C.A. §1232g. [Buckley Amendment.] (1991).

Implementing regulations 34 C.F.R. 99.3. Fed. Reg. 56, §117, 28012.

Federal Interagency Forum on Child and Family Statistics. (1999). *America's Children: Key National Indicators of Well-Being, 1999*. Retrieved 4/10/01, from the World Wide Web: http://childstats.gov/ac1999/toc.asp

Fischer, L., & Sorenson, G. P. (1996). *School law for counselors, psychologists, and social workers* (3rd ed.). White Plains, NY: Longman.

Fisher, C. B., & Hennessy, J. (1994). Ethical issues. In J. L. Ronch, W. Van Ornum, & N. C. Stilwel (Eds.), *The counseling sourcebook: A practical reference on contemporary issues* (pp. 175–185). New York: Crossroad.

Freiberg, H. J. (1998). Measuring school climate: Let me count the ways. *Educational Leadership, 56*, 22–27.

Friend, M., & Cook, L. (1992). *Interactions: Collaboration skills for school professionals*. White Plains, NY: Longman.

Friend, M., & Cook, L. (2000). *Interactions: Collaboration skills for school professionals*. (3rd ed.). New York: Longman.

Gallessich, J. (1982). *The profession and practice of consultation*. San Francisco: Jossey-Bass.

Garrett, M., & Crutchfield, L. (1997). Moving full circle: A unity model of group work with children. *Journal for Specialists in Group Work, 22*, 715–188.

Gerler, E. R., Kinney, J., & Anderson, R. F. (1985). The effects of counseling on classroom performance. *The Journal of Humanistic Education and Development, 23*, 155–165.

Gibson, R. L., & Mitchell, M. H. (1995). *Introduction to counseling and guidance* (4th ed.). Englewood Cliffs, NJ: Prentice Hall.

Gladding, S. T. (1996). *Counseling: A comprehensive profession* (3rd ed.). Upper Saddle River, NJ: Merrill.

Gladding, S. T. (1999). *Group work: A counseling specialty* (3rd ed.). Upper Saddle River, NJ: Merrill.

Glasser, W. (1998). *Choice theory: A new psychology of personal freedom*. New York: Harper Collins.

Glenn, E. E. (Ed.). (1998). Counseling children and adolescents with disabilities. [Special issue]. *Professional School Counseling, 2*.

Goldberg, M. (2000). *Town Meeting—the National Alliance of Business and School Counselors*. Speech presented at Symposium on the Role of School Counseling in Preparing Students for the 21st Century. Washington, DC.

Gonzalez, G. M., & Myrick, R. D. (2000). The teacher as student advisors program (TAP): An effective approach for drug education and other developmental guidance activities. In J. Wittmer (Ed.), *Managing your school counseling program: K-12 developmental strategies* (2nd ed.; pp. 243–252). Minneapolis, MN: Educational Media Corporation.

Gottfredson, G. D. (1988). An evaluation of an organizational development approach to reducing school disorder. *Evaluation Review, 11*, 739–763.

Gottfredson, L. S. (1996). Gottfredson's theory of circumspection and compromise. In D. Brown, L. Brooks, & Associates (Eds.), *Career choice and development* (3rd ed.; pp. 179–228). San Francisco: Jossey-Bass.

Graham, P. A. (1993). What America has expected of its schools for the past century. *American Journal of Education, 101*, 83–98.

Grassley Amendment. (1994). Sec. 1017 of GOALS 2000: The Educate America Act under the heading "Protection of Pupils." 20 U.S.C. §1232h.

Greenberg, J. M., & Shaffer, S. (1991). *Elements of equity: Criteria for equitable schools.* Mid-Atlantic Equity Consortium. Retrieved 10/18/01, from the World Wide Web: http://www.maec.org

Gronlund, N. E. (1995). *How to write and use instructional objectives* (5th ed.). Englewood Cliffs, NJ: Merrill.

Gunter, M. A., Estes, T. H., & Schwab, J. (1995). *Instruction: A models approach* (2nd ed.). Boston: Allyn and Bacon

Gysbers, N. S. (1995). Evaluating school guidance programs. *ERIC Digest* (On-line). Retrieved 11/15/01, from the World Wide Web: http://www.ed.gov/databases/ERIC_Digests/ed388887.html

Gysbers, N. C., & Henderson, P. (2000). *Developing & managing your school guidance program* (3rd ed.). Alexandria, VA: American Counseling Association.

Gysbers, N. C., Lapan, R. T., & Jones, B. A. (2000). School board policies for guidance and counseling: A call to action. *Professional School Counseling, 3*, 349–355.

Harris-Bowlsbey, J., Dikel, M. R., & Sampson, J. P. (1998). *The Internet: A tool for career planning.* Columbus, OH: National Career Development Association.

Haycock, K. (2000). *Defining the needs—Academic achievement in America.* Speech presented at Symposium on the Role of School Counseling in Preparing Students for the 21st Century. Washington, DC.

Heath, S. V. (1983). *Ways with words: Language, life, and work in communities and classrooms.* New York: Cambridge University Press.

Henderson, D. A., & Fall, M. (1998). School counseling. In R. R. Cottone & V. M. Tarvydas (Eds.), *Ethical and professional issues in counseling* (pp. 263–293). Upper Saddle River, NJ: Merrill.

Henderson, P. (1996). Providing leadership for school counselors to achieve an effective guidance program. *NASSP Bulletin, 83*, 77–83.

Henderson, P., & Gysbers, N.C. (1998). *Leading & managing your school guidance program staff: A manual for school administrators and directors of guidance.* Alexandria, VA: American Counseling Association.

Herbert, D. (1986). Career guidance, families and school counselors. Retrieved 8/15/01, from the World Wide Web: http://www.ed.gov/databases/ERIC_Digests/ed279991.html

Herring, R. D. (1997). *Multicultural counseling in schools: A synergetic approach.* Alexandria, VA: American Counseling Association.

Hibert, K. M. (2000). Mentoring leadership. *Phi Delta Kappan, 82*(1), 16–18.

Ho, B. S. (2001). Family-centered, integrated services: Opportunities for school counselors. *Professional School Counseling 4*(5), 357–361.

Hollins, E. R. (1999). Relating ethnic and racial identity development to teaching. In R. H. Sheets & E. R. Hollins (Eds.), *Racial and ethnic identity in school practices: Aspects of human development* (pp. 183–193). Mahwah, NJ: Lawrence Erlbaum.

Holmgren, S. V. (1996). *Elementary school counseling: An expanding role.* Boston: Allyn & Bacon.

House, R. M., & Martin, P. J. (1998). Advocating for better futures for all students: A new vision for school counselors. *Education, 119*, 284–291.

Hughes, R. L., Ginnett, R. C., & Curphy, G. R. (1995). What is leadership? In J. T. Wren (Ed.). *The leader's companion: Insights on leadership through the ages.* New York: Free Press.

Individuals with Disabilities Education Act of 1997. (1997). Publ. L. No. 105-17, 34 CFR 300.574.

Isaacs, M. L. (1997). The duty to warn and protect: Tarasoff and the elementary school counselor. *Elementary School Guidance and Counseling, 31*, 326–342.

Isaacs, M. L., & Stone, C. (1999). School counselors and confidentiality: Factors affecting professional choices. *Professional School Counseling, 2*, 258–266.

Jackson, D. S. (2000). The school improvement journey: Perspectives on leadership. *School Leadership & Management, 20*(1), 61–79.

Jencks, C., Bartlett, S., Corcoran, M., Crouse, J., Eaglesfield, D., Jackson, G., McClelland, K., Mueser, P., Olneck, M., Schwartz, J., Ward, S., & Williams, J. (1979). *Who gets ahead? The determinants of economic success in America.* New York: Basic Books.

Johnson, D. W., & Johnson, F. P. (1997). *Joining together: Group theory and group skills* (6th ed.). Needham Heights, MA: Allyn & Bacon.

Johnson, D. W., & Johnson, R. T. (1999). *Learning together and alone: Cooperative, competitive, and individualistic learning*. Boston: Allyn & Bacon.

Johnson, L. S. (2000). Promoting professional identity in an era of educational reform. *Professional School Counseling, 4*(1), 31–40.

Johnson, R. S. (1996). *Setting our sights: Measuring equity in school change*. Los Angeles: The Achievement Council.

Junhke, G. A. (1997). After school violence: An adapted critical incident stress debriefing model for student survivors and their parents. *Elementary School Guidance & Counseling, 31*, 163–171.

Kahn, B. B. (2000). A model of solution-focused consultation for school counselors. *Professional School Counseling, 3*, 248–255.

Kameen, M. C., Robinson, E. H., & Rotter, J. C. (1985). Coordination activities: A study of perceptions of elementary and middle school counselors. *Elementary School Guidance & Counseling, 20*, 97–104.

Kaplan, L. S., & Geoffroy, K. E. (1990). Enhancing the school climate: New opportunities for the counselor. *School Counselor, 38*, 7–13.

Katzenbach, J., Beckett, F., Dichter, S., Feigen, M., Gagnon, C., Hope, Q., & Ling, T. (1995). *Real change leaders*. New York: Random House.

Keys, S. G., Bemak, F., & Lockhart, E. J. (1998). Transforming school counseling to serve the mental health needs of at-risk youth. *Journal of Counseling and Development, 76*, 381–388.

Kormanski, C. L., & Mozenter, A. (1987). A new model of team building: A technology for today and tomorrow. In J. W. Pfeiffer (Ed.). *The 1987 annual: Developing human resources* (pp. 255–268). San Diego, CA: University Associates.

Kormanski, C. (1999). *The team: Explorations in group process*. Denver, CO: Love Publishing.

Kottman, T., Ashby, J., & DeGraaf, D. (2001). *Adventures in guidance: How to put fun into your guidance program*. Alexandria, VA: American Counseling Association.

Krathwohl, D. R., Bloom, B. S., & Masia, B. B. (1964). *Taxonomy of educational objectives. Handbook II: Affective domain*. New York: David McKay.

Kretzmann, J., & McKnight, J. (1993). *Building communities from the inside out: A path toward finding and mobilizing a community's assets*. Chicago: ACTA Publications.

Kurpius, D. J., & Fuqua, D. R. (1993). Fundamental issues in defining consultation. *Journal of Counseling and Development, 71*, 598–600.

Kurpius, D. J., & Rozecki, T. (1992). Outreach, advocacy, and consultation: A framework for prevention and intervention. *Elementary School Guidance and Counseling, 26*, 176–190.

Ladson-Billings, G. (1994). *The dreamkeepers: Successful teachers of African American children*. San Francisco: Jossey-Bass.

Lambert, L. (1998). *Building leadership capacity in schools*. Alexandria, VA: Association for Supervision and Curriculum Development.

Lapan, R. T., Gysbers, N. C., & Sun, Y. (1997). The impact of more fully implemented guidance programs on the school experiences of high school students: A statewide evaluation study. *Journal of Counseling & Development, 75*, 292–302.

Lee, C. E. (1993). *Signifying as a scaffold for literary interpretation: The pedagogical implications of an African American discourse*. Urbana, IL: National Council of Teachers of English.

Lewis, J., Lewis, M., Packard, T., Souflee, F. (2001). *Management of human service programs*. Belmont, CA: Wadsworth/Thomson.

Lippitt, G., & Lippitt, R. (1986). *The consulting process in action* (2nd ed.). La Jolla, CA: University Associates.

Locke, D. C. (1993). *Multicultural counseling*. Ann Arbor, MI: Clearinghouse on Counseling and Personnel Services. (ERIC Document No. EDO-CG-93-1).

Lockhart, E. J., & Keys, S. G. (1998). The mental health counseling role of school counselors. *Professional School Counseling, 1*, 3–6.

Luongo, P. E. (2000). Partnering child welfare, juvenile justice, and behavioral health with schools. *Professional School Counseling, 3*(5), 308–314.

Lusky, M. B. & Hayes, R. L. (2001). Collaborative consultation and program evaluation. *Journal of Counseling and Development, 79*(1), 26–38.

Lutzker, J. R., & Martin, J. A. (1981). *Behavior change*. Pacific Grove, CA: Brooks/Cole.

Mager, R. (1975). *Preparing instructional objectives* (2nd ed.). Palo Alto, CA: Fearon.

Magnuson, S. (1997). Guidance portfolios: Documenting components of children's personal and career development. *The School Counselor, 44*, 309–311.

Masten, A. S., & Coatsworth, J. D. (1998). The development of competence in favorable and unfavorable environments: Lessons from research on successful children. *American Psychologist, 53*, 205–220.

McCaslin, M., & Good, T. L. (1996). The informal curriculum. In D. C. Berliner & R. C. Calfee (Eds.) *Handbook of Educational Psychology* (pp. 622–670). New York: Simon & Schuster.

McDaniels, C. (1982). Comprehensive career information systems for the 1980s. *Vocational Guidance Quarterly, 30,* 344–350.

McFarland, L. J., Senn, L. E., & Childress, J. R. (1995). Redefining leadership for the next century. In J. T. Wren (Ed.), *The leader's companion: Insights on leadership through the ages* (pp. 456–463). New York: Free Press.

McWhirter, J. J., McWhirter, B. T., McWhirter, A. M., & McWhirter, E. H. (1998). *At-risk youth: A comprehensive response.* Pacific Grove, CA: Brooks-Cole.

Metcalf, L. (1995). Counseling toward solutions: A practical solution-focused program for working with students, teachers, and parents. West Nyack, NJ: Center for Applied Research in Education.

Meyers, J., Brent, D., Faherty, E., & Modafferi, C. (1993). Caplan's contributions to the practice of psychology in schools. In W. P. Erchul (Ed.). *Consultation in community, school, and organizational practice: Gerald Caplan's contribution in professional psychology* (pp. 99–122). Washington, DC: Taylor & Francis.

Mortenson, T. (2000a). *Defining the needs—Higher education policy.* Speech presented at Symposium on the Role of School Counseling in Preparing Students for the 21st Century. Washington, DC.

Mortenson, T. (2000b). Postsecondary education opportunity. *The Mortenson research seminar on public policy analysis of opportunity for postsecondary education, 92,* p. 11. Iowa City, Iowa: Author.

Muro, J. J., & Kottman, T. (1995). *Guidance and counseling in the elementary and middle schools: A practical approach.* Dubuque: Benchmark & Brown.

Myrick, R. D. (1987). *Developmental guidance and counseling: A practical approach.* Minneapolis: Educational Media.

Myrick, R. D. (1993). *Developmental guidance and counseling: A practical approach* (2nd ed.). Minneapolis: Educational Media.

Myrick, R. D. (1997). *Developmental guidance and counseling: A practical approach* (3rd ed.). Minneapolis, MN: Educational Media.

National Association for College Admission Counseling, American Counseling Association, The Education Trust, American School Counselor Association, Sallie Mae Foundation. (2000). *The role of school counseling in preparing students for the 21st century: policies that foster effective school counseling programs.* Washington, DC: Author.

National Occupational Information Coordinating Committee (NOICC). U.S. Department of Labor. (1992). *The national career development guidelines project.* Washington, DC: U.S. Department of Labor.

Nelson, D. E., & Gardner, J. L. (1998). *An evaluation of the comprehensive guidance program in Utah public schools.* Salt Lake City, UT: The Utah State Office of Education.

Neuman, M., & Simmons, W. (2000). Leadership for student learning. *Phi Delta Kappan, 82*(1), 9–12.

Newmann, F. M., & Wehlage, G. G. (1995). *Successful school restructuring: A report to the public and educators by the Center on Organization and Restructuring of Schools.* Madison, WI: Center on Organization and Restructuring of Schools.

Norwood, P. M., & Atkinson, S. E. (1997). Contextualizing parent education programs in urban schools: The impact on minority parents and students. *Urban Education, 32,* 411–433.

Office of Special Education Programs. (2000). Twenty-second annual report to Congress on the implementation of the individuals with disabilities act. Retrieved 10/05/01, from the World Wide Web: http://www.ed.gov/offices/OSERS/Products/OSEP/OSEP2000AnlRpt/index.html

O'Looney, J. (1996). *Redesigning the work of human services.* Westport, CT: Quorum.

Orange County Public Schools. (1999). OCPS Core Curriculum: Student Development. Retrieved 5/23/02, from the World Wide Web: http://www.ocps.K12.fl.us/framework

Ormrod, J. E. (1999). *Human learning* (3rd ed.). Upper Saddle River, NJ: Merrill.

Ormrod, J. E. (2000). *Educational psychology: Developing learners.* Upper Saddle River, NJ: Merrill

Pai, Y., & Adler, S. A. (1997). *Cultural foundations of education* (2nd ed.). Upper Saddle River, NJ: Merrill.

Paisley, P. O., & Hubbard, G. T. (1994). *Developmental school counseling programs: From theory to practice.* Alexandria, VA: American Counseling Association.

Parette, H. P., Jr., & Hourcade, J. J. (1995). Disability etiquette and school counselors: A common sense approach toward compliance with the Americans with Disabilities Act. *The School Counselor, 42,* 224–232.

Peterson, G. W., Long, K. L., & Billups, A. (1999). The effect of three career interventions on educational choices of eight grad students. *Professional School Counseling, 3,* 34–42.

Philips, S. (1983). *The invisible culture: Communication in classroom and community on the Warm Springs Indian Reservation.* New York: Longman.

Pipho, C. (2000a). Stateline: Saving public education for the new century. *Phi Delta Kappan, 81,* 341–342.

Pipho, C. (2000b). Governing the American dream of universal public education. In R. S. Brandt (Ed.), *Education in a New Era* (pp. 5–19). Alexandria, VA: Association for Supervision and Curriculum Development.

Pounder, D. G., & Ogawa, R. T. (1995). Leadership as an organization-wide phenomena: Its impact on school performance. *Educational Administration Quarterly, 31*(4), 564–589.

Pryor, D. B., & Tollerud, T. R. (1999). Applications of Adlerian principles in school settings. *Professional School Counseling, 2,* 299–305

Purkey, W. W., & Novak, J. (1996). *Inviting school success* (3rd ed.). Belmont, CA: Wadsworth.

Purkey, W. W., & Schmidt, J. J. (1990). *Invitational learning for counseling and development.* Ann Arbor, MI: ERIC/CAPS.

Purkey, W. W., & Schmidt, J. J. (1996). *Invitational counseling: A self-concept approach to professional practice.* Pacific Grove, CA: Brooks/Cole.

Rak, C., & Patterson, L. E. (1996). Resiliency in children. *Journal of counseling and development, 74,* 268–373.

Rathvon, N. (1999). *Effective school interventions: Strategies for enhancing academic achievement and social competence.* New York: Guilford Press.

Rauch, C. F., & Behling, O. (1984). Functionalism: Basis for an alternate approach to the study of leadership. In J. G. Hunt, D. M. Hosking, C. A. Schriescheim and R. Steward (Eds.). *Leaders and managers: International perspectives on managerial behavior and leadership* (pp. 45–62). Elmsford, NY: Pergamon.

Reeder, J., Douzenis, C., & Bergin, J. (1997). The effects of small group counseling on the racial attitudes of second grade students. *Professional School Counseling 1* (2), 15–18.

Remley, T. (1985). The law and ethical practices in elementary and middle schools. *Elementary School Guidance and Counseling 19,* 181–189.

Remley, T. P., Jr., & Herlihy, B. (2001). *Ethical, legal, and professional issues in counseling.* Upper Saddle River, NJ: Merrill.

Rich, J. M. (1992). *Foundations of education: Perspectives on American education.* New York: Merrill.

Riley, R. W. (1997). The baby boom echo continues. Retrieved 1/15/01, from the World Wide Web: http://www.ed.gov/pubs/bbecho/

Robinson, T. L., & Howard-Hamilton, M. (2000). *The convergence of race, ethnicity, and gender: Multiple identities in counseling.* Upper Saddle River, NJ: Prentice Hall.

Rogers, C. R. (1977). *Carl Rogers on personal power: Inner strength and its revolutionary impact.* New York: Delacorte Press.

Rogers, C. R. (1992). The necessary and sufficient conditions of therapeutic personality change. *Journal of Consulting and Clinical Psychology, 60,* 827–832.

Roos, P. D. (1998). Intradistrict resource disparities: A problem crying out for a solution. In M. J. Gittell (Ed.) *Strategies for school equity* (pp. 40–52). New Haven, CT: Yale University Press.

Rosener, J. B. (1995). Ways women lead. In J. T. Wren (Ed.), *The leader's companion: Insights on leadership through the ages.* New York: Free Press.

Rosenfield, S., & Gravois, T. A. (1993). Educating consultants for applied clinical and educational settings. In J. E. Zins, T. R. Kratochwill, & S. N. Elliott (Eds.), *Handbook of consultation services for children.* San Francisco: Jossey-Bass.

Roth, A., & Fonagy, P. (1996). *What works for whom?* New York: Guilford Press.

Sabella, R. A. (1996). School counselors and computers: Specific time-saving tips. *Elementary School Guidance & Counseling, 31,* 83–96.

Sabella, R. A. (2000). School counseling and technology. In J. Wittmer (Ed.), *Managing your school counseling program: K-12 developmental strategies* (pp. 337–357). Minneapolis: Educational Media Corporation.

Sampson, J. P., Jr., & Pyle, K. R. (1988). Ethical issues involved with the use of computer-assisted counseling, testing, and guidance systems. In W. C. Huey & T. P. Remley, Jr. (Eds.), *Ethical and legal issues in school counseling* (pp. 249–261). Alexandria, VA: American School Counselor Association.

Sandberg, D. N., Crabbs, S. K., & Crabbs, M. A. (1988). Legal issues in child abuse: Questions and answers for counselors. *Elementary School Guidance and Counseling, 22,* 268–274.

Schmidt, J. J. (1999). *Counseling in schools: Essential services and comprehensive programs* (3rd ed). Needham Heights, MA: Allyn and Bacon.

Scholtes, P. R. (1998). *The leader's handbook: A guide to inspiring your people and managing the daily workflow.* New York: McGraw-Hill.

Schwallie-Giddis, P., & Kobylarz, L. (2000). Career development: The counselor's role in preparing K-12 students for the 21st century. In J. Wittmer (Ed.), *Managing your school counseling program: K-12 developmental strategies* (2nd ed.; pp. 211–218). Minneapolis, MN: Educational Media Corporation.

Search Institute. (1999). *Search Institute profiles of student life: Attitudes and behaviors*. Minneapolis, MN: Author.

Search Institute. (2000). A positive look at today's youth. *The Child Indicator, 2*, 3.

Sears, S. (January, 1999). Transforming school counseling: Making a difference for all students. *NASSP Bulletin 83*, 47–53.

Seligman, L. (1994). *Developmental career counseling and assessment* (2nd ed.) Thousand Oaks, CA: Sage Publications.

Senge, P. M. (1999). *The fifth discipline: The art & practice of the learning organization*. New York: Doubleday.

Senge, P., Cambron-McCabe, N., Lucas, T., Smith, R., Dutton, J., & Kleiner, A. (2000). *Schools that learn: A fifth discipline fieldbook for educators, parents, and everyone who cares about education*. New York: Doubleday.

Sexton, T. L., Whiston, S. C., Bleuer, J. C., & Walz, G. R. (1997). *Integrating outcome research into counseling practice and training*. Alexandria, VA: American Counseling Association.

Shepard-Tew, D., & Creamer, D. A. (1998). Elementary school integrated services teams: Applying case-management techniques. *Professional School Counseling, 2* (2), 141–145.

Sheridan, S. M., & Welch, M. (1996). Is consultation effective? *Remedial & Special Education, 17*, 341–355.

Shoffner, M. F., & Williamson, R. D. (2000). Engaging preservice school counselors and principals in dialogue and collaboration. *Counselor Education and Supervision, 40*(2), 128–140.

Silver, S. (1995). *Organized to be the best: New timesaving ways to simplify and improve how you work* (3rd ed.). Los Angeles: Adams-Hall.

Sink, C. A., & MacDonald, G. (1998). The status of comprehensive guidance and counseling in the United States. *Professional School Counseling 2*(2), 88–94.

Sitlington, P. L., & Frank, A. R. (1993). Dropouts with learning disabilities: What happens to them as young adults? *Learning Disabilities Research and Practice, 8*, 244–252.

Sleeter, C. E., & Grant, C. A. (1988). Race, class, and gender and abandoned dreams. *Teachers' College Record* (Spring), 19–40.

Steinberg, L. (1996). *Adolescence* (4th ed.). New York: McGraw-Hill.

Sutton, J. M., & Fall, M. (1995). The relationship of school climate factors to counselor self-efficacy. *Journal of Counseling & Development, 73*, 331–336.

Taylor, D. L., & Tashakkori, A. (1995). Decision participation and school climate as predictors of job satisfaction and teachers' sense of efficacy. *Journal of Experimental Education, 63*, 217–231.

Taylor, L. M., & Adelman, H. S. (2000). Connecting schools, families, and communities. *Journal of Counseling and Development, 3*(5), 298–307.

Teaching Tolerance. (2001). *Hidden biases inventory*. Retrieved 7/7/01, from the World Wide Web: www.tolerance.org

Thompson, C. L., & Rudolph, L. B. (2000). *Counseling children*. Pacific Grove, CA: Brooks/Cole.

Tomlinson, C. A. (1999). *The differentiated classroom: Responding to the needs of all learners*. Alexandria, VA: Association for Supervision and Curriculum Development.

U.S. Department of Education. (1991). The guidance counselor's role in ensuring equal educational opportunity. Retrieved 1/15/01, from the World Wide Web: http://www.ed.gov/offices/OCR/docs/hq43ef.html

U.S. Department of Education. (1998). School poverty and academic performance: NAEP achievement in high-poverty schools—A special evaluation report for the national assessment of Title 1. Retrieved 1/15/01, from the World Wide Web: http://www.ed.gov/pubs/schoolpoverty/index.html

U.S. Department of Education, National Center for Education Statistics. (2000). *The condition of education 2000, NCES 2000-062*. Washington, DC: U.S. Government Printing Office.

U.S. Department of Education (2001). No child left behind. Retrieved from the World Wide Web: http://www.nochildleftbehind.gov/

U.S. Department of Labor. (1991). *The dictionary of occupational titles* (4th ed.). Washington DC: U.S. Government Printing Office.

VanZandt, C. E. (1990). Professionalism: A matter of personal initiatives. *Journal of Counseling and Development, 68*, 243–245.

VanZandt, C. E., & Hayslip, J. B. (1994). *Your comprehensive school guidance and counseling program*. New York: Longman.

VanZandt, C. E., & Hayslip, J. B. (2001). *Developing your school counseling program: A handbook for systemic planning*. Pacific Grove, CA: Brooks/Cole.

Vernon, A. (1999). Counseling children and adolescents: Developmental considerations. In A. Vernon (Ed.), *Counseling children and adolescents* (2nd ed.; pp. 1–30). Denver, CO: Love Publishing.

Waldo, S. L., & Malley, P. (1992). Tarasoff and its progeny: Implications for the school counselor. *The School Counselor, 40,* 46–54.

Walter, J., & Pellar, J. (1992). *Becoming solution-focused in brief therapy.* New York: Brunner/Mazel.

Webb, L. D., Metha, A., & Jordan, K. F. (1996). *Foundations of American education* (2nd ed.). Englewood Cliffs, NJ: Merrill.

Welfel, E. R. (1998). *Ethics in counseling and psychotherapy: Standards, research, and emerging issues.* Pacific Grove, CA: Brooks/Cole.

Welsh, W. N. (2000). The effects of school climate on school disorder. *Annals of the American Academy of Political & Social Science, 567,* 88–108.

Whiston, S. C., & Sexton, T. L. (1998). A review of school counseling outcome research: Implications for practice. *Journal of Counseling and Development, 76*(4), 412–426.

Wiggins, G., & McTighe, J. (1998). *Understanding by design.* Alexandria, VA: Association for Supervision and Curriculum Development.

Wittmer, J. (2000). Promoting a K–12 developmental guidance program. In J. Wittmer (Ed.), *Managing your school counseling program: K–12 developmental strategies.* (2nd ed.; pp. 306–313). Minneapolis: Educational Media.

Wittmer, J., Thompson, D. W., & Loesch, L. C. (1997). *Classroom guidance activities: A sourcebook for elementary school counselors.* Minneapolis, MN: Educational Media.

Woolfolk, A.E. (1998). *Educational psychology* (7th ed.). Boston: Allyn and Bacon.

Wrenn, G. (1962). The counselor in a changing world. Washington, DC: APGA Press.

Young, M. E. (2001). *Learning the art of helping: Building blocks and techniques* (2nd ed.). Upper Saddle River, NJ: Merrill.

Zambelli, G., & DeRosa, A. (1992). Bereavement support groups for school-age children: Theory, intervention, and case example. *American Journal of Orthopsychiatry, 62,* 484–493.

Zeichner, K. M. (1995). Educating teachers to close the achievement gap: Issues of pedagogy, knowledge, and teacher preparation. In B. Williams (Ed.), *Closing the achievement gap: A vision to guide change in beliefs and practice* (pp. 39–52). Philadelphia: Research for Better Schools and North Central Regional Educational Laboratory.

Zunker, V. G. (1998). *Career counseling: Applied concepts of life planning.* Pacific Grove, CA: Brooks/Cole Publishing.

Zunker, V. G. (2002). *Career counseling: Applied concepts of life planning.* (6th ed.). Pacific Grove, CA: Brooks/Cole Publishing.

Author Index

Subject Index